The Dons

The Dons

Mentors, Eccentrics and Geniuses

NOEL ANNAN

The University of Chicago Press

NOEL ANNAN (1916–2000) made his name as a historian of ideas with his study of Leslie Stephen. He also wrote a biography of his headmaster, *Roxburgh of Stowe* (1965), and *Changing Enemies* (1995), an account of his time as an intelligence officer in the War Cabinet Offices, and later in Germany. He is perhaps best known for his book about his own generations, *Our Age*, and his article "The Intellectual Aristocracy," which is reprinted in the book.

The University of Chicago Press, Chicago 60637

HarperCollins*Publishers*, Hammersmith, London W6 8JB

ISBN 0-226-02107-6 (cloth)
ISBN 0-226-02108-4 (paperback)

Library of Congress Cataloging-in-Publication Data

Annan, Noel Gilroy Annan, Baron, 1916–
        The dons : mentors, eccentrics, and geniuses / Noel Annan.
            p.   cm.
    Includes index.
    ISBN: 0-226-02107-6 (cloth)
    1. Universities and colleges—Great Britain—Faculty—History. 2. College teachers—Great Britain—Biography. I. Title.

LB2331.74.G7 A55 1999
378.1'2'0941—dc21

                                                                    99-046232

To Francis Haskell

Contents

ACKNOWLEDGEMENTS

I must first thank David Cannadine for taking the time to read this book in draft, and for suggesting improvements. So did my daughter Juliet, who as a publisher had many other potential books to read. That expert on the history of the University of Oxford, Michael Brock, saved me from many errors and Francis Haskell has also cast an eye over some pages. I owe a special debt to Jonathan Steinberg for making available to me his biographical material on Betty Behrens. To these and others who at times have advised me I am very grateful.

I must also thank the editors of *The Times Literary Supplement,* the *New York Review of Books* and the *New Statesman* for allowing me to reprint in part essays and reviews that I wrote for them. I am particularly grateful to Messrs Longmans for allowing me to reprint my essay on 'The Intellectual Aristocracy' and to Messrs Duckworth for permitting me to include in part a tribute paid to Maurice Bowra in a collection of essays they printed on his death.

The librarians and staff of the House of Lords and the London Library were as ever helpful and the soul of courtesy. Alan Bell, Librarian of the London Library, volunteered generously to read the book in proof. I must thank my literary agent, Gill Coleridge, for her skill in negotiation and I am naturally indebted to my publisher, Michael Fishwick, my meticulous copy editor Sophie Nelson and my picture editor Suzanne Collins. Douglas Matthews has for the third time consented to compile an index for me, as has Harriet Croxton to type many drafts of this book from my hand-written manuscript. I owe them much.

Noel Annan

List of Illustrations

INTRODUCTION

Anyone who writes about Oxford and Cambridge owes a debt to the scholars who wrote the history of those universities and of their individual colleges. But I owe a special debt of gratitude to the memorialists – those like Mark Pattison and William Tuckwell at Oxford and Leslie Stephen and the American, Charles Bristed, at Cambridge – who left us their personal impression of what life was like there in times gone by and of the dons whom they remembered. This book is not for the experts: they will know the references all too well. It is for the common reader.

I had another reason for writing about dons. Nearly forty-five years ago I was asked to contribute to a volume of essays to mark G. M. Trevelyan's seventy-fifth birthday. My subject was one which I hoped would give him pleasure: the intermarriage between some families – for instance the Trevelyans, Macaulays and Arnolds – that created what I called an intellectual aristocracy. That essay has long been out of print and not easily accessible. Furthermore, it did not sit easily with the other chapters. But if you are interested in the ramifications of these families, you will fiind the detail of their intermarriage in the Annexe at the end of the book.

Dons are so often stereotyped. I wanted to show what a variety of dons there are, all of them memorable, all exhibiting different talents. Of course, there were others it would have been right to include. G. M. Trevelyan was one. In my first term at Cambridge he invited me to tea, and at the end of my last term before I graduated he wrote me a peremptory, almost illegible note telling me to come next morning and read aloud to him the papers I had written on my special subject – he said they were illegible. Later, when I was Provost of King's and he was almost blind, I used to read poetry to him – the old favourites,

Milton, Wordsworth, Tennyson, Meredith. Sometimes, sobbing with emotion, he would join me and declaim some of the hundreds of lines he knew by heart. But David Cannadine wrote an admirable memoir of Trevelyan that says so much of what needs to be said.

Then there was Keynes, whom I got to know during the war, but no less than three biographies of him exist as well as countless articles. Indeed, I could have chosen Roy Harrod, Keynes's first biographer. At Oxford they played a game where you have to describe people in words of one syllable. The winner was the word for Harrod: 'don'. Harrod was a great writer of notes to his colleagues, within the Establishment but always willing to advance unorthodox opinions, a critic of the tutorial which, he thought, was being used for spoon-feeding; yet none was more loyal to Oxford's rituals or more insistent on a don's obligations to his pupils. A tutorial should correct 'points of style, presentation, logic, modes of criticising authorities studied etc.' His ingenious and quirky mind enlivened the high table at Christ Church.

I had an excuse for omitting two influential dons, F. R. Leavis and Michael Oakeshott, since I had written at length on each in *Our Age*. But why omit towering scientists like Florey and Todd? Or one of Oxford's most revered scholars in classics, John Beazley, who brought order into the study of Attic vases? Or socialist thinkers like G. D. H. Cole or 'Sage' Bernal? Or miraculous eccentrics such as the professor of Modern Greek at Oxford, R. M. Dawkins, remembered for his cackle of laughter and keen interest in flagellomania?

I would have liked to have included more scientists. When I returned to Cambridge after the war one of the scientists who became my special friend was Victor Rothschild. He did research on spermatozoa in the zoology lab, but although a fellow of Trinity he did not teach and left the university to become chief scientific adviser to Royal Dutch Shell. I had made a rule for myself not to write about the living and I therefore did not choose Alan Hodgkin, Nobel Prizeman and Master of Trinity, who died only as this book was ready to go to press. The others were in the molecular biology unit – Max Perutz, Sidney Brenner and Francis Crick, the discoverer, with Jim Watson, of the structure of DNA, all still happily alive. I failed to persuade Francis to allow his name to go forward for a fellowship at King's. He would not join any society with a chapel: to do so would have been to connive at error; and King's undeniably had a chapel.

Universities have endured hard times since government decided to move to mass higher education, none more so than the elite institutions I knew so well in London – University College, Imperial College and the London School of Economics – and the leading civic universities. It is these places, with Oxford and Cambridge, that are the guardians of intellectual life. Over thirty years ago I tried to put into words what such places exist to do. They cannot teach the qualities that people need in politics and business. Nor can they teach culture and wisdom, any more than theologians teach holiness, or philosophers goodness or sociologists a blueprint for the future. They exist to cultivate the intellect. Everything else is secondary. Equality of opportunity to come to the university is secondary. The matters that concern both dons and administrators are secondary. The need to mix classes, nationalities and races together is secondary. The agonies and gaieties of student life are secondary. So are the rules, customs, pay and promotion of the academic staff and their debates on changing the curricula or procuring facilities for research. Even the awakening of a sense of beauty or the life-giving shock of new experience, or the pursuit of goodness itself – all these are secondary to the cultivation, training and exercise of the intellect. Universities should hold up for admiration the intellectual life. The most precious gift they have to offer is to live and work among books or in laboratories and to enable the young to see those rare scholars who have put on one side the world of material success, both in and outside the university, in order to study with single-minded devotion some topic because that above all seems important to them. A university is dead if the dons cannot in some way communicate to the students the struggle – and the disappointments as well as the triumphs in that struggle – to produce out of the chaos of human experience some grain of order won by the intellect. That is the end to which all the arrangements of the university should be directed.

I still believe that this is the principle that should govern Oxford and Cambridge and our élite universities.

CHAPTER ONE

The Dons Create an Intellectual Aristocracy

The word 'don' carries many meanings, quite a number of them ironical. Some use it loosely to mean anyone who holds a post at a university, but well into the twentieth century it meant something more precise. 'Don' did not immediately suggest a creative scholar or a *professeur* of a particular subject, still less a *privatdozent*. A don was not expected to be an intellectual nor yet a man with a passion for general ideas. No: essentially he was a teacher and a fellow of an Oxford or Cambridge college; a teacher who stood in a peculiar relation to his pupils in that they came to his rooms individually each week and were taught by him personally. And since these pupils were men of his own college, his first allegiance was not to the university but to his college – to the close-knit society whose members had elected him. To the other fellows he was bound by ties of special loyalty and affection – sometimes, of course, by the no less binding ties of enmity and loathing which led to feuds and vendettas within the society,

It was only in late Victorian days that election to fellowships and university posts at Oxford and Cambridge began to be made on merit; and even then, merit could be determined by numbers of tests which were by no means all strictly academic. Was he, it could be asked, a good college man, sociable, willing to share in due course in the administration of the college, a potential bursar, tutor or dean? Was he a man of character as well as intellect, for he was educating the next generation who were to be the clergymen, statesmen and gentlemen of England?

In the early years of the nineteenth century before the ancient universities were reformed everything depended on patronage and few were ashamed to admit it. 'I don't know what we're coming to,' said Canon Barnes of Christ Church in the 1830s. 'I've given Studentships to my sons, and to my nephews, and to my nephew's children, and there are no more of my family left. I shall have to give them by merit one of these days.' An old fellow of Merton was urged to award a fellowship to the candidate who had done best in the examinations. 'Sir, I came here to vote for my old friend's son, and vote for him I shall, whatever the examiners may say.' To appoint by merit had echoes of the French Revolution. Had not Napoleon declared that every soldier carried a marshal's baton in his knapsack, and look what ruffians Junot, Augereau and Ney were. Wellington *per contra* defended the system of officers in the army purchasing their commissions since, as gentlemen of England, they could be depended upon to be loyal as well as brave. Patronage was the passport to getting on in life. The venerable Dr Routh, President of Magdalen, who died in 1854 in his hundredth year, was in no doubt: 'Take my advice, sir,' he said to an undergraduate destined for Parliament; 'choose some powerful patron, sir, and stick to him – stick to him always, sir, that is the only way.'* Today it is not the only way. Men and women can rise on their own merits; but, if they are honest and reflect, how many will admit that someone – a friend of their family, a teacher skilled in writing testimonials or an employer or senior colleague who took a shine to them – gave them their chance?

In the ancient universities, in which the majority of fellows were clergymen, patronage affected professorships, canonries

---

* Martin Joseph Routh (1755–1854), President of Magdalen College, Oxford (1791); remembered for his advice to a young scholar: 'Always verify your references.'

and country livings to which, if a fellow decided to marry, he could be appointed. In those days politics were more concerned with religion, and which prime minister was in office mattered because patronage was often in his gift. Readers of Trollope's *Barchester Towers* will remember how the fall of the Conservative ministry dashed Archdeacon Grantly's hopes of being made bishop and the preferment went to Dr Proudie. Tories could be expected to appoint High Churchmen, the Whigs to prefer liberals or what came to be called Broad Churchmen. But it was not as simple as that. How staunch a Protestant was a candidate? Was he stalwart against Catholic Emancipation? Routh was a High Churchman and the only head of a college to support John Henry Newman when Newman declared that Anglican beliefs were not inconsistent with Roman dogma, but he opposed Sir Robert Peel when Peel stood for the chancellorship of Oxford because Peel had finally brought himself to vote for Catholic Emancipation.*

What kind of don did this system of patronage throw up? Writing at the end of the nineteenth century William Tuckwell, a fellow of New College, thought they fell into four categories: cosmopolitan, ornamental, mere – and learned. The cosmopolitan don, intelligent but worldly, would be found in London as often as Oxford, seeing that the political interests of his friends at Westminster were reflected in elections to posts in Oxford

---

* An election to the chancellorship was a political event of importance. In 1809 the chancellorship fell vacant. The Protestant vote was split between Lord Eldon (who was Lord Liverpool's candidate) and the Duke of Beaufort, an old High Churchman. So the election was won through skilful canvassing by Lord Grenville, who had concealed until the last moment that he was in favour of Catholic Emancipation. The contest impaled the Dean of Christ Church, Dr Hall, on the horns of an excruciating dilemma. He was beholden to two patrons, Liverpool and Grenville. Liverpool, his old pupil, had procured the deanery for him. Grenville had made him Regius professor of divinity. What was he to do? Hall felt bound to tell Liverpool that he could not guarantee to deliver the Christ Church vote, where Grenville had a considerable following. Liverpool never forgave him and the canons of Christ Church, who had been appointed by Liverpool, cut him dead; his finances fell into confusion; until at last Liverpool offered him not a bishopric, but the deanery of Durham and then only on condition that he left Oxford to reside in Durham. He accepted and promptly went abroad.

and *pari passu* that patronage by cabinet ministers flowed into the right channels in the university. The ornamental don held university offices. He became a proctor and looked forward to offers of succulent benefices in the Church. He was therefore so cushioned by genial company and emoluments that further effort on his part was not required and he added nothing to learning. Preferment in the Church was what occupied his mind. But if he failed to get it he might die as senior fellow of his college, renowned for his nose for a vintage. Or he became an eccentric whom younger fellows boasted of having known.

The *mere* don referred to the bulk of the fellows, tutors who took the undergraduates in their college through Latin and Greek texts, up in arms at any attempt by the professors to deflect their pupils to attend professorial lectures. A *mere* don might well be voted in as head of a house, the compromise candidate when the supporters of the two abler rivals produced a deadlock by their intransigence. He would then preside 'with a late-married wife as uncouth and uneducated as he . . . respecting no man in the University and respected by no man out of it'. There were indeed some roughnecks among the heads or others, such as the Rector of Lincoln, Edward Tatham, a stickler for Anglican orthodoxy and hater of dissenters, whose violence of language did his cause more harm than good. In a two-and-a-half-hour sermon he declared that he wished 'all the Jarman critics at the bottom of the Jarman Ocean'. Yet there were fine heads of houses, among them Tatham's opponent, Cyril Jackson, the Dean of Christ Church, Richard Jenkyns of Balliol and later the liberal reformer Francis Jeune of Pembroke.

Tuckwell's fourth category was the *learned* don. The days had passed since Gibbon could portray the dons as stupefied by their dull and deep potations while supinely enjoying the gifts of their founder. A few were certainly learned and edited classical texts. Many more were quick and elegant versifiers in Latin and Greek. Common room talk was peppered with Latin tags;

some could even pun in Greek. Arthur Ridding not only described the Duke of Wellington lying in state as 'splendide mendax' but, seeing a wretched horse, scarcely more than skin and bones, hauling a barge along the tow-path of a canal, muttered 'to pathos' (towpath 'oss). There was the good-natured Henry 'Horse' Kett, whose long face so resembled a horse's head that undergraduates filled his snuff-box with oats. Realising that many undergraduates found the compulsory questions on Aristotelian logic beyond their powers, 'Horse' Kett wrote a book called *Logic Made Easy*. His fellow examiner Edward Copleston at once wrote a devastating riposte and headed his pamphlet with the Virgilian warning about never trusting a Greek even with a gift in his hands: *'Aliquis latet error; Equo ne credite, Teucri'* (Some trick here; don't trust the horse, Trojans). But although Oxford scholars read German commentaries on classical texts, they could not be compared to the German classical scholars, at that time the finest in the world.

Out of these learned dons there emerged an intellectual aristocracy. Dons formed dynasties. When Frederic Maitland married the sister of H. A. L. Fisher, later to be Warden of New College, he became a nephew of Julia Stephen, the wife of Leslie Stephen and mother of Virginia Woolf, and counted among his other cousins the Oxford scholars F. H. and A. C. Bradley, and the headmaster of Rugby W. W. Vaughan, a member of another clan of dons. Maitland's daughter was to marry a don.*

What was happening was that certain families of a serious cast of mind intermarried and their children became scholars and teachers, joining those at Oriel and Balliol in Oxford, or at Trinity and St John's in Cambridge. They led the movement for academic reform within the universities and became the first

---

* If you want to follow the ramifications of the intermarriage of these families, please turn to the Annexe at the end of the book.

professors of the new civic academies; and their achievements as
headmasters at Shrewsbury or Harrow or Rugby were watched
by the professional classes, eager to educate their sons well at
schools where they mixed with those of the lesser aristocracy
or gentry. When these sons in turn came to marry, what was
more natural than to choose a wife from the families of their
fathers' friends whose fortune and upbringing matched their
own?

They were a new status group. Sociologists distinguish a social
group from a social class. These families were not concerned
with the means of production and creation of wealth. What
marked them off was not wealth but standing. A section of the
Victorian middle class rose to positions of influence and respect
as a range of posts passed out of the gift of the nobility into
their hands. They naturally ascended to positions where academic and cultural policy was made. In literary life they were
the backbone of the Victorian intellectual periodicals. In public
service they were strongest in the Indian and home civil service
rather than in diplomacy, which for long was too expensive for
them and attracted the sons of the upper classes; but once
diplomats could support themselves on their salary they began
to invade the foreign service.

They were not a narrow professoriate. They could not be
when most fellowships had to be vacated on marriage or the
holder required to take holy orders. True to the traditional role
of Oxford and Cambridge, which was to educate men for service
in Church and State, they overflowed into the new professions.
The days when Addison could define the professions as divinity,
law and physic were past. Not only were the old professions
expanding to include attorneys and apothecaries, but the establishment in 1828 of the Institution of Civil Engineers to further
'the art of directing the Great Sources of Power in Nature for
the use and convenience of mankind' marked the rise of a new
kind of professional man. Members of these intellectual families

became the new professional civil servants at a time when government had become too complicated and technical to be handled by the ruling class and their dependants. They became school inspectors or took posts in the museums or were appointed secretaries of philanthropic societies; or they edited or wrote for the periodicals or entered publishing houses; or, as journalists ceased to be hacks scribbling in Grub Street, they joined the staff of *The Times*. Thus they gradually spread over the length and breadth of English intellectual life, criticising the assumptions of the ruling class above them and forming the opinions of the upper middle class to which they belonged.

This intellectual aristocracy was not an intelligentsia, a term which, Russian in origin, suggests the shifting, shiftless members of revolutionary or literary cliques who have cut themselves adrift from the moorings of family. The English intellectual élite, wedded to gradual reform of accepted institutions and able to move between the worlds of speculation and government, was stable. That it was so – that it was unexcitable and, to European minds, unexciting – was in part due to the influence of these academic families.

Why was this so? One reason was that, although they supplanted the placemen or kinsmen of the nobility and gentry, quite a number of them were in fact related to the gentry and even at a few removes from the nobility. Numbers of dons and at one time the headmasters of Eton, Radley and Rugby were connected to the Lytteltons. The Stanleys of Alderley keep cropping up in the family trees and connect with the Lubbocks and the Buxtons. The historian Hugh Trevor-Roper descends from Barbara Villiers, the mistress of Charles II, and is connected with a viceroy of India and with Robert Brand, the fellow of All Souls and member of Milner's kindergarten* after the South

---

* The group of able young men from Oxford and Toynbee Hall who helped Milner reorganise and pacify South Africa after the Boer War.

African war. Arthur Balfour, the Prime Minister and nephew of
the Marquess of Salisbury, was the brother-in-law of the Cambridge philosopher Henry Sidgwick and of the physicist and
Nobel Prizeman Lord Rayleigh; and one of his nieces married
a Trevelyan. The Trevelyans and Stracheys were cadet branches
of old West Country families with baronetcies created in the
seventeenth and eighteenth centuries. The Babingtons, who
were Leicestershire country squires, were not the only family
to trace their descent from a Duchess of Norfolk who was a
great-great-granddaughter of Edward I: so could the Cripps
family, the Venns, the Thorntons and the Plowdens – even,
improbably, among her remote descendants were Lytton
Strachey and Duncan Grant. Henry Thornton, the leader of the
Clapham Sect, smiled satirically at his brother's breakfast party
for Queen Charlotte and her daughter in his exquisitely
embellished villa. 'We are all City people and connected with
merchants and nothing but merchants on every side,' he said;
and the subsequent failure of his brother, who died under an
assumed name in New York, may have seemed like a judgement
on such luxurious display. All the same the Thorntons were
cousins of the Earl of Leven and could trace their descent to
the last of the Plantagenets, 'false, fleeting, perjur'd Clarence'.

Nevertheless they did not think of themselves, whatever their
connections, as being part of the ruling class and the established
circles of power. Nor did the nobility or upper gentry think of
them as equals. When, in one of Trollope's political novels,
Lady Mary Palliser pleads with her father, the Duke of Omnium,
to be permitted to marry Frank Tregear, she argues: 'He is a
gentleman.' 'So is my private secretary,' replies the duke. 'The
curate of the parish is a gentleman, and the medical man who
comes here from Bradstock, the word is too vague to carry any
meaning that ought to be serviceable . . .' The word 'gentleman'
became in Victorian times a subject of dialectical enquiry and
nerve-racking embarrassment. Newman and Huxley both rede-

fined it to meet the needs of their status group and the realities of a new age. To have been to a public school was not a necessary qualification; but to have been to a university, or by some means to have acquired professional status, was. Political necessity did not oblige them, as so often in France, to polarise themselves and identify with the party of order or the party of liberty; nor, as in Russia, to face the consequences of living beneath a despotism; nor, like professors in Germany, to become State officials. They formed a barrier to the jingoism and aggressive philistinism at the turn of the century. For the most part they preferred the manners of Asquith and Balfour to those of Lloyd George or Lord Hugh Cecil, though there were some stalwart Tories among them. The question of Home Rule for Ireland and later the rise of the Labour Party pushed some of the radicals among them to the right in late Victorian times.

Did these families at their zenith exert a stultifying effect upon English intellectual life by monopolising important posts? Did they exclude a new class who, unbeneficed and indignant, ate out their hearts in the wilderness? Some think so. They produced a disproportionately large number of eminent men and women, but it is also true that they produced men of sound but not outstanding ability who reached the front ranks of science and scholarship because they had been trained in their families and at school to turn their upbringing to account. The heyday of their influence probably came in the early years of this century until the 1930s, when the number of academic and editorial posts rose. As the BBC, the British Council and Arts Council, the media and other cultural institutions were set up and expanded, the number of posts multiplied far faster than the progeny of these families; and after the Second World War their members were spread very thin over the crust of British intellectual life. The charge of monopoly at any time is farfetched; but that they had influence and used it is undeniable.

What was the ethos of these families? What spiritual springs refreshed them? The first spring was evangelicalism, and though the faith in its purest form might fade, they were imbued with its principles. There was the sense of dedication, of living with purpose, or working under the eye, if not of the great Taskmaster, of their own conscience – that organ which evangelicalism magnified so greatly. They were filled with a sense of mission to improve the shining hour. They felt they had to account for their talents. They held themselves apart from a world given over to vanities which men of integrity rejected. These were the principles that inspired the Clapham Sect to which the Macaulays, Venns, Stephens and Thorntons belonged.

The second spring was philanthropy. Philanthropy linked the Clapham families with the Quaker families; the Gurneys, Frys, Gaskells, Hoares, Hodgkins, Foxes, Buxtons and Barclays had intermarried in the eighteenth century. As the Quakers became prosperous and began to play a larger part in the affairs of the world; as they turned from small traders into bankers and brewers; and as they began to own country houses and mixed with evangelical philanthropists or enlightened businessmen, many of them felt oppressed by the narrow bounds of the Society of Friends. The children of John Gurney of Earlham, a banker and country gentleman, had outgrown the simple narrow piety of their elders. They were a lively household and referred to the meeting house in Goat Lane, Norwich, as 'that disgusting Goat's'. One of the liveliest, Elizabeth Fry, suddenly experienced conversion and returned to the ways of the Society, but of her seven brothers and sisters who married, four knelt before the altar of a church. They were not alone in seceding. Mary Ann Galton left the Quakers for the Moravian Brothers, William Rathbone went over in 1805 to Unitarianism and James Wilson, the father-in-law of Walter Bagehot, ceased to attend Meeting in 1832 after marrying an Anglican. Small wonder that an appeal was made not to excommunicate members who married those of other religions.

The Quaker families also linked the evangelicals to the third group of philanthropists, the Unitarian or philosophic radical families. The Wedgwoods neither stemmed from a line of parsons nor did they breed them. Josiah Wedgwood of Maer, the son of the founder of the pottery, told his wife not to be uneasy about playing cards on Sunday, since she knew in her heart that it was not wrong. 'I am rather afraid,' he wrote, 'of Evangelicalism spreading amongst us though I have some confidence in the good sense of the Maerites for keeping it out, or if it must come for having the disease in a very mild form.' His first cousins, the Darwins, a singularly unreligious family, were equally untouched. They both belonged to the upper-middle-class world of Brougham and Mackintosh and the *Edinburgh Review*, a world which had ties with the cultivated French middle class. Their children made the Grand Tour and went to balls and race meetings. Yet if their manners were freer they were not very far removed from some of the children of Clapham; and Charles Darwin's description of his uncle Josiah as 'the very type of an upright man with the clearest judgment. I do not believe that any power on earth could have made him swerve an inch from what he considered the right course', surely suggests that they had the same temperament as the descendants of the Evangelicals or Quakers,

In the 1860s two objectives vital to their class and, as they rightly thought, vital to their country, united them. They worked tirelessly for intellectual freedom within the universities which, they thought, should admit anyone irrespective of his religious beliefs. They also worked for the creation of a public service open to talent. If they can be said to have had a Bill of Rights it was the Trevelyan-Northcote report of 1854 on reform of the civil service, and their Glorious Revolution was achieved in 1870–71, when entry to public service by privilege, purchase of army commissions and the religious tests were abolished. From then on clever men could succeed through open competitive examination. What was more Macaulay had recommended that the examination for the Indian Civil Service should be designed for those who had taken high honours at the university. The change took time. Even after Victoria's reign it was still possible to be nominated to a place in Whitehall, though one had to pass a formal examination after entry. Not until 1908 in the Home Office and 1911 in the Treasury were the values of the intellectual aristocracy – probity, loyalty, a rational system of promotion and detachment from party politics – enshrined. The workaholic bureaucrat was replacing civil servants like Trollope who expected to get three days' hunting a fortnight. By the time of the First World War no formal obstacle remained to prevent the man of brains from becoming a gentleman. An intellectual aristocracy had formed.

Was this dangerous? George Meredith, whose novels were much admired by the discerning among the intellectual aristocracy, was among the first to use the term. But he did not use it as a term of praise. He used it to highlight the dangers of a meritocracy. In 1859 he wrote in *The Ordeal of Richard Feverel*:

> How soothing it is to intellect – that noble rebel, as the Pilgrim has it – to stand, and bow, and know itself superior! This exquisite compensation maintains the balance: whereas that period anticipated by the Pilgrim, when science shall have produced an *intellectual aristocracy*, is indeed horrible to contemplate. For what despotism is so black as one the mind cannot challenge? 'Twill be an iron Age.

Meredith forgot that there are always countervailing forces in history. In the second half of the twentieth century the props that underpinned the meritocracy were shaken. Most of the grammar schools, which had so often been the first step on the ladder, became comprehensive schools; the examinations for the public service were altered to take account of the revolution in electronics and the computer age; and people learned to doubt how far scientists, economists and applied sociologists could plan and control the future.

What were these families like? It was the mark of most of them to remain almost exactly where they were placed in society. Josiah Wedgwood had a country house and had married a squire's daughter, but the Wedgwoods were not a county family and they knew it. Their fortune rested on the pottery and not on land and during the past century and a half they have neither risen nor fallen in the social scale. The families that rose by business, especially the Quaker connections, were affluent enough to enable some of their children to pursue their scholarly studies in leisure; but they had neither the wealth nor the inclination to become magnates and were always liable to need to save a brother whose affairs had failed to prosper. In any event a fortune divided among forty grandchildren did not give the cadet branches the chance to live extravagantly. The Anglican families tended to be less well-to-do. Sound commercial principles were allied to ascetic habits. Even on their meagre stipends the poorer dons thrived and, as few of them were permitted to marry, they saved. Aged twenty-six Henry Sidgwick wrote to his mother from Trinity, 'I find that I have saved £1,700 and hope to save £400 a year as long as I stay here: in spite of all my travelling, books and the extremely luxurious life that I can hardly help leading.' A fortnight later he told her that he had opposed a college ball being held because 'I consider it a most unseemly proceeding on the part of a charitable foundation for the purposes of education and of which the majority are clergymen and ... especially as it will be a great expense, and you know my miserly tendencies.' His luxurious life was evidently restrained.

Restrained because for Sidgwick, as for all of them, the purpose of life was to distinguish in conduct as well as in concept the sham from the genuine, appearance from reality. Appearances were to be exposed and these men were splendidly eccentric in Victorian society in not keeping them up. They groaned at the thought of formal receptions and preferred to wear rough clothes. The gentlemanly Arthur Benson, Sidgwick's nephew, opined that a don should be well dressed in the style-before-last and obeyed this precept by wearing shapeless flannels. Their self-confidence forbade them to ape the manners of their superiors in rank and their clothes, like their pursuits, were a protest against the pastimes of the upper classes, which became increasingly more gaudy and expensive. They neither hunted nor had the money for vast *battues* of pheasants. Most of them had lost their roots in their soil and, cut off from country sports, had become town-dwellers. But they had not lost touch with Nature, whom they sought mountaineering in the Alps or on forty-mile tramps or with their botanical satchel and geologist's hammer. Their manners lacked polish. Indeed they despised it as much as they despised the art of pleasing – that imperative accomplishment for those who enter politics or London society. But they did not become parochial or cut themselves off from London. Many of them lived there, and those who did not kept up with public affairs through dining clubs, where they met their cousins and brothers-in-law in the professions, or sometimes by themselves through participating in politics.

Their good manners appeared in their prose. At its worst it was lucid and free from scholarly jargon. They wrote with a sense of form, of drama, of the possibilities of language; and they wrote not for a scholarly clique but for the intelligent public at large whom they addressed confident that they would be understood. Moreover, their scholarly manners had an ease seldom evident in a parochial professoriate. They declined, with a few exceptions, to follow the pulverising style of German professors. Darwin and Maitland showed that it was possible to argue without breaking heads, and even such controversialists as Huxley were untainted by the *odium clericum* and distinguished between the charlatan and the wrong-headed. They valued independence and recognised it in others. Because they judged people by an exterior standard of moral and intellectual merit, they never became an exclusive clique and welcomed the penniless son of a dissenting minister as a son-in-law if they believed in his integrity and ability. Because their own proud standards were assured they tolerated a wide variety of belief. They might follow the French sociologist Auguste Comte, they were often followers of Mill, they might be agnostics, or they might continue to adhere to the Church of their fathers; but they respected each other's beliefs, however deeply convinced that the beliefs were wrong. They were agreed on one characteristic doctrine: that the world could be improved by analysing the needs of society and calculating the possible course of its development.

They could be intimidating to meet. Intellectuals often are. Their sense of responsibility to reason was too great for them to appreciate spontaneous behaviour. Spontaneity is attractive, but its lack of rational consideration irritated them. They were bored by the superficiality of drawing-room gossip, and preferred to have their talk out rather than converse. As infants they had learnt by listening to their parents to extend their vocabulary and talk in grammatical sentences – of which the best known (to an enquiry after his toothache) was the four-year-old Macaulay's 'Thank you, madam, the agony is abated.' When older they subconsciously apprehended from hearing discussions between their elders how to reason logically. They lived in houses in which books were part of existence and the intellect was prized. They developed inner resources for entertaining themselves which did not depend on the ordinary social accomplishments. Competitive examinations at the schools and

universities sharpened their minds. Children who did not
inherit their parents' intellectual talents suffered unjustly by
feeling that they had failed; children were expected to marry
according to their parents' lights. One who was on the point
of marrying an actor was safely brought back to the fold to
marry a don. The dedicated agnostic G. M. Trevelyan bore his
daughter's marriage to a scholarly clergyman like a man. But
there were limits, and he told his son: 'I want you to know that
your mother and I wish you to be free to marry whom you will.
But we will take it hard if she is a Roman Catholic.'

They had their limitations, as every close-knit class must have.
Their response to art was at best uncertain. Literature, of course,
was in their bones. The poetry and prose of Greece and Rome
had been their discipline, and that of their own country filled
their leisure hours. They were the first to admire Meredith and
Browning and to dethrone Byron for Wordsworth. Goethe and
the German poets were admired primarily for the moral pre-
cepts which their works embodied. French culture was another
matter. Lady Strachey, her children gathered about her, might
rise from her seat in the railway carriage as the train steamed
into the Gare du Nord and bow to the great city, the mistress
of European civilisation, but such a gesture was rare. Matthew
Arnold went as far as most were prepared to go in admiring
French culture and he made strong reservations. The Parisian
haute bourgeoisie combined a passion for general ideas with an
interest in the arts, the theatre and opera, in a way which was
impossible for them. Their experience of the visual arts was
meagre. Beautiful objects and elegant rooms were not to them
necessities: their comfortable ugly houses in Kensington, Bays-
water and north Oxford, rambling, untidy, full of gloryholes
and massive furnishings and staffed by two or three despairing
servants, were dedicated to utility, not beauty. Some may have
bought some good pieces of furniture, a very few of the more
prosperous may have invested in Italian primitives, others were

affected by the Pre-Raphaelites, but in the main they groped after artistic fashion in a manner inconsistent with their natural self-confidence.

To this there were exceptions. When Philip Webb, Norman Shaw and Bodley began to design houses, not in ponderous stucco or bewildering gothic, but in the potpourri of styles which came to be known as Queen Anne, some members of the intellectual aristocracy responded. Henry Sidgwick at Cambridge and the philosopher T. H. Green at Oxford both commissioned houses designed in the new style of sweetness and light, with bay windows, verandas, inglenooks and crannies crammed with a clutter of objects intended to delight the eye and interest the mind. Girton College was built as a spartan, spare building in the Tudor-gothic style of Waterhouse, everything geared to proving that women could compete on equal terms with men. But Sidgwick got his friend Champneys to design Newnham in the Queen Anne style: the students' rooms were papered with Morris wallpaper, and his wife, the first Principal, insisted that the corridors should have windows on both sides for cheerfulness. Indeed there were always a handful of them who self-consciously kept up with new styles in the visual arts which, even if the effort was not spontaneous, was a good deal better than sinking into complacent philistinism. Still, many of them inherited the old evangelical distrust of beauty as a temptress, unsusceptible to the kind of analysis of which they were accomplished masters. That distrust inhibited them in their dealings with art. A fashionably dressed wife would not only have been an extravagance but an act of submission to worldly vanity: and the Pre-Raphaelite cloaks and dresses which had been donned as a homage to beauty and a protest against the world of upper-class fashion degenerated in some cases into thick woollen stockings and flannel petticoats, which were proudly worn as a badge of financial and spiritual austerity. By the end of the century there was a slight staidness, a satisfaction, a lack of spontaneity and intellectual adventure, even a touch of philistinism in the face of new forms of art; and some of their descendants, such as Samuel Butler or the Bloomsbury group, satirised these failings.

The artist's vision was not theirs. Nor was the artist's world; critical of conventions as they might be, they emphatically did not live in Bohemia. Pleasure was identified with happiness, and happiness by both their favourite philosophers, Mill and Green, with self-realisation. There could be family jollity, but exuberance, raciness and high spirits escaped them. They were a little too far removed from the battle of keeping a job and exercising the arts of getting a better, a little too severe on inconsequential behaviour, fully to understand human nature. Nor was this surprising; those who have clear ideas on what life ought to be always have difficulty in reconciling themselves to what it is. Considering that their hearts were set on transforming the old universities into institutions of education and research, their genial and tolerant regard for the older generation of dons was remarkable. Their goals nevertheless were so clear and their purpose so single-minded that they were apt to sacrifice other valuable things to achieve them. Self-realisation was not always extended to those gifted and capital creatures their wives. Fortunately for their husbands these wives were trained to self-sacrifice.

Great as their influence was in politics and intellectual life in the middle of the century, perhaps it was even more important at the end. For then the restraints of religion and thrift and accepted class distinctions started to crumble and English society to rock as money flooded into it and affected its values. The class war, not merely between labour and owners but between all social strata of the middle and upper classes, began in earnest. The intellectual aristocracy were one of the few barriers which resisted these forces. They insisted that honesty and courtesy were valuable; and they continued to set before the young unworldly ideals. They suggested that if public life was inseparable from spiritual ignominy, another life devoted to unravelling the mysteries of mind, matter and heart was to be desired.

For them, too, it was a period of change. In the 1880s the ban on married dons was removed and many who in the past would have been forced to vacate their fellowships and pursue their studies elsewhere or find a different source of income were able to remain at Oxford and Cambridge. As a result more of them became dons. They also became relatively poorer as taxation and the standard of living rose. A young don such as A. L. Smith, who later became Master of Balliol, the son of an unsuccessful civil engineer and one of a family of nineteen surviving children, had a hard time in making ends meet. Stipends which had been tolerable for a bachelor were inadequate for a married man, especially as the agricultural depression reduced college revenues that in great part came from farm rents.

By no means all the dons mentioned in this book belonged to these families. But these families were at the heart of creating an academic profession that could match the achievements of their colleagues on the Continent and in America.

CHAPTER TWO

The Genesis of the Modern Don – William Buckland

At the beginning of the nineteenth century Oxford and Cambridge were Church of England communities in which most dons were clergymen. Oxford was regarded as a bastion of the Church at which every undergraduate had to sign on entry the Thirty-Nine Articles of faith and many expected to take holy orders on graduating. Why then were they studying Aristotle's logic instead of theology? Why, asked that liberal clergyman Sydney Smith, were tutors so afraid that 'mental exertion must end in religious scepticism'? A liberal don answered him. Edward Copleston was to become Provost of Oriel and the heart of liberal opinion within the university, a man known to be in favour of mental exertion. 'There is one province of education,' he wrote, 'indeed in which we are slow in believing that any discoveries can be made. The scheme of revelation we think is closed, and we expect no new light on earth to break in upon us.' The scheme of revelation was expounded from the pulpit. That was the point of sermons. For the first thirty years of the century all teaching, so the future tutor and Master of Balliol Jowett recollected, supported the doctrine of authority, and Oxford was another bulwark against the insidious ideas of the French Revolution. It was safer to train the mind on the writings of Greek and Latin authors. Modern studies encouraged speculation and political controversy, so the classics took priority. Science was not neglected. Posts were established and filled in chemistry, mineralogy and geology. When Thomas Gaisford became Dean of Christ Church, he insisted that all undergradu ates should attend a course on physics and be examined on it. The Regius professors of modern history lectured on political economy and a chair was created in that subject. Oriel under Copleston's influence set its own examination for fellowships, designed to test intelligence as well as syntactical exactness. Gaisford discouraged Christ Church men from entering for honours; and the future Lord Derby, who won prizes and later, while Prime Minister, translated the *Iliad*, left Christ Church without a degree.

None of these initiatives prospered. At the beginning of the century a former Dean of Christ Church, Cyril Jackson, had got the university to accept an honours system of examination in classics and mathematics. Undergraduates were classed according to merit. In 1808 Robert Peel was the first man to achieve a 'double first' in classics and maths; Gladstone followed him in 1831. The advocates of a broad education regarded the honours schools as irrelevant, but they were to be defeated. To get a first was the first step to winning your way in the world. In most colleges it was the passport to a fellowship. If it was not the dawn, it was the first light of meritocracy.

Most of the professors in science were impresarios for their subjects. They did not do experimental work; their task, they believed, was to tell their audience what had already been discovered. They supplemented the theology of the Church of England by providing new proofs of God's design – not as meticulous as those of Newton but still evidence that 'in all His works most wonderful, Most sure in all His ways', as Newman's hymn asserted. Nevertheless, there was one professor who lived in an apartment in Christ Church – which is at once a college and a cathedral – set aside for the canons, a clergyman unlike the orthodox run of canons. Christ Church was the citadel of the High and Dry party within the Church of England and this canon was a liberal latitudinarian. What was more he was a geologist. He had made his name with his research into the rocks of south-west England and his patron was no less than the Prince Regent himself, who created a special professorship for him in 1819. He was the first president of the newly formed British Association, which had been formed to publicise advances in science. This was William Buckland.

Buckland charged two guineas for attendance at his course of lectures and he drew rapt audiences. He lectured on mineralogy and palaeontology; but he was as competent to lecture on artesian wells and civil engineering. He did not despise applied science, and became chairman of the Oxford Gas and Coke Company. Buckland began lecturing in 1814, and between 1820 and 1835 his lectures were part of the Oxford scene – rather as the lectures by the controversial scholar, Edgar Wind, on the history of art became necessities for the general public in the second half of the twentieth century. But then – the common fate of many dons who are great lecturers – attendance began to drop. A rival in the shape of Newman preaching in the university church of Great St Mary's took his undergraduate audience away and in 1845 he left Oxford to become Dean of Westminster.

Buckland became a legend not so much for his scientific studies as for his remorseless application of the scientific practice of experiment and observation in his private life. He used to say that he had eaten his way through the whole animal creation and that the worst thing was a mole – 'perfectly horrible' – though afterwards he told Lady Lyndhurst that there was one thing worse than a mole and that was a blue-bottle fly. Mice in batter and bison steaks were served at his table in London. A guest wrote in his diary: 'Dined at the Deanery. Tripe for dinner last night, don't like crocodile for breakfast.' He had a Protestant's scepticism of Catholic miracles. Pausing before a dark stain on the flagstones of an Italian cathedral where the martyr's blood miraculously renewed itself, he dropped to his knees and licked it. 'I can tell you what it is: it is bat's urine.'

Like many scientists his mind subconsciously continued to work on the problems preoccupying him. 'My dear,' he said to his wife, starting up from sleep at two o'clock in the morning, 'I believe that Cheirotherium's footsteps are undoubtedly testudinal.' They hurried downstairs and while he fetched the pet tortoise from the garden, his wife mixed paste on the kitchen table. To their delight they saw that the impression left by the tortoise's feet in the paste were almost identical with those of the fossil.

Their apartments in the quad were at once a natural history museum and a menagerie. They and their children lived surrounded on all sides by specimens, dead and alive, that Buckland had collected. When you entered the hall you might as easily mount a stuffed hippopotamus as the children's rocking horse. Monsters of different eras glared down on you from the walls. The sideboard in the dining room groaned under the weight of fossils and was protected from the children by a notice: PAWS OFF. The very candlesticks were carved out of the bones of Saurians. Toads were immured in pots to see how long they could survive without food. There were cages full of snakes, and a pony with three children up would career round the dining room table and out into the quad. Guinea pigs, owls, jackdaws and smaller fry had the run of the house. The children imbibed science with their mother's milk. One day a clergyman excitedly brought Buckland some fossils for identification. 'What are these, Frankie?' said the professor to his four-year-old son. 'They are the vertebuae of an ichthyosauwus,' lisped the child. The parson retired crestfallen to his parish.

Buckland helped to establish the climate of opinion that made Darwin's theory of the origin of species within a few years irresistible. He also set a standard of integrity among British scientists. It is easy to forget today how much then the story of the earth's antiquity, the theory of evolution and the development of *homo sapiens* were founded on hypothesis and conjecture. Certainly the early geologists such as Buckland and Lyell based their theories on the facts of rock formation; certainly Darwin prevailed because no alternative explanation from the evidence that he produced was convincing. But the mass of evidence confirming and modifying their hypotheses accumulated after they wrote. It is important to remember, too, how many of the early hypotheses and theories were wrong. Buckland's story is of a man who published a book which changed his countrymen's notions of pre-history; who forced himself to acknowledge in public that the main conclusions in that book were wrong; and who failed despite his own personal success to get Oxford to introduce science into its curriculum.

The book that made Buckland's reputation in 1824 was called *Reliquiae Diluvianae* (*Relics of the Flood*). In it he linked the evidence of deposits in other caves in England and abroad with his own findings in the Kirkdale Cave in Yorkshire. This was the first fossil cave to be excavated in England. Buckland claimed that it had once been inhabited by hyenas who, it could be shown, had dragged the bodies of other animals into it, since their bones were characteristically splintered and lacked the parts which hyenas are in the habit of swallowing. These bones and teeth now lay on the floor of the cave beneath a thick layer of mud and were found all at the same level. Buckland therefore deduced that the hyenas had abandoned the cave at the onset of a great flood; and that this flood had also swept away the animals which lived about the cave and on whose carcasses the hyenas fed. It was at this stage in the argument that Buckland produced a further hypothesis. All the evidence showed that Yorkshire was once a sub-tropical land where elephants, bears and rhinoceros had roamed. All the evidence pointed to a flood. This, then, must have been the Flood described in Genesis, but it had occurred tens of thousands of years ago and not, as the seventeenth-century genealogists of the Old Testament had calculated, after 4004 BC.

When Buckland announced that it would be prudent to regard the six days of the Creation as six ages, many pious readers were in no mood to feel that the confirmation of the seventh chapter of Genesis compensated for the loss of the first. Nevertheless, there was no such outburst as greeted Darwin's great book. The evangelical movement in the churches was not so formidable then nor so well organised, and the leadership had not passed into the hands of unintelligent zealots. The Tractarians, who were to rouse Oxford and the country to new heights of religious intensity and intolerance, were still unknown young men: their campaign lay nearly ten years ahead in the future. Buckland's speculations were regarded as dangerous and daring but they were not repulsive to the Oxford of Copleston, which gave shelter to liberal theology. It was indeed this book that won him his canonry at Christ Church and his European reputation. In 1830 he was asked by the trustees of the Earl of Bridgewater's will to write under the terms of the will one of eight treatises to 'justify the ways of God to man'. Buckland spent six years on the task of explaining what geology and palaeontology told us of the earth's history and then of arguing that the Bible cannot be said to contradict these findings because it is not a scientific textbook. This elicited a flurry of pamphlets from the country parsons, one of whom spent pages deducing from the height of the Himalayas that the waters of the Flood must have risen at the rate of thirty feet per hour; and the Dean of York addressed several grave letters to Buckland. But as the Archbishop of York was a personal friend of Buckland and the two great periodicals, the *Quarterly* and the *Edinburgh*, came out on his side, he had little to fear.

Success and social eminence can easily corrupt scholars – particularly English scholars. Victorian savants found themselves petted by the influential and the great; insensibly they slid into becoming the academic defenders of the safe and the cautious; and then they found themselves expected to condemn the heretical. When *The Origin of Species* was published the geologist Adam Sedgwick, a famous contemporary of Buckland at Cambridge, used the full force of his authority to discredit it; and when the most eminent of all the English classical geologists, Sir Charles Lyell, after first hesitating announced his support, Darwin showed his appreciation of the danger that Lyell had run when he wrote, 'In view of his age and his position in society his conduct is heroic.' Buckland had in complete honesty put forward a hypothesis which enabled the story of Genesis in some sense to be reconciled with his geological discoveries. Suddenly he was challenged – and challenged by a young foreigner whom he had befriended. This young man was the Swiss naturalist Agassiz, who had corresponded with Buckland about his work and for whom Buckland had raised funds to enable him to continue his researches. Agassiz put forward the notion, commonplace nowadays, that the alluvial deposits in caves such as Buckland excavated were the relics not of the Flood but of an Ice Age. Buckland was not at first convinced. But he went to Switzerland to study glaciers with Agassiz; got him to England to go over the evidence in his caves; and then renounced his own theories, championed the hypothesis that the Swiss had put forward, and converted Lyell. The mud which had filled the hyenas' cave in Yorkshire had been brought by the melting snows on the hills, which could not disperse because the Scandinavian ice sheet was jammed up against the east coast of Britain.

This was the action of a man of character and generosity. It is also the work of a man of integrity. This kind of integrity is so much taken for granted today among scientists that is it difficult to imagine a time when it cost an effort. Perhaps it still costs an effort to the eminent when their juniors upset their conclusions, but they know well enough that it is quite hopeless to bluster. In the first half of the nineteenth century this was not so evident. Men still thought of truth as a unity. It was not Buckland's piety that made him leap to the conclusion that he had evidence of the Flood. He imagined himself simply drawing on another set of facts in the Bible which were well-attested and which fitted into the pattern of logical deductions that he had drawn from his findings in the Kirkdale Caves. It was all the more creditable then that, unlike other clergymen and members of the well-established academic circles to which he belonged, he did not fail to change his views even though they might have damaged his prospects.

In the 1830s his prospects at Oxford seemed to glow. Fluent, rapid, engaging, he would stalk up and down amid his audience brandishing a cave-bear jaw or a hyena thigh-bone. He held field days on which he demonstrated the different deposits in the countryside. His ebullience, his sharp voice, his hatred of the dishonest and the bogus, and his own learning established him as an authority. He was a popular diner-out; he would appear at a dinner party carrying his blue bag, from which he would draw fossils and bones and intrigue the company. Another don wrote him the following friendly letter:

> On our return last night I found as I thought that a spider had crawled out of the inkstand over a piece of paper; but it turns out to be a hieroglyphic from you which I so far interpreted as to perceive it was an invitation to meet some professor whose name as you wrote it looked somewhat indecent. I shall be happy to wait on you and take the opportunity of learning the Egyptian mode of writing

He had no rival in his field and might have been expected to have established a school of natural science at Oxford. Yet when he left Oxford in 1845 it was as if he had never existed.

One cause for Buckland's failure to make any impression on

the Oxford curriculum was the strength of the spirit which was embodied in the Dean of Christ Church himself. Dean Gaisford did not take kindly to the peregrinations through the college of the pets that lived in the Buckland household. He thanked God when the family departed for a holiday in Italy and prophesised, 'We shall hear no more of this geology.' Yet this was the same Gaisford who had compelled Christ Church undergraduates to study physics. He was a surly, grim, meticulous classical scholar born of an obscure family but who had married the daughter of the Bishop of Durham. Everyone quotes today a sentence which he dropped in one of his sermons to his undergraduates: 'Nor can I do better,' he concluded, 'than impress upon you the study of Greek literature, which not only elevates above the vulgar herd, but leads not infrequently to positions of considerable emolument.' He spoke from his own experience. When he was an undergraduate the then Dean of Christ Church detected his ability and told him: 'You will never be a gentleman, but you may succeed with certainty as a scholar. Take some little known Greek author and throw your knowledge into editing it: that will found your reputation.' Gaisford chose a work on Greek metres by the Alexandrian grammarian Hephaestion, and produced an edition of monumental erudition. *That* was the spirit which defeated Buckland.

In the 1830s Oxford and Cambridge were in much the same situation. Both had their naturalists and neither acknowledged the existence of science in their curricula. But whereas a century later Cambridge was famous in almost every field of science, and scientists governed its affairs as much as arts men, at Oxford science was fenced in by a shortage of college fellowships. Scientists – and especially technologists – were relegated to the backwaters of the university. However powerful the impression that Buckland made, he scarcely made a dent upon the serried ranks of classicists; and when in fact years later the curriculum broadened it was in the direction of language, law and history: few undergraduates took the science option. The studies at Oxford fit for a gentleman, fit for the ruling class, leading to 'positions of considerable emolument' were, if no longer confined to Greek literature, certainly not those that Buckland attempted to popularise. On his death his collection of rocks and fossils was swept away into an inadequate building.

In the short run, however, Gaisford was to be discomfited. For though Buckland left Oxford in due course his eldest son, Frank, came up to Christ Church as an undergraduate and for three years plagued the Dean. The principles of scientific experiment were embodied even more deeply in the son, and his father had trained him to be a keen observer. When he was eight years old a turtle had been sent to the college for the banquet which was to follow the Duke of Wellington's installation as Chancellor. His father gave it a swim in the fountain in Tom Quad, with Frank riding on its back; and the boy then watched it being decapitated in the college kitchen and noticed how the severed head bit the kitchen boy's finger. Frank was sent to school at Winchester, and there he followed his father's principles. He collected the heads of cats and rats as other boys collected birds' eggs. He taught himself to eat hedgehogs, fry mice in batter, dissect the eye of the Warden's mastiff and snare and skin the headmaster's exquisite cat. He dissected the cat's body night after night until the stench became overpowering . . . for the other boys. Dissection was his principal pastime and he was heard to remark meditatively, 'What wouldn't I give for that fellow's skull,' when a particularly dolichocephalic youth happened to saunter by.

At Oxford Frank Buckland was at last able fully to develop his hobbies. He was a large, genial, bohemian figure, often dressed in a German student's cap and a blue pea-jacket, and would make the quad resound to the notes of a gigantic Swiss wooden horn. True to family custom he lived surrounded by livestock. There were marmots, guinea pigs, snakes and a chameleon which perched on a wine glass, swallowing flies, until, to the delight of the spectators, it tumbled headlong into the preserved ginger. There was an eagle which walked into cathedral during the eight o'clock service: Dean Gaisford 'looked unspeakable things'. There was a jackal whose yells curdled the blood of nervous freshmen. Most notable of all was his young bear, named after a ferocious Old Testament king Tiglath-Pileser. Tig went to wine parties in cap and gown, watched the boats and lived a full social existence. At one party he met Monckton Milnes. Milnes was at that time known as a fashionable young versifier and man-about-town and happened to have been learning the elements of mesmerism from the well-known bluestocking Harriet Martineau. He decided to mesmerise Tig, who growled ferociously but fell in a stupor to the ground. Dean Gaisford, however, had the last word. He had already rusticated the eagle for its sacrilegious behaviour, and the jackal had also been sent down. 'Mr Buckland,' he said, 'I hear you keep a bear in college; well, either you or the bear must go.'

'My object in life, to be a high priest of nature, and a great benefactor of mankind,' Frank wrote in his diary at the age of twenty. He therefore became a doctor. But instead of turning to research after becoming qualified, as his contemporary, Darwin's great supporter T. H. Huxley did, he accepted a commission in the Life Guards as an assistant surgeon so as to be able to pursue his collection of freaks and animals. He was popular in the mess; though on one occasion he upset the solemnity of church parade when first the men and then the officers were overcome by gales of laughter on seeing Buckland, who was off-duty, stroll by on the far side of the parade ground deep in conversation with a dwarf and a seven-foot-five French giant whom he had been entertaining to breakfast. He later married and set up house near Regent's Park. Nothing could have been more cordial than the welcome the Bucklands gave to their guests, but they had to be people of strong nerves. Only one room in the house was in theory reserved for *homo sapiens*, and even this would be turned into a sanatorium for sick animals. 'Sing up, old boy,' your host would say to a piebald rat as one entered the room and, sure enough, 'melodious notes could be heard issuing from its diaphragm'. Pickled snakes would be produced for you from a tank, live ones from Frank's coat. At tea the hairy arm of the monkey would seize your muffin, while the guinea pigs nibbled your toes under the table. That incomparable memorialist, the High Church radical parson, William Tuckwell, said that 'You felt as if another Flood were toward and the animals parading for admission to the Ark.' The fellow-guests were equally unpredictable. Chinese, Zulus and Eskimos were all to be found at dinner. Delicate problems of etiquette presented themselves: should the bearded lady go down to dinner on the arm of Mr or Mrs Buckland? And which arm should you take of the four presented by the Siamese twins? After dinner you could be certain that Frank Buckland would keep the party going. He used to try the effect of chloroform on his animals and once Hag, his favourite monkey, discovered her ancient enemy the eagle almost senseless with anaesthetic: chattering with glee she proceeded to take her revenge, plucking its wings and clouting it over the head again and again. When the time came to take your leave there was no difficulty in obtaining a cab as the parrot was on duty at the front door to call a hansom. But if it was your fate to stay the night, the terrors of the small hours were scarcely endurable. A cold nose and prickles might invade your bed: it was only the hedgehog, which was let loose at night to keep down the black beetles but preferred to drink the soup in the tureen. Or you might wake in the morning to find that the jaguar had eaten your boots. Whether the servants came or left in droves is not recorded, but one supposes that only cooks of an iron constitution could remain at their post. Buckland's brother-in-law tells us that the windows slammed fast in the street and hearts sank at the house whenever a van arrived at the front door and the servants staggered up the steps bearing a cask containing a grinning gorilla or an imperfectly preserved hippopotamus, 'its lips curled in a ghastly smile'.

Needless to say Frank continued his father's gastronomic tradition. Kangaroo ham, rhinoceros pie, panther chops, horse's tongue and elephant's trunk were carved for his guests, who discovered that the best technique was to bolt a mouthful of meat and chase it with a beaker of champagne. Not all his dishes were a success. Chinese sea slugs were said to taste like calf's head and glue. But through the Acclimatisation Society and other clubs the craze spread. After the siege of Paris, when it was known how near starvation the defenders had been, rat dinners were given in London and Cambridge. At one time donkey featured on menus: one of Buckland's successors said that it was 'delicious . . . like Tyrolese venison'. But that formidable Victorian society hostess Lady Dorothy Nevill, who had a penchant for baked guinea pig, declared, 'I tried eating donkey too but I had to stop that for it made me stink.'

And yet there is something instructive and sad in this merry search for freaks and curios. Frank Buckland's career reminds one that the offspring of academic families are not by any means destined to follow their father's footsteps. The Annexe about the intellectual aristocracy (see page 304) records those who lived up to their parents' expectations, but it does not record the many who did not inherit their academic genes – or their firmness of character. Everything comes too easily to them. Frank never had to work at science, he absorbed it in childhood, he never had to work his way in the world. Winchester and Christ Church and his own good nature opened all doors; while his father kept hyenas as part of a scientific experiment, Frank assembled his menagerie for fun. He had become a typical example of the son who follows his father's calling but without the talent and inner compulsion to carve out a name for himself.

Then suddenly his life changed. For nine years he had been contributing numerous articles to the well-known periodical the *Field,* articles which formed the bulk of his book *Curiosities of Natural History.* The editors got bored and told him they had had enough. A few years previously he had failed to get the vacancy of full surgeon to the Life Guards: owing to a change in regulations, it went to the most senior man in the brigade. These two reverses made him take stock. He may also have appreciated how his father, after becoming Dean of Westminster and reaching the age when even the best scientists cease to produce their most original work, turned his mind to practical matters: the application of science to agriculture, sewage and water supply problems in London and Oxford – and the reforming of the antediluvian Westminster School. Frank Buckland got himself appointed an Inspector of Fisheries and at last began to play his role as a 'benefactor of mankind'. In the 1860s he was primarily concerned with hatching freshwater fish; in the seventies he was using all his charm and energy on a crusade up and down the country to stop river pollution, and by studying the habits of fish to learn how to make them multiply and to stop over-fishing. He was the first to predict for practical purposes the seasonal position of the shoals of fish in the North Sea. He began to study the balance of life within the sea and the effect of ocean temperature on migration. He saw to it that the inspectorate interested itself in the mesh of fishermen's nets so that fry fell back into the sea. He understood, as his predecessors had to, that to understand the life of sea fishes you must study their food and what affects its abundance. He therefore got the fishermen themselves to make observations and by a modest outlay in prizes filled log-books with their reports of fish culture in the North Sea. He fought the maltreatment of animals that often sprang from ignorance, once saving a swarm of elvers in Gloucestershire from massacre; on another occasion at the Royal Society for the Prevention of Cruelty to Animals 'made a speech about cruelty to seals. Much applauded. Deo gracias.'

In 1848 William Buckland and his wife had been injured when their coach overturned in France: Buckland was thrown out on his head and shortly afterwards he fell into a torpor for eight years, never reading a book but *The Leisure Hour* or the Bible. He directed that his body should be buried in limestone deposits and at his head should stand a slab of Aberdeen granite, one of the oldest of British rocks. The earth which had rendered so many of its secrets to him seemed reluctant to receive him in the biting frost and his grave had to be blasted by dynamite out of the ground. But his head is missing. His son had insisted on a post-mortem: the base of the brain lay in a pool of pus. Twenty-five years later, when the tubercular bacillus was discovered, the cause of death was attributed to tuberculous disease of the cervical vertebrae. Very properly in the interest of scientific medicine his skull was bequeathed to the Hunterian Museum of the Royal College of Surgeons.

CHAPTER THREE

The Charismatic Don – John Henry Newman

In the first decades of the nineteenth century there were among the Oxford colleges two centres of learning in particular: Christ Church and Oriel. Christ Church was wealthy, large and in Dean Cyril Jackson's time selected as many of its undergraduates as possible by merit. Oriel was far smaller, but Provost Eveleigh broke ranks by selecting its fellows not solely by patronage or performance in examination. He asked: did this man show intellectual sparkle? His successor, Copleston, carried on this tradition, and Oriel became known as a society of liberal intellectuals – Noetics, as they were called – who enjoyed dialectical dispute so much so that fellows of other colleges complained that the Oriel common room *stank* of logic. Thomas Arnold was one of this band until he left, later to become headmaster of Rugby. John Keble, the saintly churchman, whose hymns became part of Anglican worship, was another. The undergraduates, too, benefited from the good teaching of their tutors. When Copleston was Provost Oriel won twenty-seven first-class honours in examinations, though the far larger Christ Church won eighty-two.

Many college tutors taught the Latin and Greek texts in a perfunctory way, sometimes as baffled by their intricacies as their pupils. Some years later Leslie Stephen* at Cambridge

---

* Sir Leslie Stephen (1832–1904), fellow of Trinity Hall (1854–64), mountaineer, rowing coach, literary critic and first editor of *The Dictionary of National Biography*.

gave a satirical account of a tutor, more renowned as the coach of his college boat than as a scholar, construing a Latin text with his class: 'Easy all. Hard word here. What does it mean? Don't know? No more don't I. Paddle on all.' But the Oriel tutors were different. Among them was a rough-tongued, ill-dressed, unconventional logician, Richard Whately, who took his pupils for early morning walks and regarded them as an anvil on which to hammer out his ideas. When a shy young man from Trinity was elected a fellow of Oriel, so tongue-tied that he could not bring himself to speak to his hero Keble and the others, Copleston told Whately to take him under his wing and draw him out. He did so to such effect that four years later, in 1826, John Henry Newman was appointed a tutor at Oriel and considered to be a fine addition to the college's liberal tradition. But he was not. He spent his days discussing theology, patristics and doctrine with a group of newly elected fellows: Edward Pusey, Robert Wilberforce and above all with Hurrell Froude, a militant High Churchman. It was Froude who sowed in Newman's mind the seeds of a hatred of Protestantism. The Oxford Movement was forming and it was to change the face of Oxford.

The first sign of this moral intensity soon appeared. In the Oriel tradition a tutor should help his men to construe Greek and Latin texts: it was up to them to make something of what they read, not for him to tell them what they should believe. But this was what Newman thought it was his duty to do. More than that, he held himself responsible for his students' conduct. He was unique in treating them as friends, and those who responded hung on his every word. On the other hand the well-born fellow commoners who took the sacrament at Holy Communion and chased it with a champagne breakfast were anathema to Newman. He and his fellow tutors reduced the numbers of these aristocratic sprigs by half, and turned away stupid candidates. They next proposed that undergraduates should be divided into the clever and diligent and the thick and idle. Each group would follow a course of lectures appropriate to their talents. At this point the new Provost, Edward Hawkins, took fright. Were all men of good family to be turned away? Was it not the duty of tutors to give as much attention to less able students as to the high-fliers? Hawkins was disturbed to hear that Newman proselytised his pupils, and Copleston supported Hawkins. Oriel had always set its face against cramming for exams. The dispute rumbled on until Hawkins refused to allot any pupils to Newman or to Froude and Wilberforce. They resigned. Hawkins appointed safe men in their place – and the decline of Oriel as an intellectual power house began. Little did Hawkins realise that his own election as Provost had given Newman a position far more influential than a tutorship. For on his election he resigned as vicar of St Mary's in the High Street, where the university sermon was preached each Sunday – a living in the gift of Oriel – and Newman was appointed in his place.

No don has ever captivated Oxford as John Henry Newman did. For ten years or more every pronouncement he made, every direction towards which he seemed to be veering was scrutinised, interpreted and criticised and those luminous eyes scanned to see if they expressed praise or censure. What was it on this day to make him petulant and on that honey-tongued and caressing?

> Who could resist the charm [asked Matthew Arnold] of that spiritual apparition gliding in the dim afternoon light through the aisles of St Mary's, rising into the pulpit, and then in the most entrancing of voices, breaking the silence with words and thoughts – subtle, sweet, mournful? I seem to hear him still saying: 'After the fever of life, after wearinesses and sicknesses, fightings and despondings, languor and fretfulness, struggling and succeeding; after all the changes and chances of this

troubled, unhealthy state – at length comes death, at length the
white throne of God, at length the beatific vision.'

There were other famous preachers in his time. At Cambridge
Charles Simeon in Holy Trinity commanded a congregation as
large as that of Newman and for longer. But Simeon was a
moderate Evangelical and not in any sense an intellectual. Newman appealed to intellectuals and scholars as well as to devout
religious enthusiasts. They were never sure what new interpretation would be put on the Scriptures, what doctrine would be
reinterpreted to bring it into line with whatever position Newman in his spiritual pilgrimage had reached. When his readings
of the Fathers revealed schisms and heresies in the early Church,
Newman asked himself whether these depravities were not being
repeated today in the Church of England. He spoke seemingly
to every individual in his congregation because he reminded
him he was a sinner. At the heart of his sermons, as much when
he went over to Rome as before, was the overpowering sense
of sin – and of its consequences. For Newman hell was a reality.
The fear of the Lord, said the Psalmist, is the beginning of
wisdom, and he strove to inculcate holy dread among his
listeners. His voice was quiet and musical, with a 'silver inton-
ation', as one contemporary put it. The pauses, the charm, the
change of tone, all the arts of rhetoric were at his command.
Long though it is, the passage below, imagining the horror of
a soul that finds itself condemned to eternal punishment –
taken from a sermon he preached when a Roman Catholic –
illustrates his power.

> 'Impossible,' he cries, 'I a lost soul. I separated from hope and
> from peace for ever. It is not I of whom the Judge so spake!
> There is a mistake somewhere; Christ, Saviour, hold thy hand –
> one minute to explain it. My name is Demos: I am but Demos,
> not Judas, or Nicolas, or Alexander, or Philetus, or Diotrephes.

What? hopeless pain! for me! Impossible, it shall not be.' And the poor soul struggles and wrestles in the grasp of the mighty demon which has hold of it, and whose very touch is torment. 'Oh, atrocious,' it shrieks in agony, and in anger, too, as if the very keenness of the affliction were a proof of its injustice. 'A second! and a third! I can bear no more! stop, horrible fiend, give over; I am a man and not such as thou! I am not food for thee, or sport for thee! I never was in hell as thou, I have not on me the smell or taint of the charnel-house. I know what human feelings are; I have been taught religion; I have had a conscience; I have a cultivated mind; I am well versed in science and art; I have been refined by literature; I have had an eye for the beauties of nature; I am a philosopher or a poet, or a shrewd observer of men, or a hero, or a statesman or an orator, or a man of wit and humour. Nay – I am a Catholic; I am not an unregenerate Protestant; I have received the grace of the Redeemer; I have attended the Sacraments for years; I have been a Catholic from a child; I am a son of the Martyrs; I died in communion with the Church; nothing, nothing which I have ever seen, bears any resemblance to thee, and to the fame and stench which exhale from thee; so I defy thee and abjure thee, O enemy of man!'

Alas! poor soul, and whilst it there fights with that destiny which it has brought upon itself, and with those companions whom it has chosen, the man's name, perhaps, is solemnly chanted forth, and his memory decently cherished among his friends on earth. His readiness in speech, his fertility in thought, his sagacity, or his wisdom are not forgotten. Men talk of him from time to time, they appeal to his authority, they quote his words; perhaps they even raise a monument to his name, or write his history. 'So comprehensive a mind! Such a power of throwing light on a perplexed subject, and bringing conflicting ideas or facts into harmony!' 'Such a speech it was he made on such and such an occasion; I happened to be present, and never shall forget it,' or 'It was the saying of a very sensible man' or 'A great personage, whom some of us knew' or 'It was a rule of mine, now no more' or 'Never was his equal in society, so just in his remarks, so versatile, so unobtrusive', or 'I was fortunate to see him once when I was a boy' or 'So great a benefactor to his country and his kind!' 'His discoveries so great' or, 'His philosophy so profound'. O vanity! vanity of vanities, all is vanity. What profiteth it? His soul is in hell . . . Vanity of vanities, misery of miseries! They will not attend to us, they will not believe us. We are but few in number and they are many, and the many will not give credit to the few . . . Thousands are dying daily; they are waking up into God's everlasting wrath.

That passage, so profuse in examples, so exquisite in variations of pace, so dramatic in the change of tone from the condemned's protestations to the pitying dispassionate observer who retails how worldly judgements of a man's worth are trivial and absurd when set against eternal judgement, plays upon the mind. And then comes the end, so bitter and characteristic of Newman's self-pity and anger that he and his minority of believers are scorned by the great and the good and by the multitude who, regardless of his warning, are, perhaps, destined themselves to eternal torment.

Newman came by his sense of sin honestly. He was brought up an Evangelical, and the Evangelical party in the Church more than any other explained how that terrible sense of sin can be assuaged and the sinner find comfort provided that he throws himself on Christ's mercy, repents and finds grace in his new-found faith. The drama of Newman's spiritual pilgrimage from Evangelicalism to the Church of Rome is all the more ironic since his first break with the culture of the Oriel Noetics came over the issue of Catholic Emancipation. He opposed it.

For centuries Roman Catholics had been subject to disabilities. They were not permitted, for instance, to sit in Parliament. In the seventeenth century they were regarded as a fifth column in the service of England's enemies, Spain and France. James II, a Catholic king, had been deposed. Nor had opinion changed after the Napoleonic Wars. England remained solidly Protestant. But Ireland was another matter. For years Roman Catholic Ireland had been regarded as England's Achilles' heel – a country in which the French might consider they could successfully land and strangle British trade. Yet here was a country whose population was largely Roman Catholic, who were compelled to finance the established Protestant Church of Ireland and whose political leaders were debarred from sitting in Parliament. Agitation to repeal the anti-Catholic laws met obdurate resistance, not least from the King. What changed the minds of the Tory ministers was the state of public opinion in Ireland, which by 1829 seemed likely to burst into open rebellion. The Duke of Wellington and Robert Peel, who had both opposed Catholic Emancipation, now caved in; and they forced George IV, slobbering in tears, to give his assent.

Peel was the member of Parliament for Oxford University and, in view of his U-turn, scrupulously resigned his seat and stood for re-election. He was defeated, had to find another constituency, was denounced as a traitor and apostate. His defeat as the university's burgess was brought about by a coalition of outraged Evangelicals and the old High and Dry party of the Established Church, composed of heads of houses and clergy united by the slogan of 'No Popery'. Prominent in this coalition was Newman. He even carried the majority of the younger fellows of Oriel with him, leaving the Provost, Hawkins, isolated and his old mentor Whately fuming. Whately realised that Newman had broken with the liberal party for ever and with delicate malice saw to it that at a dinner he was placed between the most obtuse, port-swilling High Churchman and the most violent Evangelical: he asked him how he liked his new allies.

Meanwhile the government had been trying to lighten the burden of Church rates and taxes upon the Irish peasantry. How could this, in part, be financed? The Established Church of Ireland was sustained by four archbishops and eighteen bishops, somewhat excessive for the number of Irish Protestants. Why not therefore suppress ten bishoprics? It was Whately who had taught Newman to deplore Erastianism – the acceptance that the Church was a dependency of the State, a ministry of morals, whose bishops were appointed under Crown patronage by the Prime Minister. Even more questionable was the Prime Minister's practice of choosing clergymen who would vote for his party in the House of Lords. By singular irony Whately had become Archbishop of Dublin and the opportunity was too good to miss. Newman wrote a devastating snub to his old teacher.

At this time Newman's stock was high among the Oxford dons. Like the vast majority of the bishops he opposed the introduction of the Reform Bill, which was finally passed in 1832. The Whig reforms generated a new wave of opposition. The reforms in Ireland beggared the Protestant parish clergymen, and did not do all that much for the Roman Catholic peasantry. Nor, in the opinion of Oxford, were the reforms to lighten the burden of Church rates and other disabilities on the Dissenters any better. Yet it was at this moment that another attempt was made to enable Dissenters – Methodists, Baptists, Congregationalists, Quakers and the like – to enter Oxford and Cambridge. If Roman Catholics and Dissenters could now sit in Parliament, why should they not be permitted to become students at Oxford and Cambridge? This was the view which Provost Hawkins and other fellows of Oriel held. Among them was Renn Dickson Hampden. He had been appointed professor of moral philosophy when Newman himself had hopes of being elected, and had written a pamphlet supporting the proposal to relax the rule requiring undergraduates to subscribe to the

Thirty-Nine Articles. Pamphlets flew about. Once again Newman triumphed when the proposal was voted down.

Worse was to follow. In 1836 the Regius professor of divinity
died and the Whigs were still in power in London. Melbourne
naturally consulted the Archbishop of Canterbury but he sent
the Archbishop's list of eight names to Whately and Copleston
for comment. They advised him to reject all eight names and
appoint the new professor of moral philosophy, Hampden. Newman and the young professor of Hebrew, Edward Pusey, petitioned the Hebdomadal Council (composed of the heads of
the colleges) to appoint a committee to examine Hampden's
writings – in particular the Bampton Lectures he had delivered
a few years previously. Were they or were they not heretical?
The committee found Hampden guilty of rationalism. Amid
growing excitement, with one set of proctors vetoing a vote,
and their successors permitting it, various indignities and pro-
hibitions were heaped on Hampden. The virulence of the language used infected the undergraduates, who at one point
stormed the Sheldonian Theatre denouncing Hampden.

Newman had now become a different kind of don. He had
become a university politician. But he remained a puzzle,
because he was not playing politics along the recognised party
lines. Not for him the reform of the curriculum or the structure
of university committees. His concern was the orientation of the
Church of England; and since nearly all dons were clergymen in
holy orders, what he said concerned them. By now he had
turned against science and political economy as subjects fit for
Oxford. He deplored the decision to hold the British Association meeting in the university. The aim of Oxford should be
to guide and purify the Church. Using all his gifts of charisma
and rhetoric Newman provoked an era of controversy, bitterness
and intolerance which hung like a cloud over Oxford for the
next thirty years. Religion – doctrine, theology, the interpretation of the Bible, the liturgy, fasting, celibacy, the sacraments

– became topics of unbridled dispute. Newman had come to regard Evangelicalism as a faith that fostered spiritual pride, a faith that was vulgar and hostile to the intellect, too liable to foster sects that broke away from the Anglican Church, too sympathetic towards those enemies of the Church, the Dissenters, and above all too self-confident that all that a soul needed to be saved was to experience conversion. Evangelicals regarded the Church of England as less important than the Invisible Church to which the elect of all sects belonged. But Newman argued that a good Christian should not consider that one single experience – his conversion – absolved him. Newman preached holiness, not conversion. Holiness was a state of mind in which day by day you sought to live a better life, a more disciplined life, under the Church's guidance. Evangelicals were content to convert individuals but Newman wanted to convert the nation.

To Newman the independence of the Church was more important than anything else in the world. The Church – did not the Apostles' Creed say so? – was a Catholic church, a reformed, not a Protestant church: Roman abuses had been reformed, but not the Church itself. No government, no sovereign, no Parliament, could reform God's Church, and Erastianism – the Prime Minister exercising ecclesiastical patronage – was as evil as Protestantism. To disestablish bishoprics in Ireland was sacrilege: whether the Irish were or were not Anglicans was irrelevant. The word of God required authoritative interpretation and priests alone could interpret it because they were directly descended from the Apostles by the laying-on of hands at ordination. The Church interprets the Bible and the rubrics of the Prayer Book and looks to the Early Fathers for guidance. The old High and Dry party, centred on Christ Church, supported the Established Church. But for Newman the Church was not established by the State. It was sanctified because the Church was a holy body descended from the twelve Apostles.

These were the tenets of the Oxford Movement and Newman was its leader. Among his allies was his senior, John Keble, who preached a sermon on National Apostasy denouncing the proposal to suppress the Irish bishoprics. More influential was the young Edward Bouverie Pusey, appointed in his twenties to the Regius professorship of Hebrew by Wellington on the advice of the Dean of Christ Church. (The Duke's supporters were mightily offended: the Bouverie family had made bitter speeches against the government; but the Duke replied against the grain of the times: 'How could I help it when they told me he was the best man?') Pusey's prestige as a scholar, an Eton and Christ Church man, his aristocratic connections, gave weight to the cause. Young disciples, such as Robert Wilberforce (son of the great Evangelical opponent of the slave trade), Frederick Faber, Henry Manning, joined Newman; but one man in particular captivated Newman. That was Hurrell Froude.

Froude was a handsome, dashing young man of a well-born Devon family and Newman fell in love with him. There are always some dons who like to shock and Froude was one of them. He was a fanatic. Coming from a High Church family, he hated Protestantism, detested the Reformation and ridiculed the Thirty-Nine Articles. So did Newman's brother-in-law Tom Mozley, who declared that the Catechism was like a millstone round the neck of the Church. The Puseyites, as they began to be called, spread their teaching through pamphlets they called 'Tracts for the Times' – tracts which later became learned treatises. Many of the tracts were designed to show how many medieval practices, long since abandoned, should be revived. The first tract Pusey wrote was on the spiritual benefits of fasting.

In 1836 Froude died of tuberculosis and Newman wrote a preface to his *Remains*, in great part a transcription of his diaries. No young man who is earnest and has a mission in life should allow his diaries to be published. Froude's descriptions of his ascetic practices, and his self-examination of his deeds, his thoughts, his motives, revealed him to be a prig; but far more damaging were his praise of clerical celibacy, his devotion to the Virgin Mary, his contempt for the heroes of the English Reformation – Froude once said that the best thing about Cranmer was that he burned well. Before the year (1838) was out, the irrepressible champion of Protestantism, Charles 'Golly' Golightly, got up a subscription to raise a memorial in Oxford to the Protestant Martyrs, and impaled Newman and Pusey upon a dilemma: to contribute or not to contribute? They havered; and then withdrew. From then on they were suspect.

Dons are apt to give way to a temptation that afflicts many of us. They cannot resist ridiculing their opponents. Newman pulverised his. When a professor preached against Froude, and went on to doubt whether Newman and Keble were sound men, Newman sat up all night fashioning a reply that twitted the professor from pillar to post. He was to do the same years later when, in the first chapter of his *Apologia*, he turned Charles Kingsley into a figure of fun. But dons who possess the gift of writing devastating reviews of other scholars are often sullen and prickly when they themselves are attacked. Newman wrote indignant letters to his adversaries and to old friends.

The habit of rebuking those whom he considered were betraying the Church grew on him. What others called intolerance he called adherence to principles. He was jeered when he refused to conduct the marriage of a parishioner called Jubber because she was the daughter of a Baptist pastry-cook and had not been baptised according to the rites of the Church of England. Arnold, by now headmaster of Rugby, was a special target for his jokes – Arnold had once published an ill-judged book on reform of the Church so that Dissenters (but not Quakers, Unitarians or Roman Catholics) might be deemed to be in communion with Anglicans. Newman was reported as saying – his throwaway lines were quoted everywhere – 'But is Arnold a

Christian?' He had not in fact quite said that. Someone had said of a German theologian who the Tractarians suspected was unorthodox, 'Arnold said he was a Christian': to which Newman replied with a laugh, 'Arnold must first show that he is a Christian himself.' After Newman's campaign against Hampden an article came from the School house at Rugby. It was titled 'The Oxford Malignants', and it stigmatised Newman and his followers as persecutors.

By 1839 Newman had lost the support of the old High and Dry party. In 1841 he scandalised Oxford beyond hope of redemption. That was the year when he published Tract 90, just before his fortieth birthday. In it he declared that the Thirty-Nine Articles in the Prayer Book, though they were conceived in an uncatholic age, could be 'subscribed by those who aim at being Catholic in heart and doctrine'. Newman still believed that the Church of Rome was wrong in practice. But in dogma? Even though some of the articles expressly condemned Roman beliefs, Newman argued that a way could be found to reconcile the two churches. Indeed the articles required re-casting. 'Let the church sit still,' he wrote, 'let her be content to be in bondage . . . let her go on teaching with the stammering lips of ambiguous formularies.' The time would come, so Newman's reader inferred, when the Church would be reunited with Rome.

Tract 90 confirmed what High Churchmen as well as Evangelicals had feared. It convinced them that Newman was a popish agent infiltrating the Church of England to bring it over to Rome. All but two of the heads of houses condemned it, bishop after bishop penned charges denouncing it. The row was not a theological dispute alone. It penetrated to the heart of academic life. The Provost of Oriel refused to write testimonials for those candidates for ordination known to admire Newman and Pusey. The new brand of High Churchmen had little hope of being elected to fellowships. Colleges changed the hour of hall dinner on Sunday to prevent their undergraduates from attending St Mary's, where Newman preached. Tittle-tattle about the latest Tractarian perversions replaced urbane conversation. A lady in an omnibus turned to the clergyman next to her and asked him whether he realised that each Friday Dr Pusey sacrificed a lamb. 'My dear Madam, I am Dr Pusey, and I assure you I do not know how to kill a lamb.' Tell-tale informers flitted about the streets insinuating, intriguing and whispering that so and so was unsound, another a known Romaniser, a third had been seen going to Littlemore, where Newman was conducting a retreat in which each day was governed by monastic discipline from Matins and Laud to Vespers and Compline. Newman had become the most notorious don in Oxford.

In 1842, the year after Tract 90 was published, Newman in effect retired as a don. He moved to Littlemore, a village outside Oxford, to lead a life governed by monastic rules and even penances such as hair-shirts and whips. The country, as well as Oxford, waited for him to convert to Rome. They waited for three years. Then at last he took the fatal step.

When Newman went over to Rome, the effect was cataclysmic. Dozens followed him – to the grief and fury of their families. He left behind him far more who felt betrayed. They believed he had found in Anglicanism the *via media* between vulgar Protestantism and Roman idolatry. For him, too, it was tragic: Keble and old Dr Routh, the President of Magdalen, did not shun him, but many of his closest friends broke with him for ever. Of his own family all were estranged except for one sister.

Yet Newman had one further contribution to make as a don. Some years later as a Roman Catholic priest he was appointed President of the new Catholic university in Dublin. Was that university to be a denominational university for Roman Catholics as one bishop wanted? Or was it to be, as another wanted, solely for Irishmen and a spearhead against the English ascendancy? Newman wanted neither. He soon resigned but the experience inspired him to write his academic utopia, *The Idea of a University.*

'For all the complicating effect of its religious setting,' wrote Anthony Quinton,* 'there is still no more eloquent and finely judged defence of intellectual culture than Newman's.' Pater thought it perfection in its own sphere, just as *Lycidas* was the perfect poem. G. M. Young considered that all other books on education could be pulped so long as we were left with Aristotle's *Ethics* and Newman's *Idea.*†

The university, Newman argued, was a temple for teaching universal knowledge. Students should study the sciences that advance knowledge and the arts and professions relevant to everyday life. But not vocational subjects; nor subjects that lack general ideas – antiquarianism is not history. The university did not exist to *create* knowledge. Its purpose was to disseminate 'the best that is known and thought in the world', to use his admirer Matthew Arnold's words. Of course, the teachers should 'study', but the notion of systematic research did not swim into Newman's ken. Originality, discovery, students dedicated to a single branch of learning, were contrary to his idea of a university. He accepted that some scholars want to devote themselves exclusively to study: let them do so – but in an institute. Nor did he sanction students studying whatever took their fancy – what the Germans called *Lernfreiheit.*

Students will graduate cack-handed unless they are taught how to relate their own specialism to every other and what the meaning is of the totality. That is why everyone must study philosophy. Philosophy will teach them the difference between scholarship and 'viewiness', i.e. journalism or the kind of edu-

---

* Anthony, Lord Quinton, life peer 1982, fellow of All Souls (1949–55), New College (1955–78), President of Trinity College, Oxford (1978–87); philosopher.
† G. M. Young (1882–1959) fellow of All Souls, civil servant in the Board of Education, scholar of the Victorian era and author of *Portrait of an Age* (1936).

cation – so Newman and most Oxford dons considered – the University of London offered.

Learning is not the sole function of a university. It is also a milieu, a place where a spell is cast over the student that binds him to it for the rest of his life. The college inside the university was the sorcerer that cast the spell. Without the spirit of a college, run by tutors who regarded their office as a calling and not another step in the journey to rich livings or benefices in the Church, a university becomes a mere examining machine. A university is nothing unless it is a place where a student lives, eats and converses with other students, learns to socialise, to understand human beings other than himself. If you specialise and grind away at a subject you may become egotistical, self-centred, uncivilised. The true university taught a man to be a gentleman, one 'who never inflicts pain . . . avoids whatever may cause a jar or a jolt in the minds of those with whom he is cast . . . guards against unseasonable allusions or topics which may irritate. If he be an unbeliever, he will be too profound and large-minded to ridicule religion . . .' A university is an assemblage of learned men [who] 'adjust together the claims and relations of their respective subjects of investigation. They learn to respect, to consult and to aid each other.'

The satirical will observe that this was hardly a description of the role Newman had played in Oxford; what is more Newman did not hesitate to call the habit of mind that he was advocating 'liberal' (a word which in his Oxford days was synonymous with sin). It was a habit that inculcates 'freedom, equitableness, calmness, moderation and wisdom'. It will not be acquired unless the student first learns the idea of rule and exception, and the scientific method of assessing evidence. Nor will he acquire it merely by reading books. The cultivation of the intellect is a goal in itself. Newman had no fear in accepting science as a fit study, whereas Michael Oakeshott's utopia of a university (published in 1949) dismissed science as a subject that had scarcely been able to detach itself from vocational training. But then came the all-important qualification. Knowledge has to be guided and purified by religion.

The American scholar Sheldon Rothblatt* unravelled the subtlety of the qualification. The scholar or scientist, wrote Newman, should be 'free, independent, unshackled in his movements', untroubled by any threat that he was going too far or causing a scandal. But then no one surely could argue that a scientist would be shackled if he accepted that he would not use his science to contradict the dogmas of faith. Nor would such a scientist be unaware that among his students were those with immature minds; and he would naturally avoid scandal at all costs. The cultivation of the intellect is not enough. Without religion it is but a sounding brass or a tinkling cymbal. The filthiest Catholic beggar woman, if she be chaste and receives the sacraments, has a better chance of reaching heaven than the most upright gentleman if all he has to exhibit at St Peter's gate are his virtues. Knowledge has to be guided by religion. Did not this qualification torpedo the lovely vessel he had built?

Newman loved to needle. 'It would be a gain,' he once said, 'to the country were it vastly more superstitious.' G. M. Young noted that Newman's mind was forged and tempered in the schools of Oxford where Aristotle's logic was practised: a mind 'always skimming along the verge of a logical catastrophe and always relying on his dialectical agility to save himself from falling: always exposing what seems to be an unguarded spot, and always revealing a new line of defence when the unwary assailant has reached it'. Kingsley was the unwary assailant and his denunciation of Newman provoked Newman's *Apologia*, a masterpiece of spiritual autobiography. Yet, Young adds,

---

* Sheldon Rothblatt, professor of history at the University of California, Berkeley since 1963 and some time Director of the Center for Studies in Higher Education.

If the public, or the modern reader, said 'Never mind all that:
what we want to know is, when Dr Newman or one of his pupils
tells us a thing, can we believe it as we should believe it if the
old-fashioned parson said it?' I am afraid that the upshot of the
Apologia and its appendices is No. What is one to make of a man,
especially of a preacher, whose every sentence must be put under
a logical microscope if its full sense is to be revealed?

Today it is no longer possible to define a university in terms
of a single idea. British universities differ vastly. Some still pursue
original enquiry and, unlike Newman's utopia, engage in fundamental research. Others contain departments for specialist learning and act as a service centre for vocational, professional and
technological demands made on them by government. Whether
it was wise to call them all universities is another matter. Nevertheless Newman's ideal was not all that far from the distinguished
liberal arts colleges in America, and some new universities in
Britain tried to set up separate colleges within the campus. For
many years Newman's *Idea* was cited as the justification of the
Oxford and Cambridge colleges and of the special status of
Oxbridge as distinct from other universities. To this day Oxford
and Cambridge colleges scarcely doubt that, from whatever class
their students come, they exist to educate Newman's elite.

'*Credo in Newmanum*' was not an idle joke. His magnetism
lasted long after he disappeared from Oxford. He haunted
those who knew him in their dreams. His disciple W. G. Ward,
who in turn had to resign from his lectureships at Balliol and
then was degraded to the status of undergraduate for publishing
The Ideal of a Christian Church, dreamt that he was talking to a
veiled lady and telling her that her voice fascinated him as
Newman's once had done. 'I am John Henry Newman,' she
said, throwing back her veil. Another dreamt he was travelling
in a first-class carriage and talking to an elderly clergyman whom
he suddenly recognised as Newman and who said to him in a

tone of surpassing sweetness, 'Will you not come and join me in my third-class carriage?'

Newman's charisma was unmatched. As knowledge became more specialised and Oxford and Cambridge grew larger, no don could hope to appeal to the whole university as Newman was able to do. Some thought Ruskin might do so; and T. H. Green, who appeared as Mr Gray in Mrs Humphry Ward's novel *Robert Elsmere*, intrigued so many students that Jowett feared he was indoctrinating them. But neither of them rivalled Newman. Although brilliant lecturers over the years bewitched their audience few could expect many students from faculties other than their own to attend. Scientists often regarded the head of the lab, 'the prof', with awe and affection; but no mass audience of undergraduates hung on the utterances of Rutherford or Florey. To see charisma at work in the twentieth century you had to go to a smaller institution such as the London School of Economics. There Laski* exerted a pervasive influence among generations of students, particularly those from India; though perhaps the truer charismatic figure was R. H. Tawney, the famous socialist historian, recognised by colleagues and students alike as something of a saint. Tawney held out hopes of a better world to come, and he possessed a quality that impressed all who met him: purity of heart. The Cambridge philosopher G. E. Moore possessed this quality and so, in a fierce, uncompromising way, did Wittgenstein. But though everyone knows of Moore's influence on Bloomsbury, the numbers these Cambridge philosophers spoke to, immured as they were in a tiny faculty that spoke to none other, were sparse. At Oxford it was different. Philosophy was integral to Greats (the second part of the degree in classics) and in Modern Greats (the degree in philosophy, politics and economics). In the mid-

---

* Harold Laski (1893–1950), professor and teacher on politics at LSE for thirty years; prominent Fabian Society member and publicist for socialism.

century Ryle, Ayer and Austin, the Robespierre of linguistic philosophy, held audiences agog. But no one thought of comparing any of them to Newman.

Perhaps the don in recent years who reminds one of Newman was F. R. Leavis in Cambridge. Leavis used some of Newman's tactics to create a following. Like Newman he was proud to be both persecutor and persecuted. He accused his colleagues in the faculty of English of betraying the true principles of literary criticism, insinuated they were dullards or featherweights, and was aggrieved when those who were in fact excellent critics, but were not crusaders, were promoted and he was not. He was more successful than Newman in persuading a wider public that he had been ill-treated and embodied the true ethos of Cambridge. Each number of *Scrutiny* which he edited was a 'Tract for the Times'. That he was an outstanding literary critic was beyond question. What is more he declared that criticism, not philosophy (let alone theology), was to be queen of the sciences. Leavis claimed to reveal not just the meaning of literature but the meaning of life. He told the young which values to praise and which to denounce and who, present as well as past, was to be despised.

That was why his disciples were as ardent as Newman's. They admired his austerity and his unremitting seriousness. They were fortified when he toppled poets and novelists of long-established reputations – why waste time on them, he declared, when those whose vision of life was supremely important beckoned? Writing about Newman, Owen Chadwick* judged that the Oxford students flocked to hear him because he was a revolutionary. They admired him precisely because he enraged the heads of houses, the proctors, the tutors and other symbols of authority in the university. Leavis, too, made himself

* Owen Chadwick, OM, Regius professor of modern history (1968–83), Master of Selwyn College (1956–83).

an outcast, embattled, friendly and helpful to those who accepted him and sat at his feet and correspondingly hostile to those who did not accept that there is in the end only one way to live and only a handful of great poets and novelists who teach one how to do so.

To regard Newman solely as a don would do him monstrous injustice. Newman changed the face of the Church of England. The Oxford Movement brought back the mystery of the sacraments, and the beauty of worship. He understood the romance of Oxford, the dignity of its buildings, its gardens and the flowers in them, whose *genius loci* cast a spell of lasting loyalty over its alumni. The university ceased to be merely a corporate body with endowments and privileges. It became, as Sheldon Rothblatt puts it, 'a thrilling emotion-laden higher order conception of higher education', and the colleges centres of aristocratic culture linked to certain schools, grammar as well as public schools, which fed them with pupils. Newman did not go quite as far as Pusey, who asserted that it was no part of a university to advance science, or make discoveries 'or produce works in Medicine, Jurisprudence or even Theology': though he agreed with Pusey that a university existed to 'form minds religiously, morally, intellectually, which shall discharge aright whatever duties God, in his Providence, shall appoint to them'. Newman considered the university's role was to *teach* universal knowledge. Let the scientists and their laboratories go elsewhere. That is why, Rothblatt noted, Victorian researchers were more famed for the learned societies, the botanical gardens, the museums, libraries and other specialised institutions they created, than for the publications by which their German confrères made their reputation.

Newman breathed a new spirit into a university that had become complacent and becalmed. But 'the voice that breathed o'er Eden' was not the gentle Keble's voice. It was the voice of a doctrinaire – indubitable, incontestable; and the reverberations were disagreeable. Accusations of heterodoxy flew about and the atmosphere of the university became sour and embittered. The tempest-tossed seas that charismatic dons leave behind them take some time to subside, and Newman's career was to trouble the man who, more than any other, gave meaning to the word don: Benjamin Jowett, tutor and Master of Balliol College.

CHAPTER FOUR

Benjamin Jowett and the Balliol Tradition

For a century and a half Balliol has been one of the most splendid colleges at Oxford or Cambridge. It sent a host of distinguished graduates into all walks of life; its successes in the schools were proverbial; its junior common room provided a scene of animated intellectual life which few other undergraduate societies could rival. It was a society with a history of academic distinction and the nursery of statesmen, pro-consuls, scholars, lawyers and men of letters. When Harrovians sang, 'the Balliol comes to us now and then', they acknowledged that a Balliol scholarship was prized higher by headmasters than that of any other college – because the winner would have had to have faced the stiffest competition. How did this come about? The answer is that it was the work of Benjamin Jowett.

No famous institution owes its quality merely to one man. The foundations of Balliol's success were laid by two former masters, Parsons and Jenkyns. Their reforms made possible the election of fellows on their merits: Jowett was elected while he was still an undergraduate. When Hawkins got rid of Newman, Froude and Robert Wilberforce as tutors, Balliol supplanted Oriel. But whereas Oriel had offered fellowships to men from other colleges, and by this means overcame the insularity of the past, Balliol found a less spectacular method of finding scholarly candidates for fellowships. Less spectacular but simple – the method was to teach the undergraduates well and train them in the traditions of the college. This was Jowett's doing. No doubt he was helped by historical accidents – by his senior, Tait, a Balliol tutor, going to Rugby as headmaster in succession to Arnold, and sending the new breed of high-minded public schoolboy to his own college. No doubt he was helped by Balliol's Scottish connections, so that hard-working, hard-headed Scots came there to irritate the gentlemanly idlers. But it was Jowett who directed the energies of both breeds – and those of the idlers. His own parents had been spendthrift failures; his family, once rich, had fallen on evil days. As a result he was haunted by the spectre of wasted lives and determined that his pupils should not waste theirs. 'Usefulness in life' was his yardstick, and he observed how often men of great ability failed because they were shy, awkward or ill mannered. His enemies declared that his only criterion was worldly success – that he felt that a pupil who had failed in life had somehow personally insulted him – that Balliol had been let down. The Warden of Merton put it differently: 'He never affected or specifically admired an "unworldly" character ... he was always disposed to regard worldly success as a test of merit ... he hoped that his pupils would not like those of another great teacher "make a mess of life".' (The other 'great teacher' was, of course, Newman; and Jowett considered that those who went over with him to Rome or were bewildered and deserted, as Arthur Hugh Clough found himself, had 'made a mess of life'.)

Jowett taught his men the secret and the delight of hard work. 'The object of reading for the Schools,' he said, 'is not primarily to obtain a first class, but to elevate and strengthen the character for life.' 'You are a fool,' he said to one. 'You must be sick of idling. It is too late for you to do much. But the class [in examination] matters nothing. What does matter is the sense of power which comes from steady working.' By power, Jowett meant the power over oneself, the 'power in a man to control and direct his own life instead of drifting on the currents of fortune and self-indulgence'.

He used this power over himself. He was small, shy, and in his youth looked like a cherub; but he turned his shyness into an educative weapon by maintaining devastating silences followed by still more devastating remarks. After walking for three hours in silence his undergraduate companion, as they passed by a bridge, ventured to say, 'That is a fine view.' The silence continued until Jowett said, 'That was a very foolish remark you made an hour ago.' When a man showed up with an indifferent copy of Greek iambics, Jowett asked him, 'Have you any taste for mathematics?' He would dictate a passage from English literature and expect, poker in hand in front of his fire, his pupils to extemporise *viva voce* into Latin or Greek. To be able to do so 'gave more promise than knowing the whole of Tennyson and Wordsworth'. At all times of day and night his door was open – but for study, not talk. He was not popular as a tutor. He once rebuked a fellow for being too familiar with the undergraduates. He hated slang and insisted on giving a little girl a shilling every time she said 'awfully' until she was ashamed. Newman had been the first to regard his duties as a tutor to be pastoral. But, as his one-time disciple and later Rector of Lincoln Mark Pattison said, Newman would have turned Oriel into a priestly seminary whereas Jowett never imposed his own beliefs on anyone.

There are few occasions more likely to produce bad blood in a college than the death or retirement of the head and the election of a successor. At Lincoln Mark Pattison had been an outstanding tutor; but outstanding tutors all too often fail to be elected head of the college – they have offended too many colleagues. Pattison was harsh, severe and sardonic; always willing to wound and never afraid to strike. Yet it looked as if he would be Rector until, by a discreditable intrigue, a non-resident fellow was brought in to vote and Pattison was outvoted. To his fury he had to connive in the election of a boorish nonentity. He threw up his tutorship and left for Germany.

At Balliol in 1854 it was different. The younger fellows voted for Jowett, the elderly for the future Archbishop Temple. The votes were equal. Then Temple's supporters suborned two of Jowett's party; would not Robert Scott make a suitable Master? He was part author of the standard Greek lexicon 'Liddell and Scott'. After all, he was known to be on friendly terms with Jowett. So the deal was struck. Jowett was mortified. He did not leave for Germany, nor did he resign his tutorship. But he sulked. He no longer appeared in common room and when a dinner was given to celebrate the consecration of the new chapel, Jowett sat with the undergraduates. Some consider he was rejected on grounds of unorthodoxy. More likely he was thought to be inflexible. He bided his time and after eleven years elections to the fellowship gave him a majority and Scott was reduced to a cipher.

Jowett lived at a cataclysmic time in the history of the Church of England. The intense inter-party disputes between Tractarians, Evangelicals and the old High and Dry and Low and Slow parties in the Church were as nothing to the more menacing developments in Germany. Scholars there began to apply to the Bible methods of criticising sources that were used in historical research. Clever dons were not perturbed that William Buckland and the geologists had disproved the literal truth of Genesis; but what of the thousands who went to church each Sunday and believed every tale in the Bible to be true? Clever dons, however, were appalled when they appreciated what the 'higher criticism', as it was called, was doing in Germany, where professors in the classroom mocked the miraculous doings in the Old Testament; and thus anyone suspected of being influenced by German scholarship was assumed to be unorthodox. The years of Jowett's maturity were years marked by a series of rows, disputes, accusations of treachery and reproaches for bigotry.

It was the age of the row over *The Origin of Species* and of the colonial bishop, John Colenso, who admitted that the questions of the simple natives to whom he ministered had shown him that the literal truth of the Bible was unsustainable. They were years when those who, however tentatively, tried to reinterpret Scripture were bound to be attacked by, for example, Henry Liddon, who became the leader of the Tractarian party. Liddon declared that if Jesus believed Moses to be the author of the first five books of the Bible, anyone who doubted this – or that Jonah lived in the belly of the whale – called Christ a liar and could not be a Christian.

Before he failed to be elected Master of Balliol Jowett had been among those reinterpreting Scripture. He and his friend Arthur Stanley published commentaries on several of St Paul's Epistles. The leading biblical scholar of the day, Lightfoot, at Cambridge, dismissed Stanley's work as readable, inaccurate and superficial. He thought better of Jowett. Jowett was more skilful, said Lightfoot, at destroying accepted interpretations than at forming a new one, but he praised Jowett for challenging received opinions. Jowett had set himself to reinterpret the doctrine of the Atonement. Sunday after Sunday in Evangelical and Low Church pulpits the congregation was told why Christ died for all mankind on the Cross. He died to atone for their sins. But there was a proviso. He made this bargain with God the Father provided that the sinner 'closed with the offer' – who must proclaim his faith that he was saved. Jowett found this offensive. Was the redemption of mankind to be compared to a huge commercial transaction? Jowett determined to sanitise this version of the central Christian dogma. He had visited Germany and consulted the renowned biblical critic Lachmann. That was enough for the traditionalists. Having humiliated Newman over the Martyrs Memorial, 'Golly' Golightly now determined to humiliate Jowett.

The year after Jowett's defeat for the mastership Dean

Gaisford died and Palmerston appointed Jowett to the Regius professorship of Greek. Golightly dug up an old statute and forced Jowett to sign the Thirty-Nine Articles in front of the Vice-Chancellor. Jowett did so with contempt. He interrupted the Vice-Chancellor, who began a sententious speech to remind him what an awesome occasion this was, and stalked from the room. He met with further injustice, this time at the hands of the Tractarians. The Regius chair was worth only £40 a year and Jowett lost money by accepting it. The stipend was paid by Christ Church. Why should Christ Church, asked Pusey as a canon of Christ Church, finance a university professorship held by a man whose orthodoxy was suspect? Such was the legacy of Tractarian zeal.

To do Pusey justice he tried various devices to increase Jowett's salary but every attempt was foiled by Jowett's foes – and sometimes by his friends. It became more difficult when in 1860 *Essays and Reviews* was published. This was a book of contributions by churchmen, some of whom were trying to come to grips with the critical analysis of the Bible by German theologians. They were a distinguished lot: Temple and Pattison among them, but also four, including Jowett, who had become notorious for their unorthodox views. The book created yet another scandal. Two of the contributors were prosecuted and found guilty in the ecclesiastical courts. One of them was condemned for doubting whether the wicked would suffer Eternal Punishment in hell. In the end the Judicial Committee of the Privy Council acquitted. But the judgement had a more serious consequence. It meant that the State, not the Church, would decide whether individual clergymen were unorthodox. The rows continued to the end of the century. Good, earnest dons brought up to see themselves as defenders of the faith believed that it was their duty to protest at deviations from what had until yesterday been regarded as true; and equally good but enquiring dons believed it was their duty to show how it was

possible to reconcile Christian belief with the most recent discoveries of scientists and of historical and textual research. The
Privy Council's judgement stopped dozens of priests from being
ejected from their livings and the Church from being torn apart
by faction.

Jowett did not escape censure. Pusey launched proceedings
in the Vice-Chancellor's court to convict Jowett of having published doctrines contrary to those of the Church. The pros-
ecution failed but never again was Jowett to express his
theological opinions in public. What exactly did he believe?
Pusey was not the only one to ask that question. As the years
passed the rationalists looked at him with suspicion. Frederic
Harrison, the Positivist follower of Auguste Comte, and Leslie
Stephen the agnostic, both considered that the only course
open to Jowett was to become a layman. Certainly there are
passages in the official biography of Jowett which suggest that
he believed neither in a personal God nor in a corporeal resur-
rection. The best that can be said for him, Stephen suggested,
was that Jowett was only following Mill's advice to liberal clergymen, which was to stay in the Church and throw their weight in
favour of tolerance in order to prevent the Church falling into
the hands of fanatics. Shortly after *Essays and Reviews* appeared
Stephen gave up his fellowship at Cambridge because he could
no longer believe in the truth of Christianity; and so, a few years
later, did Henry Sidgwick, whose reputation as a scholar was far
higher than that of Jowett. Stephen thought Jowett should have
followed his example. Should he have done so?

A don ought to revere the intellect and believe in the power
of reason. Jowett didn't. His perplexity about Christian dogma
seems to have affected his attitude to the whole of knowledge.
He was interested in Hegel – indeed was among the first in
England ever to study him. That was as far as it went. 'Logic,'
he used to say, 'is neither a science nor an art but a dodge.'
Maybe: but the aphorism showed that he did not think anyone

could write anything valuable. 'How I hate learning!' he once exclaimed. He disliked 'useless learning', yes – but this grew into contempt for research. To say as Jowett did, 'One man is as good as another until he has written a book,' was a typical piece of dreary donnish irony. Leslie Stephen's most biting sentence on Jowett runs: ' "He stood," said one of his pupils, "at the parting of the ways," and he wrote, one must add, "No thoroughfare" upon them all.'

Yet no one who reads his letters or his works can doubt that he believed himself to be a Christian, and many sincere Anglicans believed far less than he did. He was less concerned with the truth or the all-importance of Christianity than with the inadequacy of the forms and the words in which to express it. It is not fair to brand him with moral cowardice and infer that he would not stand up for what he believed to be true. In his wisdom Jowett realised that he himself had not the genius to redefine Christian doctrine; and this being so it would be better to remain silent rather than add to the din raised by Tractarians. He thought little of the best liberal theologian, F. D. Maurice: what had he done but substitute one form of mysticism for another? But the Church owed more to Maurice than to Jowett's attempts to strip Christianity of its eschatology, its mysteries, its paradoxes and perplexities. He knew that his reputation did not rest on his published work: 'What I do is by sparks and flashes and not by steady thought.' His lectures were called 'Glimpses of the Obvious'. He left his pupil T. H. Green to pursue Hegel and become the most influential philosopher in Oxford in the seventies (Jowett admired and deplored Green and was buried next to him). Augustine Birrell* put forward a worldly apologia: 'Why should men sell out of a still-going and dividend-paying concern when they have not the faintest idea

---

* Augustine Birrell (1850–1933), man of letters and liberal minister for education and later Chief Secretary for Ireland (1907–16).

where to look for another investment for their money? Where was Jowett to go if he gave up Balliol? . . . So he stayed where he was and Balliol . . . turned out a number of excellent young fellows warranted to come and go anywhere except to the gallows and the stake.' It was not an explanation that would have satisfied Leslie Stephen. But it satisfied George Eliot and Tennyson.

The tide had at last turned for him when in 1870 he met Gladstone and they had a long talk about Ireland. Jowett disagreed with the line Gladstone took, but Gladstone was impressed. Could he do something for Jowett? he asked one of his cabinet colleagues. He did the one thing that Jowett wanted – he got Scott out of the Master's Lodgings by offering him the lucrative deanery of Rochester. Jowett was at last Master of Balliol, and rumours mounted about impending reforms. The ceremony of grace at hall dinner was modified and a new head chef was appointed. That was all.

Jowett was no reformer. In the early fifties he had been one of the few to applaud Gladstone for supporting university reform, though sad that Gladstone (wisely) appointed commissioners to see that the colleges gave effect to the reforms proposed by the Royal Commission instead of trusting the dons to reform themselves. At one time he advocated creating more professorships, but when Mark Pattison put forward a scheme for endowing research, Jowett opposed it. His remark that study for its own sake was a waste of time drew from Pattison the comment that Oxford resembled a lively municipal borough.

Pattison was a singularly unattractive figure. When he became a theist he spurned his sisters, who adored him, and married his wife not for love but to look after him. She was twenty-seven years his junior. Her selfishness took the form of self-righteousness; his, self-pity. Both were hypochondriacs – as John Sparrow noted – she the more resourceful and experienced of the two. Pattison blamed her frigidity for the estrangement, but when she later married Charles Dilke* (at a time when the scandal that was to drive him from public life was beginning) Dilke never complained that she was sexually inadequate. Pattison had learnt in exile to admire German universities and their outstanding contributions to learning. Having been a champion of the tutorial system and an opponent in the fifties of increasing the professoriate, he now wanted, when at last he became Rector of Lincoln, to abolish colleges, religious tests and pass degrees. He hated the new Oxford of prizes and firsts in the schools. He was the ally of the medieval historian Freeman, who as a guest at a tutors' dinner exclaimed, 'I have come to see the crammers cram.' He considered a don should devote himself to learning. Oxford should become a centre for advanced studies and colleges should become specialised departments as in civic universities.

Jowett stood for the college and the tutorial system. He made enemies. No one of his character could fail to do so. The conservatives among the dons were as jealous of his success as the liberals indignant at his hostility to research. The historian and fellow of All Souls Charles Oman called him 'a noted and much detested figure' representing 'modernism, advertisement and an autocratic pose, a tendency to push the importance of the college beyond the limits of its undoubted merit'. Trollope characterised him as Mr Jobbles in *The Three Clerks*, and W. H. Mallock mocked him as Dr Jenkinson in *The New Republic*. Oman, Freeman and Pattison considered a don's first duty was to research. On the other hand, the then Dean of Christ Church, while accepting that tutors as well as professors should write books, considered the tutor's first duty was 'to look after his men'. The result too often was that tutors didn't write books.

---

* Sir Charles Dilke (1843–1911), Liberal minister for local government (1882), withdrew from public life after Mrs Crawford (his sister-in-law) declared she had committed adultery with him – which he denied. Married Mark Pattison's widow in 1885. Returned as an MP in 1892 until his death.

Jowett was to be remembered for ever as a character. Undergraduates appeared before him – he saw two or three every day – and the idle were slain by his sarcasm. By now he had learnt to sympathise with their pleasures. As early as 1879 Balliol held a ball and as Vice-Chancellor he defended the Oxford University Dramatic Society against the sourpuss dons like Freeman who spoke of the 'portentous rage for play acting'. At the end of his life Jowett said, 'At one time I was against the boat, and cared little for its success, but now I think very differently.' He became known as 'The Jowler'. The terrible silences disappeared so that even Pattison could say, 'There's affability for you.' He was now positively genial towards the young. One of them said he tried never to quarrel: if a man insulted him he asked him to dinner. 'You'll do, dear boy,' laughed Jowett. 'You'll do.' It was said that if you were a peer, a profligate or a pauper, the Master would be sure to take you up. Jowett was not the first don to institute reading parties in the vacation, but he was the first head of house to know something about all his men, and a great deal about some of them. The list of Balliol graduates in 1873–8 included Asquith, Curzon, Gell, Milner, Baden-Powell, Leveson-Gower and W. P. Ker. As undergraduates they would have been invited to meet the Master's guests – among them Turgenev, George Eliot and G. H. Lewes, Bishop Colenso, Archbishop Tait, Lord Sherbrooke and Tyndall. He made a point of mixing the different types of undergraduates at his parties – 'Jowett's Jumbles', they were called – yet Balliol was judged to be the most cliquey of all colleges.

Swinburne as well as George Eliot stayed in the Lodgings. Jowett asked Swinburne to look at his translation of Plato's *Symposium* and when the poet suggested a sentence could be construed differently Jowett's eyes widened: 'Of course that is the meaning. You would be a good scholar if you were to study.' Swinburne was set down in an adjoining room to continue the good work, and a friend talking to Jowett was interrupted by a cackle from next door. 'Another howler, Master.' 'Thank you, dear Algernon,' said Jowett as he shut the door. Jowett's translation of Plato's *Republic* was his most lasting contribution to learning. For years it was the most popular translation, much read in schools.

He liked the well-born and the famous. When the Crown-Princess of Prussia ('little Vicky') called on him to talk philosophy he thought her 'quite a genius' – and certainly she would have made a better showing than most of her women contemporaries, other than George Eliot. But he also encouraged poor men to come to Balliol and did nothing to impede the concern with working-class education and poverty that T. H. Green and Arnold Toynbee initiated and for which Balliol became so well known under the mastership of A. L. Smith and Alexander ('Sandy') Lindsay.

He continued to hold sharp opinions. 'No writer,' he said of Carlyle, 'had done or was doing so much harm to young men as the preacher of tyranny or apologist of cruelty.' 'Comtism destroys the minds of men, Carlyle their morals.' He was outraged that Governor Eyre's* expenses should have been paid by the State. 'A generation ago we should have hanged him.' He hated Euripides: 'he is immoral when he is irreligious and when he is religious, he is more immoral still.' Staying in Scotland to deliver two lectures on Socrates he was accosted after dinner by Professor Blackie of Glasgow University, who said, 'I hope you in Oxford don't think we hate you.' 'We don't think of you at all,' was the reply. The snub was deserved; the professor had sung a song, unasked, called 'The Burning of the Heretic', which Jowett may have considered was a dig at him.

In 1882 Jowett became Vice-Chancellor for four years. Charles Fortnum again offered his collection of antique and Renais-

* Edward Eyre (1815–1901), Governor of Jamaica, put down riots by the black population in the island with great brutality: defended by Carlyle, prosecuted at the instigation of J. S. Mill, Huxley and Herbert Spencer.

sance works of art to the Ashmolean Museum, and Arthur Evans, the prime excavator of Minoan civilisation in Crete, maintained that Jowett did his best to refuse the gift by masterly inactivity and much dissembling. In his biography Geoffrey Faber defended Jowett against this charge and pointed out that no Vice-Chancellor can accept a gift without considering what it will cost the university to accept it. Evans was young and high-handed: Fortnum, like other benefactors, hinted that his bequest could go elsewhere unless Oxford fell in with his wishes. Furthermore Jowett had always recognised that something had to be done for archaeology and for the old Ashmolean collections. Nevertheless, he acquired a reputation as one who was determined to have his way. It was said of him, 'Parnell is not in it with him for obstruction.' When supporters of a scheme he opposed got it put first on the agenda at the last meeting of Council, Jowett declared that no one could discuss so important a matter so late in the term and left the chair. His mode of governance lived on. Years later Lindsay, when Master of Balliol, found himself in a minority of one at a college meeting and remarked, 'I see, we are deadlocked.'

And love? He was devoted to a giant Scotsman, Robert Morier, one of his earliest pupils who later became ambassador in St Petersburg. In the sixties he was tempted to marry the daughter of the Dean of Bristol; but when another fellow was appointed to the only fellowship in the college open to a married man, Jowett's interest flagged. No wonder: he had fallen for Florence Nightingale. The friendship grew: he annotated three vast volumes she had written entitled *Suggestions for Thought*. He was impressed by her vitality, originality and by her caustic comments on the religious and social life of the day. She corresponded with him and he wrote interminable replies. Then some instinct told him that if he continued to answer her requests and some of her commands, he would wear himself out – as indeed Clough and Sidney Herbert had done. Years later the irrepressible Margot Tennant asked him outright whether he had ever been in love; and when he said he had once been very much in love she persisted and asked what she was like. 'Very violent, my dear, very violent.'

There was another kind of love that was to confront Jowett. Disillusioned in his attempts to sustain Christianity by liberal theology, Jowett turned to Plato. Gladstone had spoken of the 'shameless lusts which formed the incredible and indelible disgrace of Greece', and Ruskin wondered at the 'singular states of inferior passion which arrested the ethical as well as the formative progress of the Greek mind'. But the Aesthetic Movement began to get under way in the seventies and soon Pater's mellifluous sentences began to be quoted and John Addington Symonds extolled the phallic ecstasy in Aristophanes. Indeed there was a falling-off of candidates for Greats and a shift towards law and the modern history school, where William Stubbs lectured (usually to classes of four or five undergraduates) on the safe subject of Parliament in the Middle Ages and never ventured later than the Thirty Years War. Greats was to recover in the eighties, when it scored twice as many firsts as history. Swinburne left no one in doubt where Jowett stood. He declared that it was impossible to confuse Jowett

> with such morally and spiritually typical and unmistakable apes of the Dead Sea as Mark Pattison, or with such renascent blossoms of the Italian Renaissance as the Platonic amorist of blue-breeched gondoliers who is now in Aretino's bosom. The cult of the calamus, as expounded by Mr Addington Symonds to his fellow calamites, would have found no acceptance or tolerance with the translator of Plato.

The translator of Plato did indeed on one occasion take action. A Balliol undergraduate, William Hardinge, sent Pater sonnets praising homosexual love. Pater responded by signing himself

'Yours lovingly'. Jowett was told: confronted both, expelled Hardinge from Balliol and never spoke to Pater again.

Jowett left two legacies. The first he could not have foreseen, a legacy that influenced higher education throughout the twentieth century. Those who have read the most famous of all public school novels, *Tom Brown's Schooldays*, will remember that at supper after the football match in which School house has defeated the School, young Tom hears the captain, 'old Brooke', say in his speech, 'I know I'd sooner win two schoolhouse matches running than get the Balliol Scholarship any day.' Of course other colleges offered scholarships but by ancient statute they might be confined to those who could claim descent from the founder of the college: 'Founder's Kin'. Or they were reserved for those from a particular school – at New College for Wykehamists or at King's for Etonians. Or at Trinity and all other colleges at Cambridge they were awarded after an undergraduate had been in residence for a year or more. But by the end of the century the colleges, in response to the commissioners' criticism that poor men of talent could not afford to enter the ancient universities, offered scholarships for the less well-to-do. The requirements for entry to the university remained as unexacting as possible: few wanted to frighten away the sons of the well-to-do, whose fees kept the colleges afloat.

The scholarship exam in each college did more than provide a bursary for poor undergraduates. It became the blue riband for the public schools and the grammar schools. Schools prided themselves on winning one or more each year. Later Oxford and Cambridge established examining boards that granted exemption from the modest university entrance exam. You were exempt if you obtained five credits in the School Certificate – a test that an intelligent fifteen-year-old or a clever fourteen-year-old could pass. What were schoolboys and -girls to do for the last three to four years at their school? The answer was to work for the scholarship exam in classics, or maths, or science, or history, or modern languages. When the Oxbridge examining boards set up a new sixth-form exam, the Higher Certificate or Advanced Level (A Level, as it was later called), it followed the pattern of the scholarship exam. Of course the colleges insisted that ancillary subjects must be taken as well as papers in the specialism that the candidate had chosen. A history specialist had to be tested in Latin and French and one other foreign language; a scientist in maths; but everyone knew that those who shone in their specialism were those who won the prize.

And so the notorious English specialism in secondary schools took root. Boys and girls chose which way they would jump as early as fourteen; and at fifteen opted either for maths and science or for the humanities. If for the latter, they never opened a maths textbook again. The system suited the dons: boys and girls arrived at the university knowing something about the scholarly debates in their specialism. It suited the professions: after leaving school a doctor could qualify in seven years, a lawyer in six. It suited the Treasury because the first degree took only three years. Boys and girls were content: no longer would those with a mathematical block have to try to master the calculus.

But did it suit the nation? During the twentieth century the complaints grew. Industry complained that graduates in science and engineering had such narrow minds, and commerce that arts graduates were innumerate. Even the Civil Service at last rebelled. They rebelled because critics argued that the skills which a civil servant needed at the end of the twentieth century were not tested by the kind of examination so dear to the hearts of the dons. In the nineteenth century the dons had got government to agree that entry to the public service should be met by a competitive examination on the same lines as the final examination in the universities. At one time all you had to do was to reproduce in the Civil Service or Foreign Service exam

those qualities that had won you high honours in the university;
though it must be said, you had to pass an interview. From time
to time variations were introduced; and your examiners, who
were dons themselves, might not sympathise with the spin that
you put on your answers to questions. (When Keynes sat for
the Civil Service exam he got his lowest mark for economics
and as a result entered the India Office and not the Treasury.)
No one dissented from the principle. It seemed self-evident –
to Macaulay, to Charles Trevelyan, to Jowett and the younger
dons. So indeed it seemed until the very end of the twentieth
century.

The second legacy was the primacy of the tutors. Jowett's
reign saw the end of the old catechetical college lecture (in
reality a class construing a text) and the rise of the tutorial. In
1869 the History Tutors Association formed: they arranged the
lectures, supplied the examiners and determined what was to
be taught. The professoriate was outflanked. Clerical fellowships
declined: colleges did not want fellows who had an eye on the
next benefice on offer.

There grew up in Oxford and Cambridge a posse of dons,
often young bachelors, who like Jowett knew something of all
of their men and a lot about some of them. At Balliol, it was
noted, it was 'possible for a tutor without taking Orders to be
virtually a minister of religion'. An observer writing in the *Church
Quarterly Review* thanked God for the work of John Conroy, a
science tutor at Balliol, and for H. O. Wakeman, tutor at Keble;
and at Balliol T. H. Green and Nettleship were renowned mor-
alists.

Not everyone saw college tutors as deutero-clergymen. 'They
sit in their comfortable rooms and do nothing except cram
in Latin and Greek for examinations,' wrote one critic in the
Nineteenth Century, and another in the same year, 1895, depicted
the modern don as 'an open derider of religion'. All was not
well with Oxford, and the university had its critics in London.

In 1866 Jowett was lamenting that not a twentieth part of the ability of the country came to the university, and Pattison two years later echoed him. An odious comparison was made between Oxford and the Grandes Écoles, in which Oxford was compared to 'a great steam-hammer for cracking walnuts'. But then, as the *Saturday Review* observed, what was one to say when the Provost of Oriel said that Oxford existed to provide curates, not solicitors or surgeons? With the collapse of college incomes in the eighties fellowships became less attractive. Those formerly devoted to research were diminished or abolished. This in turn led to dissatisfaction among the college tutors, who now saw themselves as less well-paid than public schoolmasters with little leisure to pursue learning, compelled every year to begin teaching the same subjects to a new set of students. When in the past young dons taught for a spell and then left to fill college livings, they did not grow stale; but after twenty years the college tutor became dull and dispirited.

For a moment it looked as if the pendulum might swing back against the tutorial system. When Jowett died his natural successor in the college was not chosen. The Balliol dons imported a Scots philosopher, Edward Caird. But fourteen years later, when Caird resigned, the natural successor came in. He was, like Jowett, a bachelor. Strachan-Davidson had been senior Dean for thirty-two years and was the idol of the undergraduates, particularly of those whose frolics and way of life, so different from his own, he tolerated. Balliol was to become the home of many tutors famous in their day, such as Cyril Bailey, though perhaps the best known was Francis 'Sligger' Urquhart, at whose austere chalet in Switzerland reading parties met in vacation. Urquhart was not an intellectual. He emanated a stream of gentle sympathy that brought others out. At the end of Lindsay's twenty-five-year mastership of Balliol Lindsay said, 'The place exists and I hope always will exist, for the young men.'

CHAPTER FIVE

The Don as Scholar – Frederic Maitland

Trinity is the greatest and grandest of all Cambridge colleges and in science the intellectual power-house of the university. It was the home of Newton and of those formidable classical scholars Bentley and Porson. But though Cambridge was spared the bitter divisions that split Oxford, it too became embroiled in similar political and religious controversy. By tradition Cambridge was a university of the Whigs, but in 1831, as the nation was rocked by the debates on the Reform Bill, the true sentiments of the dons became clear. The Whigs – a young Cavendish who had become second in the mathematical tripos, and young Palmerston – lost their seats in Parliament. The Master of Trinity, Christopher Wordsworth, deprived Connop Thirlwall, the outstanding young theologian of the day, of his assistant tutorship. Thirlwall had come out in favour of admitting Dissenters to Cambridge and had questioned the merit of compulsory attendance in chapel. Wordsworth did not stop there. He let it be known that, had he had the power to deprive Thirlwall of his fellowship, he would have done so. That was too much for the fellows of Trinity. They gave Wordsworth such a hard time that he found life in the Lodge as Master unendurable. But Wordsworth was not a man to give an inch to his enemies. He timed his resignation skilfully. The mastership of Trinity is a Crown appointment, and Wordsworth was determined that he should not be succeeded by the notable liberal and popular professor Adam Sedgwick. Watching the smoke signals from Westminster as keenly as any bushman, Wordsworth perceived that Melbourne's administration was tottering and he waited until Peel formed a Tory government. Peel did not disappoint him. He nominated William Whewell as the next Master.

Whewell was a polymath. He introduced analysis into Cambridge mathematics after a visit to Germany, where he picked up crystallography and – after he had been appointed professor in the subject – mineralogy. A treatise on gothic architecture was tossed off, as was a work of considerable importance on the theory of tides and how they affected the British Isles. He was not an experimental scientist. He described science and became famous for a vast treatise on the history and philosophy of the inductive sciences. He had unbounded energy and boundless arrogance. Built like a prize-fighter, he was a bully. But he was not a die-hard and was generous on the rare occasions he suffered defeat. He bounced the university into accepting the Prince Consort as a candidate for the chancellorship, brought him home in a contested election and supported his plans for increasing the number of professorships. Whewell spoke in favour of establishing a natural and moral sciences tripos and put forward a not very practical plan for reforming the curriculum.

For intellectual distinction Trinity had a rival. Next door was St John's, where Wordsworth found his sleep disturbed by Trinity's loquacious clock and pealing organ where in the ante-chapel the statue stood

> Of Newton with his prism and silent face
> The marble index of a mind for ever
> Voyaging through strange seas thought, alone.

The Master of St John's, William Bateson, was a more vigorous reformer than Whewell and considerably more genial. The

Johnian mathematicians clocked up a record of successes in the tripos that surpassed even those of Trinity. The first chemistry laboratory in Cambridge was set up in St John's under George Liveing; the moral science teachers included the economist Alfred Marshall; and skilled classicists from Shrewsbury School flocked there to be taught by a notable reformer, Heitland, and by T. E. Page, whose Latin texts for many years every schoolboy had to master. They were the successors of those whom William Wordsworth praised when he went there in 1787, 'whose authority of Office serv'd, To set our minds on edge'. On the other hand the mathematicians at St John's tended to be an unimaginative lot, the successors to Wordsworth's

> Men unscoured, grotesque
> In character, tricked out like aged trees
> Which, through the lapse of their infirmity
> Give ready place to any random seed
> That chuses to be rear'd upon their trunks.*

Undergraduates studied either for a pass degree or for honours, i.e. the tripos. In the first half of the nineteenth century the pass men regarded the tutors as mere schoolmasters. They were rowdy. The reforming headmasters of the public schools got their boys under control by delegating the problem of discipline to housemasters and prefects and by promoting games. The tutors had no such resources. Their pupils were irritated by the intolerable numbers of petty university and college rules which may have been appropriate three centuries earlier when undergraduates were fifteen years old. To carry an umbrella while wearing cap and gown was an offence. So

---

* The contrast between German professors, enthusing students with their original research in seminar, and the plodding English don is often made. Yet Theodor Fontane recognised both of Wordsworth's models among the Prussian professoriate: the excellent Professor Schmidt in *Frau Jenny Treibel*; and the egregious Professor Cujachius in *Der Stechlin*.

were pigeon-shooting, attendance at prize-fights, dinners in pubs – even, in one case, sporting a moustache. The college tutors were there to din into their heads the rudiments required for a pass degree – if they were in residence. It was said that you knew it was term-time in Cambridge if you saw Whewell, when he was tutor at Trinity, at the Athenaeum. Whewell knew none of his undergraduates: he argued that if he knew them he could not be an impartial examiner. He once rebuked his gyp (college servant) for not telling him when one of his pupils died.

The men reading for honours were equally dismissive of their tutors. Few of the 350 fellows taught them. If you sat for the mathematical or classical tripos you hired a coach (who had taken high honours in his time). He would charge you £7 or, if you settled for being taught once a day, £14 a term. The tutor was your enemy, fining or gating you for breaking a college rule. The coach was your friend. You paid him and his job was to get you as high a place as possible in the tripos list; in both classics and mathematics marks were awarded for each question and an exact order of merit was published in the class list. The coach would be an expert crammer adept at forecasting what the examiners might ask that year. He might even be a professor. Henslow, the professor of botany at Cambridge, was so ill-paid that he had to cram students for five to six hours a day. Undergraduates made their name by being classed senior Classic, or among the top Wranglers (i.e. mathematicians).

One of the obstacles to change was the existence of small colleges. Who was to teach new subjects such as science or history when the few fellows were able only to teach mathematics or classics? When the future historian G. G. Coulton came up to St Catharine's in 1877 the senior tutor was such an inadequate teacher that Coulton paid to be taught classics by the junior tutor. The Dean was omniscient – that is to say he knew, if challenged on the spur of the moment, the price of a wooden leg and the added cost if it was tipped with brass. Five other fellows completed the list, three of whom were non-resident; and in order to keep out any younger man the old guard elected yet another non-resident in 1880.

There were, of course, a number of dons who were determined to bring about change. The impetus came from Trinity and St John's. The reforming dons disliked the coaches because so long as they reigned supreme it was difficult to reform the tripos and bring into the classical curriculum philosophy, history and philology, or establish science as a separate tripos. The reformers finally undermined the coaches – though it took years to do so – not only by extending the curriculum but by abolishing the tradition of ranking candidates in the tripos results. The narrowness of the curriculum and the premium it put on memory as distinct from critical intelligence had been criticised outside more than inside the university. The Prince Consort let it be known where his sympathies lay, though he was careful not to suggest that German universities were superior to Cambridge in scholarship. When John Seeley gave his inaugural lecture, succeeding Charles Kingsley as Regius professor of history, he used the opportunity to criticise the narrowness of the classical curriculum and the pedantry of the great coach Richard Shilleto. It was this that drew from Hepworth Thompson, who had succeeded Whewell as Master of Trinity, the remark, 'I never could have supposed that we should so soon regret the departure of poor Kingsley.'

Yet Thompson was one of those who did his share in reform. The statutes of all colleges were archaic, and when Lord John Russell's commissioners appeared and numbers of colleges at first refused to cooperate, Whewell – despite reservations – was helpful. Twenty years later the junior fellows of Trinity again determined to revise the statutes and found themselves supported by Hepworth Thompson. Thompson had to keep reminding the fellows that the question was not how the statutes were to be reformed but how they were to be *altered*, that is to say redrafted to give effect to the changes the reformers wanted. It was at one of these interminable meetings that Thompson made his immortal dictum: 'We are none of us infallible, not even the youngest.' The revised statutes were passed to the Privy Council – which under Gladstone's influence rejected them. Gladstone had a more comprehensive plan. He wanted to set up another Commission on Oxford and Cambridge, and the commissioners incorporated Thompson's work into their recommendations.

Thompson was helped by three fellows in particular – Henry Jackson, Coutts Trotter and Henry Sidgwick. Coutts Trotter got the college to accept that candidates for fellowships should submit a dissertation; and that the tripos should not be considered as the sole guide to their intellectual promise. Henry Jackson became renowned as a great teacher and threw open his classes on Plato to the whole university. He was behind the removal of religious tests, the abolition of Greek as a requirement to enter the university, and he and Sidgwick supported the foundation of colleges for women. The third, Henry Sidgwick, was the outstanding utilitarian philosopher in the tradition of Mill. It was he who invited Michael Foster to teach physiology and become the first professor in the subject; and it was he who taught Frederic Maitland, who won a first in philosophy.

Trinity was the nest of Cambridge's philosophers: of the Idealist M'Taggart, then of G. E. Moore and Bertrand Russell, and later of Wittgenstein – and also of the notably less original C. D. Broad. In history both G. M. Trevelyan and Steven Runciman* were able as men with independent means to retire from Trinity when young to devote themselves to research and writing. But Trevelyan returned in 1926 as Regius professor of modern his-

---

* The Hon. Sir Steven Runciman, CH, born 1903, fellow of Trinity (1927–38), historian of Byzantine civilisation and of the Crusades.

tory and in 1940 accepted at Churchill's insistence another Crown appointment, the mastership of Trinity.

The most famous scholar in classics was a Trinity don: Housman believed that the first duty of a classicist was to apply himself to textual criticism. He despised those who tried to explain why Greek and Latin poetry were so moving. Yet he was profoundly moved by poetry; and on one occasion he let the mask of rigid fidelity to textual criticism slip and at the end of a lecture on Horace he read his translation of what he considered the most poignant of all the odes, *Diffugere nives*'. He refused to allow his name to go forward for a higher degree of Doctor of Letters on the grounds that he was not the equal in textual criticism of those Trinity scholars, Bentley and Porson. (As a result no other classical don dared put in for the degree.) His austerity, his determination to *nil admirari* became a tradition in Trinity. Andrew Gow, a classical scholar in the Housman tradition, was a friend to numbers of undergraduates, particularly if they were interested in painting. His colleague Gaillard Lapsley, the American-born medieval historian, asked Gow to look at a painting by Allan Ramsay he had bought and waited on tenterhooks for the connoisseur's judgement. 'Not a very good Allan Ramsay, is it?' Pause. 'But then Allan Ramsay wasn't a very good painter, was he?' When Housman deigned to review a fellow of Trinity's history of Louis Napoleon and admitted that some of the epigrams hit the nail on the head, he could not resist adding, 'the slang with which Mr Simpson now and then defiles his pen is probably slang he learnt in his cradle and believed in his innocence to be English: "a settlement of sorts for example . . ."'

As befits a great college Trinity had its share of eccentrics: the Russian mathematician Abram Besicovitch came high on the list. But none could excel Housman's target, F. A. Simpson. Simpson was a clergyman whom Trevelyan had found writing history in his Cumberland parish and had brought to Trinity to teach history. He published two of his four projected volumes on Louis-Napoleon. The second got roughly handled in *The Times Literary Supplement* and, worse still, a charlatan, a flashy, journalist Philip Guedalla, who had written about the Second Empire, sneered at it. That was enough for Simpson. He would write no more. He continued to lecture until the Second World War on theories of the modern state, excellently on the utilitarians and Hegel, whose ethical theories, he pointed out, could not account for the actions of the Good Samaritan. He never mentioned Marx.

Eric James, at one time chaplain of Trinity, compiled an entrancing memoir of this oddity. Simpson ruffled many of the fellows. Gow loathed him. When Simpson was knocked down outside the Great Gate – not surprising as he plunged across the road and waved his stick at the traffic and expected it to stop – Gow's only comment was, 'but it hasn't done him much good'. Vile and humiliating to the college servants, importunate in his demands for different and better food in hall, he was told by the Vice-Master, Winstanley, 'You'll have to rough it a bit in heaven.' His war work consisted in gathering honey in the countryside which he ate himself. He refused to firewatch – unless an armchair was placed for him on the roof of chapel. Kitson Clark, the impetuous, talkative director of studies in history, asked Simpson to give some tutorials as he was left single-handed. Simpson refused: so Trevelyan stepped into the breach. Yet when Trevelyan lay old and blind, Simpson refused to visit him, telling Kitson Clark that it was too far for him to walk – though Trevelyan's home was only three hundred metres further than the University Library, to which Simpson regularly went. Needless to say he despised Kitson: 'He thinks he's popular with the undergraduates because he appears so often in their light verse.' Almost any day he could be found, secateurs in hand, snipping any plant presumptuous enough to have overgrown; and in summer he frequented the men's bathing sheds on the river. Yet he gave the young generous gifts, and fought the examiners to allow Enoch Powell, too sick to leave his rooms, to take his finals papers in Trinity. This monster of ingratitude and selfishness was the finest preacher in Cambridge, cherished for his extraordinary eccentricities, and indulged by the chaplains of Trinity. They admired his discrimination in matters of doctrine and morals and the content of his sermons. He was the friend of other rebellious spirits in the Church such as Mervyn Stockwood. Stockwood had been translated from being vicar of Great St Mary's in Cambridge to Bishop of Southwark, and Eric James's account of getting Simpson to London to preach the sermon at Stockwood's consecration – a sermon that left the Archbishop of Canterbury gobbling like a turkey-cock with anger – is a minor masterpiece.

Trevelyan may have persuaded the Trinity Council to appoint Simpson to teach history because he hoped to prolong the tradition of narrative history of which he was such a master. But it was at a time when historians were becoming more analytical and more absorbed by the techniques of their subject. Very many dons are described with justice as fine scholars. They work on a particular subject or an era, they examine the archives, they work in the field or in libraries, they can seek the relevant primary and secondary sources, they decipher and check texts and weigh evidence. They may have to learn palaeography, diplomatic usage, philology and obsolete languages. Nor is this the end of the techniques they have to master. But the reading public understandably has only a sketchy idea of what scholarship entails. The common reader appreciates the labour that must have gone into the works of John Elliott on classical Spain or Hugh Thomas on modern Spain or Denis Mack Smith on Italy or John Plumb on the years after 1688, or Hugh Trevor-Roper on topics ranging from the Reformation to Hitler, or Eric Hobsbawm's analyses of society in the nineteenth and twentieth centuries. Historians often ask of other historians: has he or she changed the way in which we regard the past as the German and French historians did in the nineteenth century, or as Namier did for eighteenth-century politics, or as Steven Runciman did when he suggested that the Crusades were the last of the barbarian invasions in Europe that destroyed the only remaining link, Byzantium, with the civilisation of the ancient Greek-Roman Empire. The common reader expects that the results of research should be at his disposal, whether they take the form of narrative history written by G. M. Trevelyan or Simon Schama, or analytical history such as Braudel's classic work on the Mediterranean in the time of Philip II of Spain.

At the end of the nineteenth century Frederic Maitland changed the way historians studied the Middle Ages – and indeed suggested how constitutional history should be studied.

He faced a formidable predecessor. The Tractarian Movement – and even more so the Romantic Movement – awoke interest in the Middle Ages. William Stubbs was for years Regius professor of history at Oxford and ended his days there as a bishop. Stubbs spent his life editing medieval ecclesiastical and legal documents. *Stubbs's Charters* became a standard work for the examination in history at Oxford. Stubbs wrote the constitutional history of England from Anglo-Saxon times to the reign of Edward I and carried the story through to the end of the Middle Ages. This bald account gives no conception of the hundreds of documents which he edited and elucidated in his introduction to the text.

Stubbs and his great ally Freeman saw medieval history as a gradual process in which parliamentary and liberal politics evolved. Back in the Middle Ages one can find the eternal English concern for muzzling the power of the Crown and establishing constitutional government. Unkind tongues intoned the rhyme:

Ladling butter from alternate tubs
Stubbs butters Freeman, and Freeman butters Stubbs.

Maitland did not write a history of the constitution nor narrative history like Freeman. He thought that Freeman and most English historians (but not Stubbs) were insular. They had not learnt the German way of interpreting history. It should not be interpreted through their rulers, the battles they had fought and the treaties they had made. It should be interpreted through the origins of their land, their institutions, their language and their folk tales and myths. He did not, like Marx, invest an all-embracing theory that would explain the inseparable processes that determined the direction in which society must move. He showed that our medieval ancestors thought differently from us and used words and legal terms in a different sense from us. Maitland wrote a series of works explaining what certain documents meant and what the men who wrote them thought they meant.

The very titles of his works are enough to make the common reader flinch: *The pleas of the Crown for the County of Gloucester before the Abbot of Reading, 1221*; *Township and Borough*; *Trust and Corporation*; the three volumes on the Eyre of Kent; *Three Rolls of the King's Court* – the texts he edited with introductions are legion. Perhaps his most renowned editions were the three-volume *Bracton's Note-Book* and the Year Books from the reigns of Edward I and Edward II, which were compilations of notes made by students in court (though he mistakenly believed they were semi-official collections of cases for the use of judge and counsel). His introduction to *Memoranda de Parliamento* put the study of parliamentary origins on a new level. But all he claimed to be doing was 'to provide materials for the formation of opinions'. As Edward Miller said, 'He was introducing a set of documents and not rewriting the history of Parliament.'

Maitland was doing more than that. He was telling us how men thought in the past. When men in the twelfth century spoke of their liberties, they were not using that word as we would today. Whereas Freeman wanted to prove that the Anglo-

Saxons cared as passionately about freedom as Gladstonian liberals, Maitland showed that medieval men reasoned in ways foreign to us. When we today perceive a wrong, our instinct is to say that the law must provide a remedy. Maitland deduced that in the early Middle Ages men argued that if no remedy existed no wrong had been committed.

The chips that fell from his hammer were as inspiring as the finished statue itself. Suddenly you find him telling you why the men of Kent were not bound by the law of primogeniture, but preferred the law of gavelkind, by which all offspring, and not just the eldest, inherit land. Or, in discussing the terms 'sake' and 'soke', he will add in an aside that sake 'is still in use among us; although we do not speak of a sake between two persons, we do speak of a man acting for another's sake, or for God's sake, or for the sake of money'. He rarely had theories; he preferred to give suggestive warnings. He warned against the prevailing practice of interpreting history in terms of unilinear progress. In some localities medieval customs survived for centuries, whereas in others they disappeared never to be revived. He warned that special precautions are needed when studying the early Middle Ages and the activities of those 'who are still learning to say what they mean'.

To do what he wanted to do he had to learn new techniques. Most of the materials that enable historians to reconstruct medieval history are the records of the law and the courts, and you have to master, as Maitland put it, 'an extremely formal system of pleading and procedure' and 'a whole system of actions with repulsive names'. Maitland, who soon gave up the law and returned to Cambridge, had to do more than that. He read enormously in several languages, taught himself palaeography to decipher the Gloucester roll of 1221 ('anyone who knows some law and some Latin will find that the difficulty disappears in a few weeks'), and produced a grammar of Norman French. He understood the limitations of the records and also what, with squeezing, they could yield: he also warned that much of the evidence historians use is suspect.

The secret of his reputation was that he wrote in a different style from other medieval historians. He went for a stroll with his reader, explaining the landscape, cutting a path through the thorns, and warning him of pits and bogs along the way. He avoided circumlocutions and illustrated abstract notions by showing how in practice they affected ordinary men and women. He was courtesy itself to those whom he found to be in error. Maitland treated Bishop Stubbs, twenty-five years his senior, with decent respect even though he was undermining the foundations of the Bishop's history of the constitution, and only the medievalist, the horrible Horace Round, who in controversy had the manners of a ferret, ever felt the edge of his tongue. He was a master in puncturing those who evolve theories to explain how the whole of society works. For years schoolboys were taught that in the Middle Ages there was a form of government, the feudal system, that was more or less stable as parliamentary democracy. If this was so, the feudal system, said Maitland, with tongue in cheek, attained its most perfect state of development in the eighteenth century. Scholarship, alas, he concluded, has revealed the differences rather than the similarities between one century and another and between England and the Continent, so that 'it is quite possible to maintain that England was the most, or for that matter the least, feudalized; and that William the Conqueror introduced, or for that matter, suppressed the feudal system'.

Scholars may illuminate subjects which have never before been examined in detail, but how good were these great scholars themselves? How has their work, which appeared in their time to have broken new ground, stood up to the criticism of the generations to come? For years historians genuflected whenever Maitland's name was mentioned. This irritated a scholar of repute who had himself spent thousands of hours in the archives, taking a field – Tudor history – that had been tilled until one would have thought the soil was exhausted. He produced a work that put him in the front rank of contemporary historians. Geoffrey Elton transformed our understanding of Henry VIII's reign, of Tudor rule, and of Parliament. It was Henry's servant, Thomas Cromwell, who was the first to realise that the machinery of state could be used to make a stronger society. French and Spanish kings recognised how powerful a central state could become, but they used their insight so that they could make war more efficiently. In England Cromwell imposed new duties on courts and institutions to improve central and local government.*

Determined not to add to the hagiography which surrounded Maitland's name, Elton warmed to his task. Why did Maitland imagine that towns began as garrisons, not as centres of trade? In saying so Maitland 'never proved himself more the lawyer than in his relative neglect of economic influences'. (True: but then how little economic history at that date had been written.) Maitland misinterpreted the law of trespass; he ignored the ability of a plaintiff to petition the Crown for a grievance although this was often done in Henry III's reign – a period that was an open book to Maitland. When Maitland poked his nose into Elton's terrain and used the term *Rex Legia* to mean Tudor despotism, a notion Elton spent his life trying to destroy – worse still when he allowed his readers to deduce that Henry VIII considered that the common law had ossified and therefore set up new courts, Chancery and the Star Chamber – he gave an opening to his contemptible successor Holdsworth, whose sixteen-volume history of English law, according to Elton, 'has for years been as much an obstacle as an aid to the correct understanding of the themes he created'.

---

* G. Elton, *The Tudor Revolution in Government* (1953), was challenged by Lawrence Stone, J. P. Cooper and Joel Hurstfield. But Elton's interpretation is generally considered to be the most convincing even if his dismissal of 'Tudor despotism' is still questionable.

For Elton the supreme test was the view a historian takes of Parliament. Stubbs followed the seventeenth-century lawyers, who declared that Parliament had been an assembly of the estates of the realm (nobility, clergy and commons). According to him the King called them to discuss and advise on the great affairs of the nation. Here, for Stubbs, was evidence of the genesis of Parliament. But when Maitland came to examine the medieval writs summoning men to Parliament he found they were commanded to discuss 'certain matters touching our affairs.' Nothing great about these affairs: they were often petitions by private persons. Parliament was not the expression of the political power of the nation. It was simply yet another court in which justice was dispensed because there was no other appropriate court where it could be dispensed. Parliament did not hear petitions. It was a session of the King's council and its committees heard petitions.

Maitland may have made mistakes but it was not he who argued that Parliament's role did not change. On the main issue Maitland was right to hold that the King did not call Parliament to shackle him. Even today only 'politicians ignorant of history and historians untutored in politics' believe that Parliament rules. Certainly Parliament today shackles arbitrary rule by a clique. But Queen in Council or, in practice, the Cabinet and its committees and ministers rule: Parliament enables ministers to claim that they rule by consent.

Elton praised Maitland for being a don who did the things dons do – he examined, lectured, and sat on committees. His patience was such that he even accepted membership in the Council of the Senate (the most important committee of government in Cambridge), 'a body designed to teach men the mortification of the spirit'. Elton's work is peppered with such sardonic observations and he sets about other scholars with glee. The hitherto revered authority on Tudor history, A. F. Pollard, was a 'careful avoider of manuscripts', who treated

Parliament with 'massive as well as repulsive insularity'. Charles Duggan was foolish to criticise Maitland for a view he did not hold, and Canon Malcolm MacColl had the effrontery of a numskull. G. M. Young, who wrote a glowing tribute to Maitland, which he reprinted in *Daylight and Champaign*, is referred to as a 'self-confident, non-scholar'.

Well, Young was certainly not a professional historian, but that is an odd description of one who could quote from Blue Books by heart, inspired two generations of Victorian scholars, and whose *Portrait of an Age* a Cambridge historian, George Kitson Clark, thought worth editing and identifying Young's allusions with the help of thirty-eight contributors. It would have been wiser, too, for Elton not to refer to Young's book as 'Daylights and Champagne' as if it were the recollections of a roué nursing a hangover.

An unwholesome suspicion seizes one that Elton was more interested in writing about Elton than about Maitland. He saw it as an opportunity to pay a tribute to himself. He wrote scalding criticisms of other scholars; but the most modest criticism of his own work would bring down upon the reviewer an avalanche of abuse. He once accused David Cannadine of having been paid by Lawrence Stone to write as he did. He despised nearly all branches of history that were not concerned with the politics of power in past societies. Not to put that first was to have no sense of history at all. He was uninterested in personality and loathed biography. What we wanted to know about Thomas Cromwell, in his opinion, was the number of pieces of paper that crossed his desk in a particular month dealing with a particular region. So when he wrote about Maitland we are simply told that 'he was a reasonably uncomplicated man of honour, good humour and general kindness'. He found Maitland's passion for Blake's poetry 'the only fact about him that I find incomprehensible'. Odd, too, that Maitland was not more trenchant, truculent and trouncing when he came across error in other men's work. Lamentable that he was a Liberal. 'The Boer War . . . brought out his profound distrust of Joseph Chamberlain (a very conventional attitude).' (No doubt, but quite a good attitude.)

Indeed it is when Elton writes of Maitland as a man that some reservations about Elton's accuracy as an historian need to be made. Some of his Victorian references are inaccurate. It is not true that the only subjects to be studied when Maitland became an undergraduate in 1869 were classics and mathematics. The natural and moral science tripos had been established in 1851. The Apostles do not *debate* topics: they *discuss* them. Nor is it a club. He even manages to mis-spell the name of Maitland's eldest daughter, marvellously called Fredegond. Elton reminds us that in Victorian times manners were more formal and men addressed each other by their surnames. 'One never used first names; only members of the family, and that included brother-in-law Herbert Fisher, were ever so addressed. At all other times Maitland used surnames . . . Maitland's letters to Leslie Stephen in Fisher's memoir are printed without address or subscription.' But they aren't. In C. H. S. Fifoot's collection of Maitland's letters two letters to Stephen are printed, both beginning 'My dear Leslie', and both are in the Cambridge University Library. (All Elton's references to Fifoot's volume went haywire.) In fact Maitland could express emotion when he felt it. Virginia Woolf, who always referred to Maitland as Fred, said that he wrote one of the few letters worth keeping about her father and was one of the very few who wrote something that she thought true and inspiring about her brother on his death.

In the end Elton acquits the prisoner at the bar without a stain on his character. What was it that made this remarkable scholar adopt such a pugnacious attitude to his fellow-historians? It was not that Elton lacked deeper emotions. As a child he knew no word of English, yet never failed to recall the emotion he felt as a young refugee at seeing the white cliffs of

Dover. Like Namier* he loved England and was convinced, as all good ultras are, that things could only get worse. His last public lecture when appointed Regius professor was a tirade against his colleagues for abandoning the requirement that every undergraduate studying history should be examined in the constitutional history of England in its entirety.

Yet you feel that he is in the grip of that tradition of *nil admirari* that inhibits his finer instincts when he writes of Maitland. Hepworth Thompson blighted the initiative of his younger colleagues by his cutting sarcasm, and A. E. Housman carried *nil admirari* to such lengths that he cast a blight upon classical studies in Cambridge for a generation. You feel Elton is treating Maitland as if Maitland was answering questions in an examination paper and Elton marking them with those magical symbols – alpha minus, beta minus query query alpha, alpha gamma – which Cambridge dons use with such self-confidence to describe the exact nuances of ability or ineptitude that their students display in examinations. In the biographical chapter is there not some quality lacking that every biographer should have: a compassion, an empathy with the man or woman, an understanding of his or her faults and limitations, successes and distinctions, and also of the frustrations or achievements we all experience during our encounter with our times? It is a faint disappointment to be handed a balance sheet.

Is scholarship worth it? That is the question which bureaucrats anxious to curb public expenditure on universities ask, and even dons themselves, when vitality is low and the year at an ebb, sometimes doubt. Scholarship resembles reproduction. Millions of spermatozoa are needed before an egg is fertilised, and hundreds of articles have to be written by different hands

---

* Sir Lewis Namier (1888–1960), professor of history at Manchester University; revolutionised the study of Parliament by his contention that political ideas are the rationalisations men use to mask their interests and that it is only by studying the lives of individual MPs that we can understand why events took the shape that they did.

before a major work on a topic that revolutionises our understanding of that topic can be written. It would be comforting to picture all the articles published in learned journals piling up and contributing to truth at compound interest: but it is not so. Even with the most sophisticated techniques of information retrieval, scholars today cannot winnow the chaff from the wheat or master more than a fraction of what is available.

It is these articles that provide the stones used by the great synthesisers and innovators to build their castles. Yet how many scholars, as the day of their retirement comes round, and the speeches and presentations are made – perhaps even a *Festschrift* in their honour, articles by their former students or colleagues are pressed into their hands – wonder whether the contributions they have made to learning will still be used by scholars fifty years hence? Indeed in pursuing one goal scholars almost inevitably neglect other goals. Elton declared that one must study the sources of power and the way that men are governed. With insufferable arrogance he dismissed as unimportant the way that men reason about power and discuss its limitations.

But Maitland did not dismiss it; and it was his long and dazzling introduction to Otto Gierke's *Political Theories of the Middle Ages* that made me first realize what the history of ideas could be. When Leslie Stephen's wife died Maitland wrote to him, 'I have an irrepressible wish, however foolish and wrong it may be, to touch your hand and tell you in two words what I think of you.' I have the same foolish and irrepressible wish about Maitland.

CHAPTER SIX

The Pastoral Don –
The Ethos of King's

In 1950, in his last year as Master of Trinity, G. M. Trevelyan spoke at Founders Feast at King's. King's, he said, was the home of the Muses – the college that cared for poetry, music and drama; a college, so it was reported, which celebrated the Bump Supper after the May Races by the Boat Club and its supporters marching over the lawns singing the chorus of a Greek play. At any rate, Trevelyan added, if it was not true, no one would have told the story about any other college. In his day as an undergraduate, he added, he used to say that the intellectual life of Cambridge turned on the hinge of the side-gate of King's – the shortest route between it and Trinity. Trevelyan was an Apostle: and at that time the Kingsmen among the Apostles began to outnumber those from Trinity.

No college changed character more in the nineteenth century than King's. It was the only college to welcome the commissioners in the fifties and was ready with a revised set of statutes. Until then King's had admitted only Etonians, some of them from college at Eton who were elected scholars of King's and moved, if they so wished and there were vacancies, into fellowships. King's undergraduates did not have to sit the tripos exams: they were awarded degrees automatically. This put them at a disadvantage when prestige and posts went to the Wranglers and the firsts in classics. Under Provost Austen Leigh the college opened the gates to non-Kingsmen and financed scholarships and open fellowships to attract them.

The transformation of King's from being a purely Etonian enclave whose undergraduates became Master of Arts without taking any university examinations into a mixed society took time. It was in 1861 when King's voted to admit non-Etonians; and after 1871, when Nonconformists could be admitted to the university, many came to King's. For forty years many of its best-known fellows came from Nonconformist families and schools. To give non-Etonians equal rights and opportunities fellowships had to be suppressed to find funds to provide scholarships for them and rooms to house them had to be built. The agricultural depression reduced college income. In 1870 a fellow was paid £280–300. In 1895 he was paid £80. The figure was so low because the fellows voluntarily gave up emoluments so that more rooms for undergraduates could be built and scholarships could be financed for non-Etonians. These heroic days of self-sacrifice seem long ago. Dons no longer follow a calling: they belong to a profession. Yet without such idealism (which was not confined to King's) would the English conception of a university have developed as it has done?

At Cambridge there were in effect two kinds of undergraduate: those who read for a pass degree, and those who read for honours. To enter the university everyone had to pass an exam but a very simple exam, deliberately simple because the colleges needed the fees. In fact to become a junior member of a college one did not in some cases even have to pass that. One could play in the college football or cricket teams or row for the university while still trying to pass the exam for university entrance after a failed first attempt. Only after the Second World War did colleges ask about A Level results – sometimes not even then. An Etonian, Bamber Gascoigne, came up to King's in 1953 for an interview and was asked what books he had read during the past year. To his dismay he could not recollect a single one. What did he do in the holidays? He hunted. Anything else? Well, he did a bit of shooting. King's did not give him a place. So he applied next to Magdalene. The Master opened the interview by asking him whether by any chance he was related to an old friend of his, Sir Julian Gascoigne. 'He is my uncle, sir.' 'Thank you, Mr Gascoigne. We look forward to seeing you here next October.' Mr Gascoigne got a double first in English.

There was, however, one significant difference between the undergraduates of Trinity and King's. At King's no one was admitted unless he read for an honours degree. At Trinity numbers were admitted who intended only to read for a pass degree or were content to take a third class in the tripos. There was also another difference. At King's there was a natural intimate relationship between the younger dons and the undergraduates. After all at Eton you might have been in college with a boy who had now become a fellow. There had always been some dons in many colleges who made a point of being available for talk or walks with undergraduates and sought them out. At Trinity Hall there had been Joseph Jowett, great-uncle of the future Master of Balliol; at Jesus, the tutor J. G. 'Tommy' Watts; and in the fifties Leslie Stephen was coaching the Trinity Hall boat and promoting athletics. Most of these were bachelors. Although compulsory celibacy was abolished in 1881, many dons could not afford to marry. Young dons found they could just manage on what they could earn in addition by teaching; but to set up an establishment with a wife would be beyond them. They gave up their time to become ciceroni to the young and helped them to grow up intellectually. They introduced them to books and music that they had never heard of in their philistine public schools.

The earliest, the most bizarre, and yet the best-known of this new school of dons – or at least the best-known in London and abroad (to the dismay of his colleagues) – was Oscar Browning. He went, as the custom was, from Eton to King's and then, after taking a fellowship as of right, returned to Eton to teach and

became a successful housemaster. He also became a trying colleague, testy, touchy, vain and insubordinate. The pattern
throughout his life was always the same. At first eager enthusiasm, self-congratulation that his merits had been recognised,
then resentment and suspicion followed by wild accusations of
intrigue, conspiracy, malice and unfair treatment. In committee
he praised his own far-sightedness and deplored his colleagues'
ineptitude.

He revolutionised the role of the pedagogue. He led the
parched minds of schoolboys out of the desert of iambics and
pentameters into the meadows of English poetry. He was also
the first to protest against the tyranny of games. Mid-Victorian
schoolmasters were either lofty or remote, or ruled through
fear and sarcasm like the harsh-voiced Temple or Kennedy at
Shrewsbury screaming abuse at his sixth-form. Browning made
friends with the boys – too openly in the case of the young
Curzon, a boy not in his house. Hearing of this, the headmaster
seized on a trivial matter of entering too many boys to his house
to sack him. Curzon's father was outraged: not by Browning but
by the headmaster. He approved of the friendship. Browning
returned to King's and there blossomed.

He was not a scholar. History for him was politics. During a
tutorial he would slumber, red bandanna handkerchief over his
face, and then, so my father used to tell me, would begin: 'You
must pay particular attention to what I say, dear boy, for you won't
find it in any book or in the lectures you attend. Count Cavour –
a charming man, I knew him well . . .' He wrote voluminously:
twenty volumes of which not one, but two, were histories of the
world. Naturally he applied to be a Doctor of Letters: naturally
he was turned down. Among his fellow dons he invited ripostes.
Dining at Trinity he said he hardly knew what to do with his books,
the number grew so fast: why not read them? asked Joseph Prior.

Always known as O. B., no set of adjectives describes him.
'Falstaffian, shameless, affectionate, egotistic, snobbish, demo-

cratic, witty, lazy, dull, worldly' are some of those chosen by
one of his earliest protégés, the King's don Goldsworthy Lowes
Dickinson. A few days after Dickinson arrived as a freshman he
came rollicking into his rooms, took stock of him, dropped
him, and then, hearing Dickinson speak in some society, came
up and said, 'I didn't know you were such a clever fellow.' He
had the power of making a young man believe in himself. In the
history society he founded 'we felt we were men and history a
serious subject' – so unlike the 'dreary, meaningless stuff' they
had to translate from Greek. The worldly called O. B. a snob and
no lion-hunter was more avid than he. At a garden party he said,
'Hello Tennyson, I'm Browning.' 'No you're not,' replied the
Poet Laureate. He was unabashed because even more than celebrities he hunted royalty. The royal Tecks (Queen Mary's family)
were partial to him and he amassed crowned heads ('The nicest
Emperor I know'). When his colleague Waldstein brought the
Crown Prince of Prussia to King's, O. B. trumped him by producing the Duchess of York (later Queen Mary).

But he was not a snob among the young. It was the non-
Etonians he sought out at King's. They were often shy and came
from Nonconformist homes – Sheppard, a future Provost of
King's, was one of them. O. B. had to telegraph Sheppard's
father for permission to take his son to the theatre with him;
and later took him to Bayreuth. ('Look, Jack, isn't it just like
an aquarium?' he observed of the Rhinemaidens.) He opened
their minds by making them mix with the elegant sprigs. He
educated the sprigs, too, by puncturing their ideas of good
form. Class differences evaporated in his rooms, where at his
parties one would find foreign professors, diplomats, apprentice
teachers, merchant seamen and soldiers in full regimentals. He
would strum Wagner on the piano and Desmond MacCarthy*

---

* Sir Desmond MacCarthy (1877–1952), literary and dramatic critic; an Apostle and friend
of G. E. Moore and the Bloomsbury group

remembered how after he had sung *'Voi che sapete'* a Tommy in scarlet uniform picked him up and spanked him for singing false notes. He was senior treasurer to dozens of undergraduate societies, including the Union. It was he rather than Seeley who got the history school in the university afloat and it was he who first set up a teacher training college and became its principal. (One of its staff, covering for several sick colleagues, begged to be excused writing a weekly report. 'Certainly not, my dear fellow. When I get your reports I feel like Napoleon reading the reports of his Marshals.')

Browning left behind him 10,000 letters, of which 2,000 were from soldiers or sailors and some from a few shady characters. He never concealed his interest in young men and wrote an ode in alcaics to the penis ('Partner of our days, King potent over men, Troublesome author of anxieties you are . . .'). Some Victorians were privately less shocked by demonstrations of homosexual affection than their successors and were even indulgent towards spooning and swooning over choristers. As a boy Browning had been revolted by the scenes of animal lust in college at Eton and there was never any evidence that he stole even a kiss from the undergraduates he befriended. Nor indeed from the dozens of poor boys whom he put on the road to a steady job. His most recent biographer, Ian Anstruther, who unearthed his correspondence, admits that there were a few bad hats among those he helped and their jocular, mocking letters could suggest that he went to bed with them. But there was never a hint of blackmail or threats in the letters that importuned him for money. He gave them money but also practical suggestions, sympathy and advice, was never shocked by what they told him and never preached. Nicholas Furbank* remarked that he was not a seducer but a jilt. You might bask in the sun,

* P. N. Furbank, professor of English at the Open University and biographer of E. M. Forster.

and it would suddenly go down; and no tears or entreaties to be restored to favour would work.

His self-importance, his high-handedness and his delight in quarrels and protest – three letters in one day was par for the course if a fellow opposed him on the governing body of King's – determined institutions one after another to get rid of him. Whatever club, society or venture he founded he tried to become the sole ruler; and nothing pleased him better than a row. After twenty-one years he was eased out of the treasurership of the Union. After Browning had taught history for twenty-nine years, King's invented a retiring age of seventy. True, a third of the undergraduates read history and O. B. inspired them to analyse the past; but he taught them nothing. He had his consolations. Curzon, when Viceroy of India, invited him to stay and O. B. basked in the aura of curtsies and salaams. Years later, when Curzon was Foreign Secretary, he wrote to him suggesting that he should be made a KBE. Curzon did not miss his opportunity. He got O. B. made OBE. O. B. was delighted.

In colleges where decisions are taken by votes there will always be groupings or even parties, usually vague but occasionally virulent. C. P. Snow's well-known novel *The Masters* reflected accurately the divisions which existed in Christ's before and after the war. (Five years after it was published, in an election to the bursarship of the college the historian and later Master, Jack Plumb, was defeated by one vote after much clandestine intrigue with all the bitterness of personal feeling portrayed by Snow.) This did not happen in King's. To take up a predetermined political position would have been thought to indicate an unregenerate mind. Impossible to predict the votes on any issue: good reasons – well, at any rate, reasons – could always sway votes.

Nevertheless, parties were bound to form at some moment of tension; and in late Victorian days they can be said to have resembled the two cricket teams that used to play at Lords, the

Gentlemen and the Players: those to whom the Eton connection was paramount and those who wanted to broaden the college's horizons. The 'Best Set' in King's were the Etonians, led by A. C. Benson and Arthur Tilley: they decided who from other schools might be admitted to the Best Set and were well-dressed, cultivated, Christian gentlemen. The Players, like Nathaniel Wedd, E. M. Forster's mentor, bubbled with subversive ideas. When Robert Ross was an undergraduate he took his lead from them and in his first year published in *Granta* an unflattering account of the college deploring the Etonian ascendancy and advocating that Oscar Browning should be made Vice-Provost – a proposal palpably inspired by O. B. himself. The tutor of the college, Tilley, suggested to some of the Best Set dining with him that they should throw Ross into the fountain. This they did, and in those days they were doing nothing peculiar. What was peculiar was the reaction in King's. The sense of outrage at this lack of tolerance was such that Tilley was compelled by the college council to make a public apology at hall dinner; and he later had to resign his tutorship. From that time barbaric behaviour in King's was despised and eccentric behaviour, however bizarre, tolerated.

The Players were in fact captained by Etonians. Bradshaw*, the descendant of the regicide who presided at the trial of Charles I, was the epitome of the tolerant, hospitable scholar. Like Oscar Browning he encouraged shy, mistrusting freshmen from minor schools and was an ally of the Scallywags. The Players were not ideological. Bradshaw was a spiritual man but he was the friend of Karl Pearson who, as an undergraduate, had compelled the college to abolish a freshmen's exam in divinity. O.B. kept a crucifix on his door to 'frighten the agnoggers'; but when an undergraduate presented a petition in hall dinner to the high table 'in the name of Jesus Christ our Lord',

---

* Henry Bradshaw (1831–86), bibliographer and University Librarian.

the sweating silence was broken by O.B.: 'Would you mind passing the potatoes?' In 1889 Provost Austen Leigh made a speech deploring the existence of any Best Set. (The Eton era finally came to an end when Provost Durnford died in 1926, the last of the old order who became a fellow, returned to Eton as a beak and then came back to King's – in his case as Provost – which he celebrated by appointing his nephew as Domus bursar, a post for which the nephew lacked some essential abilities, even when, as he put it, he 'had his foot in the saddle'.)

The man who set his face against the Best Set was an Etonian who belonged to it. He had been heard to say that no wonder the boat was bumped in the May Races when the cox was an agnostic from a grammar school. This was Montague Rhodes James. Lord Acton, the most ecumenical historian of the day – who published little but whose vast library ended up in the University Library – was puzzled by him. Was it true, he asked, that James spent the day entertaining undergraduates to lunch and his evenings playing games? How then did he manage to be the third or fourth authority in Europe on manuscripts? 'We have not yet found out' was the reply. As a boy at Eton James had found in the library an unknown fragment of Plutarch and published it. He became a pioneer cataloguer of manuscript collections, was fluent in five European languages, edited eleven volumes published by the Roxburghe Club; and was one of the early members of the Order of Merit. He balanced these accomplishments by being a skilled mimic, who could sing cockney music hall songs and was a merciless player of the nursery card game Racing Demon. The secret was his impeccable memory and the ability to compose articles on trains. He won the affection of all he met and praise for his fairness. It was he who eased O.B. out of the college, but against opposition got Browning a generous pension.

That cox of the boat, Nathaniel Wedd, had by now become a fellow and when the provostship became vacant he went round saying, 'We don't want James as Provost, James doesn't care for the intellect.' He didn't. He took against a young Turk among the fellows, Maynard Keynes, who upset him by moving what were in effect votes of no confidence in the financial adminis-tration of the college. (But he had voted for Keynes to be elected a fellow against his friend, an antiquarian near to his heart, Stephen Gaselee.) His friend Arthur Benson said – in the way that some friends do – that he had the mind of a nice child. (Benson, a catty don if ever there was one, even stood against him at the last moment in the election for Provost: he got two votes.) Benson forecast that just as James had no policy in run-ning the Fitzwilliam Museum, he would have none as Provost. In fact he had a policy of unthinking conservatism. He refused to allow *The Dream of Gerontius* to be performed in the chapel: it was popish. He hated baroque churches, James Joyce's lan-guage, science and the Irish. He opposed degrees for women, and the abolition of compulsory Greek for admission to the university. He joined in the persecution of conscientious objec-tors in the war. When in 1925 the scientist J. B. S. Haldane was arraigned for adultery, he voted for his dismissal. Whenever undergraduates began to discuss serious topics at his parties he turned the conversation to gossip. (In this he was like another brilliant colleger at Eton when he became a don at Trinity, Oxford – Ronald Knox.) A century later not only his opinions but his scholarship began to be attacked by the termites. He was praised in a biography by a scholar of medieval manuscripts for his pioneer work and extraordinary range of knowledge. But a younger admirer found his catalogues full of faults. He was not a dull enough man; he devoured manuscripts too fast; and reliability, after all, is the one quality one hopes for in a catalogue.

James took part in the first archaeological dig in Cyprus, organised by the British School at Athens; and in the first vol-ume of its annual James assured readers that the bones that had been disinterred had been reverently reburied. Perhaps this was the genesis of the book for which for the past century he has been most startlingly remembered – the ghost stories which he read to undergraduates and to the King's choristers over Christmas. They were not perhaps as unsettling as *The Turn of the Screw* by James's famous namesake; but they make the flesh creep. He had in fact an agreeably macabre sense of humour. Of a murderer who buried his wives under the kitchen floor he said: 'Marry in haste, cement at leisure.'

The don who was most remarkable in treating undergraduates as his equal studied political thought. This was Goldsworthy Lowes Dickinson. Unlike Monty James he stood for the life of the mind. In common with other dons at Oxford and Cambridge in the last decades of the century he was preoccupied by ethics and published a Socratic dialogue entitled *The Meaning of Good*. A year or so later he wryly watched his junior, G. E. Moore, sweep aside his offering and refute the metaphysics of his friend M'Taggart, which until that time had captivated Cambridge intellectuals.

Despite the difference in philosophical discourse and method, these three Cambridge philosophers came to almost identical notions of value. For Moore the states of mind that were produced by the pursuit of truth and knowledge or by the contemplation of beauty were excellent; but even more excellent was the state of mind achieved by communion with the beloved. McTaggart dismissed as illusions the existence of God, material objects in Space and the self-contradictions of Time; but – though it went against the grain to do so – he admitted that *something* existed, and by the process of deduction concluded that the universe consisted of souls in ecstatic communion with each other. Lowes Dickinson too put the love of friends first. Human beings in love come nearer than in any of their other experiences to what we might conceive as absolutely good.

Whatever Reality may ultimately be, it is in the life of the affec
tions with all its confused tangle of loves and hates, attractions,
repulsions and, worst of all, indifferences, it is in this intricate
commerce of souls that we may come nearest to apprehending
what perhaps we shall never wholly comprehend, but the quest
of which alone, as I believe, gives any significance to life . . .

This belief that the love of friends transcends all other values
demanded total truthfulness in personal relations. Hypocrisy
about one's feelings, or jealousy of other people's success in
love, were cardinal sins. It became natural to expect that you
would go to bed with someone you loved. But friendship might
entail being hard on friends. The two opiates to be avoided at
all costs were love of success and a preoccupation with money.
Lowes Dickinson's most famous pupil was E. M. Forster, who
in his novels took Dickinson's ideas a stage further; and he
summarised the King's ethos by saying that it was a place that
'taught the perky boy that he was not everything and the limp
boy that he might be something'.

As may be expected Lowes Dickinson was a natural member
of the Apostles. In the most characteristic paper he read to the
Apostles he imagined a meeting of the Society taking place
in heaven. The celestial Apostles were emphatically not Peter,
Andrew, James and John, but Goethe, Hegel, Turgenev and
Victor Hugo. They are discussing – as the Apostles on earth
often did – whom to elect and the question they are facing is,
'Shall we elect God?' For a number of reasons they are disposed
to think it would be unwise, but before the question is put to
the vote there is a knock at the door and God enters. He tells
them their doubts are mistaken. They cannot refuse to elect
him. He is all they believe in, all they see, all they deny, all they
affirm. He is the doubter and the doubt and the founder of
their society. They are still unconvinced and, since his face is
hidden by his hat and cloak, they ask him to reveal himself. As

he does so they all recognise him and each calls him by his name – Goethe *'Das Schöne!'*, Turgenev *'La Verité!'*, Hugo *'L'Idéal!'*, Hegel *'Das Absolut!'*

The college that Monty James presided over was a curious affair. The Vice-Provost had no roof to his mouth but radiated geniality. The oddest was Nixon, an amicable eccentric classicist, kind in particular to poor undergraduates and patron of the choristers. He had only one eye and one hand, and the legend was that two dons had been involved in a railway accident and Nixon was put together with what was left. He would say, 'I threw up my hands in amazement,' rode a tricycle and was often thrown by it, and outdid even O. B. in the length and number of his interventions at college meetings. He would begin by saying that he must 'most strongly protest' against whatever was being proposed and when he worked up to his peroration concluded, 'Yes, a thousand times, yes, or rather No, a thousand times no.' He once proposed a motion, spoke for it at unendurable length and later in the discussion asked leave to speak against it. A fellow who left a meeting of the governing body went outside to smoke a cigarette and asked through the window what was happening. 'Johnny Nixon is up for the seventeenth time' was the reply. At the end of the twentieth century nothing had changed.

But there was one fellow who reminded the college that there were other goals that dons should pursue. This was George Prothero, who twice was runner-up for the Regius professorship of history (once to Acton and once to J. B. Bury: 'history is a science, no more, no less'). In 1877 he reminded King's that it had no university professor, ignored the natural sciences and could not hold a candle to Trinity or St John's in academic distinction. During the next fifty years King's produced some scholars, usually in what were then fringe subjects such as metallurgy and tropical medicine; but Joseph Bancroft emerged in physiology, and C. G. Barkla won a Nobel Prize for X-ray physics; and in the humanities there was the musicologist Edward Dent, in the history of art Roger Fry, in economic history John Clapham and in ancient history F. E. Adcock.

But the spirit of O. B., Monty James, Lowes Dickinson and Nathaniel Wedd ensured that a rival tradition prevailed. This was the tradition that all fellows, certainly all directors of studies and tutors, should try, as far as they were able, to become the guide, philosopher and friend of those they taught; or, in the case of tutors and deans, of the whole undergraduate body. The ideal teacher realised that his task was to teach men, not subjects – with the result that tutorials might begin by discussing whatever written work the undergraduate had brought but could drift into a discussion about Dante or Napoleon or Plato. The don who embodied this tradition – and invented many others to sustain it – was the future Provost John Tressider Sheppard.

Sheppard had begun his career by winning all the undergraduate prizes for classics and obtaining a fellowship, though one of his referees commented, 'Mr S has an unfortunate lightness of touch. This might be cured by a year in a German seminar.' He inherited a touch of buffoonery from Oscar Browning, but in his case it took the form of acting in public whatever he was describing: in a lecture on *The Oresteia* he would become 'each character in turn now reproducing the actual words in Greek and English . . . conveying to an audience the feeling of witnessing the drama not merely being told about it while having it interpreted at the same time'. When Housman arrived in Cambridge he said to Sheppard, 'I hear your lectures are well attended, so I know they must be bad.' He was – rightly – twice defeated for the post of Regius professor of Greek and in tutorials bad grammar went uncorrected: but the pieces he chose for translation or composition were literature, not exercises in syntax. By constant visits to schools and colleges and by his productions in Greek of the dramas, he kept Greek literature alive and postponed its decline. His pupil Patrick Wilkinson, the chronicler of the college of this period, found him baffling to describe: how to convey

> the attraction of his personality; the almost hypnotic power of those slightly protruding eyes, which could have been sinister if it had not been so patently benevolent: the dignity wilfully varied with clowning; the histrionics and rhetoric; the splendid sense of humour and fun; the shrewdness streaked with naivety; the constitutional toughness masquerading as senile debility; the inexhaustible interest in people and desire to help them; the egoism which yet did good by stealth; the total devotion to the college which was yet an extension of the ego . . .

His generosity took more practical forms. He would take an undergraduate on a Hellenic cruise, or pay surreptitiously for a boy to come to Cambridge. Every Sunday night he was at home: no food or drink; only conversation, sometimes long silences and those who broke them were often snubbed 'until some remark would strike his fancy and he would be off on a trail of inspired fantasy.' When Provost he saw to it that fellows and undergraduates sat together at lunch and steered benefactions in the direction of the undergraduates.

During his time as Provost he became a legend. He pranced about with a stick, his white hair flowed, he accosted strangers, he welcomed anyone from overseas. He was at once half a dozen characters from Dickens and also Dickens himself. Like Dickens, he adored acting and dramatising his own situation: he was simultaneously the brothers Cheeryble and Miss Miggs. Although he might shock his old agnostic friends by his religiosity and weary his colleagues by the dilatory way in which he conducted college meetings, maundering from anecdote to anecdote, he was in fact clever at getting his own way. The wealth that Keynes created and hoarded gradually began to be used – and Sheppard saw that it was used for the benefit of the undergraduates. Prizes, travel grants, scholarships and studentships multiplied; hostels were built for them; studentships for the Commonwealth countries were created; amicable concords with colleges at Yale or in London were struck.

He could be cruel, petulant, and in committee a time-waster on a prodigious scale. Under Monty James the annual general meeting of the fellows when the accounts were read over lasted from eleven in the morning until seven in the evening; with Sheppard it was much the same. Every Saturday he regarded meetings of the Council as an agreeable way of filling the day until dinner in hall approached. 'The impartiality of a chairman did not come naturally to him,' wrote Patrick Wilkinson.* 'Indeed it hardly came to him at all.' But he knew all his students and sat in on the scholarship exams, and invited the schoolboys to the Provost's Lodge, crawling round the floor to talk to each one. With his head of white hair and Edwardian clothes he was a character. Every student knew him, often because he gave them money to go abroad or buy books. He wanted the college to be something distinctive and different from the university. When he was young he was friends with Keynes, Strachey, Bell and the Bloomsbury group, worked hard at new interpretations of Homer and the Greek dramas, scoffed at Christianity, was something of a dandy – a late riser shaved each morning in bed by the celebrated barber Beatty. Later he forgot his radical days, wore a cassock, denigrated research and developed an antipathy to the natural sciences – they did not fit in with his idea of a humane education. Keynes, who retained an affection for him and as bursar managed the finances of the college, indulged some of Sheppard's foibles because Sheppard cared for the arts – and few other dons in Cambridge did. His provostship of twenty years culminated in entertaining the King and Queen

* L. P. Wilkinson (1906–1985), Vice-Provost of King's and literary critic of the poetry of Horace and Ovid.

and in being knighted for making classical literature live for the common reader.

By Sheppard's time the old parties of Gentlemen and Players had dissolved. They were replaced by two parties, whose division was less social than moral, and could be described as the Green Ties and the Black Ties. The Green Ties stood for the virtues of intellectual adventure, gaiety, pleasure, vitality; they also stood for sexual disreputability. They descended from both Oscar Browning and Lowes Dickinson and their leaders were Sheppard and Keynes. The Black Ties were respectable, *bien-pensant* and the guardians of orthodox scholarship. Their leader was the economic historian 'Honest John' Clapham, and the staider more conventional fellows followed him, as did the older scientists. The height of their intellectual ideal was ability in solid research, whereas the Green Ties were always looking for promise . . . Promise of what? Of dazzling literary ability, of new heterodoxy, of flights in pure mathematical analysis. At their best they sought to discover a genius, the scholar who revolutionises his subject and makes a breakthrough – as Keynes himself did when, after thirty years in economics, he published the *General Theory*. At their worst they confused promise with the art of being what was called 'a natural Kingsman'. The Green Ties cherished personality. They wanted attractive, if possible good-looking, witty, fascinating young fellows – or if not witty and amusing, then full of heart and sensibility – above all devoted to the undergraduates. The tradition of Bradshaw, O. B. and Lowes Dickinson of treating undergraduates as equals developed still further when, after the First World War, the undergraduates at King's began to call the younger dons by their first names.

The party of the Green Ties was associated inevitably with homosexuality. Yet readers of David Newsome's life of A. C. Benson will know that the typical kindly Victorian don, however romantic his language, never laid a finger on any young man.

Oscar Browning was outraged when he was forced to leave Eton with the imputation that his motives for befriending Curzon were suspect. Sheppard, when a young fellow, was no different even if he went about proclaiming his infatuation with various handsome young men and tried to convince Lytton Strachey that to fall for a philistine was not necessarily evidence of a bad state of mind. Lowes Dickinson was different. He fully understood his temperament, submissive and ardent, regarding himself as crippled by his homosexuality but distinguishing between his condition, which by the laws and conventions of his country was tragic, and his actions, which were not, he thought, base. He had five great loves with whom he sought a kind of physical satisfaction in different ways which the coarse will find comical and the sensitive full of pathos. When in 1931 he read to the Apostles a paper arguing that passionate love as distinct from deep friendship was not something to be ashamed of, he noted that the Society thought it was a lot of fuss about nothing.

In fact undergraduates who were practising homosexuals were not a post-First World War phenomenon. Alfred Brooke, the charming and sweet-natured brother of the poet, was notably promiscuous, but after the war the dons changed too. In both Trinity and King's bachelor dons flourished, but with a difference. In Trinity the susceptible were divided into 'good Trinity', old-style admirers rather than participants, and 'bad Trinity', a tiny and discreet band. In King's things were more flamboyant. It would be an anachronism to imagine that some Kingsmen steeled themselves to 'come out' with all the overtones of unctuous heroism that the phrase conveys; but it is certainly true that those who were active homosexuals did not much mind who knew it or what they said. 'Most of the participants,' Patrick Wilkinson commented, 'got married soon after going down.' Much of the notoriety was gossip, innuendo and high spirits and most King's undergraduates passed through the college either oblivious of anything untoward or not much disposed to mind if they noticed. Nevertheless, in the early twenties, when Provost Durnford died, the Black Ties had to be conciliated, and Keynes, who at that time had been living openly with the ballerina Lydia Lopokova, withdrew from the contest. The Green Ties thereupon declared that at no price could they consent to Clapham moving from the tutorship to the Lodge. When, however, the *tertium quid*, Rupert Brooke's uncle, resigned in 1933 there was little debate. Sheppard was elected and the Green Ties triumphed.

Yet it was Sheppard who more than any other man destroyed the Green Ties. His irritability with intellectuals, his monologues against science and research, his preference as he grew older for illusion to truth, grew with the years. Between Sheppard and Keynes there had always been a tension. Keynes thought that the intellect and its exercise mattered more than anything else in academic life. He once clashed with Wedd, who said to him, 'You want the college to become Alexandria. I want it to become Athens.' Keynes brought an aura of worldliness with him. 'How many of the fellows,' he once asked, 'will find a place in the *Dictionary of National Biography*?' Whereas Sheppard once shocked a group of Etonians by reminding them that the founder of Eton and King's, Henry VI, was a failure; and the failures among their contemporaries, shy, inarticulate creatures, should not be despised: who was to know what they might be in the future?

After the Second World War some of the younger fellows began to ask whether the ideals of the Green Ties were adequate. Why did King's have so low a reputation in science? Why did those fellows elected on promise publish so little and so few become professors? The college lavished its wealth on the welfare of the undergraduates but what did it do for research? Was it right that 69 per cent of its entry came from public schools? Easy to justify because year after year King's got a higher percentage of firsts than any other college: but would that record stand unless the college recruited from not merely the famous direct grant schools but maintained grammar schools such as Maidstone? Should King's not create fellowships for university lecturers who had no fellowships elsewhere?

These and many other anxieties coalesced into a debate about the size of the college. The then senior tutor, Patrick Wilkinson, wanted to reduce the size from 300 to 240 undergraduates, with sixty-five fellows. I argued for 270 and eighty respectively. But there was a party that wanted to expand yet further and when they pressed their case to a vote I, as Provost, read out a letter sent to me by E. M. Forster, an honorary fellow who had rooms in college:

> The contact – particularly social contact – between the old and the young is eminently desirable for the old, and may save them from becoming too pompous and frowsty. Such contact still exists in King's, although it has been impaired for various reasons during the past ten years. It will be further impaired if we get larger. The arguments in favour of expansion are not convincing. Our 'national need' is pleaded, and quite correct if one accepts the Whitehall definition of National Need. I don't. For me our need is the production of civilised individuals, and I believe that we are more likely to produce them if we stay at our present size than if we expand. The suggestion is also made that by expanding we shall demonstrate our vitality, but I think that those who make it may be confusing a college with a commercial enterprise and even with a newspaper. It seems true that a business concern must either get bigger or get out. But an institution over 500 years old may respond to other laws and have other means of proving that it is alive.

But the impersonal forces which were expanding nearly all academic institutions, including Cambridge itself, were too strong. The social composition of the undergraduate body changed and so did its ethos. The increase in the number of the fellows in order to provide, among other things, more opportunities to young scholars at a time when universities were expanding, together with the desire to give high table rights to anyone who taught for the college and to the cohorts of eminent scholars passing a year in Cambridge, created a situation where at dinner in hall it was the rule rather than the exception to find oneself sitting next to strangers on either side.

But it is time to look at another institution that had an intellectual life of its own and owed little to the colleges: the laboratory.

William Buckland
carrying his blue bag
(after a portrait by
Richard Ansdell, 1843).

John Henry Newman,
1847 (after a painting
by W. C. Ross).

Benjamin Jowett, 1889 (portrait by G. F. Watts).

Mark Pattison, 1884.

Oscar Browning,
*c.*1900.

Goldsworthy Lowes
Dickinson, 1920.

John Tressider
Sheppard, *c.*1920.

William Whewell,
*c.*1860.

Frederic Maitland,
1906 (portrait by
Beatrice Lock).

J. J. Thomson, the young Fellow of Trinity, 1885.

Ernest Rutherford, Cavendish professor (photograph taken after the award of the Order of Merit, 1926).

Alan Hodgkin,
on election to a
Fellowship at
Trinity, 1936.

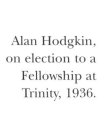

Cyril Bailey, 1939
(drawing by William
Rothenstein).

CHAPTER SEVEN

The Trinity Scientists –
J. J. and Rutherford

Great scientists can kill their subject. Newton killed physics in Cambridge. What, it was asked, was there left to do? As a result the advances in sciences and technology on the Continent were ignored. So were Faraday in London and William Thomson (Lord Kelvin) in Glasgow. Obsessed by the belief that an undergraduate must learn what was true, Whewell opposed the study of modern science: he argued that not until a century had passed could we be certain that scientific theories were true.* No wonder Robert Peel remarked, 'Are the students of Cambridge to hear nothing of electricity?' Gradually heat and hydrostatics seeped into the mathematical tripos, but in the new natural sciences tripos men studied only botany, chemistry and anatomy. After more than twenty years of fly sheets, votes in the Senate House and arid discussion it was at last decided in 1868 to set up a committee on the teaching of experimental physics. It recommended establishing a chair and a laboratory. But how to pay for the laboratory? The next year William Cavendish, by then Duke of Devonshire and Chancellor of the univer-

---

* In the 1940s J. A. Ratcliffe, one of Rutherford's research students and later professor of the radio ionosphere group, proposed the establishment of a new tripos, a 'Science Greats' which would enable those in the humanities to understand modern science. His proposal was opposed by, among others, his colleague in the Cavendish laboratory, Brian Pippard, who in an elegant speech in the Senate House said that while a lecture by Professor Ratcliffe would indeed be worthwhile hearing, students might be lulled into thinking that what he said was *true*. and that could not be the case since many scientific hypotheses could be only provisional.

sity, offered to pay the whole sum. This enlightened industrialist – who built railways and Bessemer plants to make steel – had the luck to see that the first holder of the chair was a genius. James Clerk Maxwell had shown that electricity and magnetism were the same thing. In his inaugural lecture he declared that students have to be taught how to conduct experiments by demonstrators. And, second, that the professor and staff must engage in experimental research. They must keep in touch with work on physics abroad: physics was not just mathematical measurement of what was already known. Are we, he asked, so sure that there is nothing more to be learnt about the molecule?

Still, Clerk Maxwell was more of a theoretician than an experimentalist, and the impetus to upset conventional scientific and philosophical theories came from the mathematicians. One of them at Trinity, William Kingdon Clifford, foreshadowed some of the most abstruse theories of twentieth-century physics.

Clifford was that rare bird, a mathematician who was interested in general ideas – as well as being a gymnast who once hung by his toes from the weathercock of a church tower. He challenged Kant's answer to Hume. Hume had argued that no proposition could be said objectively to be true since all our knowledge is based on our own or past experience. Kant disagreed: there was one branch of knowledge, mathematics, that was universally true. If you measure space you will find that the angles of every triangle add up to 180 degrees. Had man never existed that would have been true. Clifford was the first to realise that the non-Euclidean geometry which had just been invented by Lobachewsky and Riemann – in which the sum of the angles of a triangle was either more or less than 180 degrees – destroyed Kant's argument. Euclid's geometry had now to be regarded as just one of a number of systems of measuring space: the axioms of geometry, as Clifford put it, 'are convenient assumptions: and not *a priori* necessities of thought and perception'.

Clifford went further. In attacking the concept of continuous space he foreshadowed elements of quantum theory; and when he applied Riemann's geometry he deduced that space was curved and anticipated Einstein. He wrote with wit, clarity and passion. When he and Sidgwick disputed at the Grote Club, the conversation sizzled. 'Rules of philosophy,' he wrote, 'are admirable if two conditions are satisfied: first you philosophise before you make your rules: second you publish them with the fond and feverish hope that no philosopher will attend to them.' Of another philosopher he wrote: 'He is writing a book on metaphysics and is clearly cut out for it; the cleverness with which he understands things and his total inability to express what little he knows will make his fortune as a philosopher.'

Clerk Maxwell died when only forty-seven and his successor, Lord Rayleigh, stayed for only five years. The next holder of the chair, however, turned the Cavendish into the most prestigious department of experimental physics in the world. He helped to answer questions that concerned chemists: namely, what are molecules and how are the atoms that form them glued together? This was J. J. Thomson.

Thomson had come up the hard way. He was born into the minor mercantile class in Manchester. His father died young (his mother was left impoverished), but not before he had introduced his son to Joule, Manchester's most famous scientist who framed the first law of thermodynamics. Thomson managed to get a place at Owens College, which was to become the University of Manchester, and from there won a scholarship to Trinity. He read mathematics and became second Wrangler. In so doing he joined a remarkable band of those who came second in the mathematical tripos: Whewell, Clerk Maxwell, Kelvin, W. K. Clifford, William Cavendish and the economist Alfred Marshall. On the strength of a number of papers during three years after becoming a fellow of Trinity, he was elected fellow of the Royal

Society in his twenties and, to the astonishment of his fellow-scientists as well as the sceptics in the humanities, he was elected to succeed Rayleigh in 1884 at the age of twenty-seven. In the judgement of Lawrence Bragg, who years later held the chair, he more than any man transformed Victorian physics into the physics of the twentieth century.

Thomson worked on the conduction of electricity through gas. German physicists believed that the stream of faint blue light coming from the negative electrode – the cathode ray – was a form of radiation. The English physicists thought they were negatively charged particles. In 1896–7 Thomson succeeded in deflecting the particles by both magnetic and electric fields, and he published a paper showing that the cathode ray stream was made up of particles with a mass of a smaller order of magnitude than an atom. Each particle carried an electric charge and they were different from any atoms known to exist. These particles were soon called electrons. The atom was no longer the smallest unit of matter.

J. J., as he was always called, looked meek and mild but he got what he wanted. He was told by his tutor not to try for a Trinity fellowship after only one year's work; he did so and was elected. His wife-to-be told him she would not leave her father; he replied he was intending to tell her father that he wanted to marry her. He married into the Cambridge intellectual aristocracy. His father-in-law, Sir George Paget, was Regius professor of physic (i.e. medicine), but he was without social pretensions and refused a peerage because he did not think he was rich enough to merit the title. Soon a stream of the most brilliant students flocked to work under J. J. at the Cavendish, including some who had qualified for science research scholarships for overseas students. (Rutherford came to England on such a scholarship; and so did Oliphant and Philip Bowden.) Nobel Prizes descended regularly on the Cavendish scientists: Rutherford, Francis Aston, Charles Wilson, Lawrence Bragg, Owen

Richardson, Edward Appleton and J. J.'s son George were all Laureates.

He took a genuine interest in everyone's work and in the man himself. 'Every one of us felt a certain pleasure within ourselves,' wrote a foreign researcher, 'on hearing a footstep that every Cavendish man recognises solely as J. J.'s.' He thought enthusiasm even more important than originality. He never attempted to direct research: although most were working on X-rays and electrons, some worked in other fields. Nothing pleased him more than to relax with his colleagues during the afternoon tea-break. He paid for the tea and milk (but not for the buns). Once a year the lab held a dinner at Trinity at which J. J., and later Rutherford with J. J. at his side, presided beaming. There were facetious speeches and tributes to new triumphs and traditional songs, one to the tune of 'Clementine':

> There the atoms in their glory
> Ionise and recombine . . .

The triumphs owed as much to ingenuity in building apparatus as to scientific induction or intuition. J. J. fought hard to get funds from the university, but most of the apparatus was hand-made – in the proverbial manner of sealing wax and string. The smell of burning Bank of England red sealing wax pervaded the building. The glass jars containing shrimp paste for sandwiches on grander occasions were used – when empty – to make cheap high-voltage batteries. For years scientists had been trying to create a vacuum and for years they never quite succeeded. The brilliant young German Heinrich Hertz came to some wrong conclusions about cathode rays because his vacuum techniques were inferior, and it was Thomson's skill in devising better apparatus that enabled him to discover the electron. His son, George Thomson, admitted that J. J. was not good at putting the apparatus together but

He had the physician's gift of diagnosis and could often tell a research worker what was really the matter with an apparatus that a man had made and struggled with miserably for weeks. His own apparatus was simply designed and constructed without necessary refinement. The phrase 'sealing wax and string' with which a later generation described the Cavendish apparatus of his day is an exaggeration of course but not a great one; judged by modern standards at least there was a slightly amateurish air about it . . . Yet this rather odd collection of glass and brass did in fact play a major part in producing a change in men's ideas of the nature of matter and energy that has occurred since 1896.

James Aston described how a researcher in the Cavendish might be reduced to baffled despair when the apparatus he had built failed to work and then

along would shuffle this remarkable being, who, after cogitating in a characteristic attitude over his funny old desk in the corner, and jotting down a few figures and formulae in his tidy handwriting, on the back of somebody's Fellowship thesis, or on an old envelope, or even the laboratory cheque book, would produce a luminous suggestion, like a rabbit out of a hat, not only revealing the cause of trouble, but also the means of cure. This intuitive ability to comprehend the inner working of intricate apparatus without the trouble of handling it appeared to me then, and still appears to me now, as something verging on the miraculous, the hallmark of a great genius.

Thomson visualised his experiments: they owed nothing to theory, or indeed to mathematics, which was for him 'merely the language', as his son put it, 'which described the physical and spatial concepts in his mind'.

In 1918 J. J. was appointed Master of Trinity and died there

in 1940. He was not a don who went for walks in the Lake
District or sailed on the Norfolk Broads. Gardening, gentle lawn
tennis and golf (often by himself as a way of solving problems)
were his hobbies. He liked talk, watching rugger matches, reading Dickens, Scott and Jane Austen and going to chapel – he
was a devout attender. He was a classic absent-minded professor.
Finding her husband's trousers lying on his bed, Lady Thomson
in a frenzy phoned the Trinity porters to enquire if he had
forgotten to put on a new pair.

Women were welcomed in J. J.'s lab. Rose Thomson had been
a research student in the Cavendish when the young professor
wooed her. Eleanor Sidgwick had been recognised as a co-
author with Rayleigh of three papers presented to the Royal
Society; and J. J. sent Helen Klasien's work on resistance curves
to the Royal. Rose was inordinately proud of her husband, but
she developed into something of a tartar. When Enoch Powell
and the (later) Nobel Prizeman and Master of Trinity Alan
Hodgkin were elected fellows, Powell said to her how proud he
was to be a successor in classics to the greatest of all Masters of
Trinity, Bentley. Lady Thomson had no doubt in her mind who
was the greatest Master, and later in the evening came up to
Hodgkin and said, 'Mr Powell, I thought it was disgraceful the
way that Mr Hodgkin talked about the Mastership,' and swept
on before Hodgkin could disclaim his new identity. He was
never invited to the Lodge again. Hodgkin treasured the story
that when W. B. Yeats was brought to dine in hall, J. J. turned
and said, 'Been writing much poetry lately, Mr Keats?' It was
on the election of new fellows that J. J. at times displayed an
odd way of welcoming them. When Lord Rothschild was elected
he made a point of saying that race, creed, great wealth and
social standing counted for nothing in the deliberations of the
electors: true, but somewhat dampening. On another occasion,
when Anthony Blunt was elected, he said, 'This is the first time
we have elected a Fellow in art-history and I very much hope it

will be the last.' No one minded; and he was regarded with unassailable affection.

J. J.'s successor as head of the Cavendish was one of the geniuses of the twentieth century. Ernest Rutherford was a pioneer in the study of radioactivity. He was the first to disintegrate the nucleus of the atom artificially and the first to discover that the structure of the atom resembles a planetary system. His model of the atom contradicted the laws of classical electrodynamics. His work on radioactivity contradicted the law of the conservation of energy. And these conclusions he justified by his experiments, not by spinning theories.

No one could have been less like J. J., blinking through his spectacles and talking through his false teeth. Rutherford was generous, hot-tempered, hearty, big, boastful and boisterous. He was born on a farm in New Zealand and when he came to Cambridge found himself disparaged as a colonial. He spoke with an accent – all his life. In fact he had an excellent education there and among his teachers in college at Christchurch was a curio, who later became a crank, but who encouraged him to research. He at once made his name in a paper on the magnetisation of iron by high-frequency discharges, quoting Thomson, Oliver Lodge and Hertz with respect; but then arguing that they were all wrong. Not the usual preamble to a paper by a young scientist. Later he worked on radio waves and it was this that won him one of the 1851 Exhibition scholarships that the Prince Consort had set up. In fact the awarders in London put a New Zealand chemist first – an indication that chemistry still outranked physics; but the chemist withdrew, and Rutherford wrote asking J. J. to accept him as a research student.

Thomson not only accepted him, but he and his wife found Rutherford lodgings and were especially kind to him. Not so the demonstrators in the lab, who high-hatted him for his first two months when he was lonely and had no friends. But, Rutherford wrote to his fiancée in New Zealand, they changed their tune when they heard him give his first paper to the Physical Society on his radio-wave detector. In his first year in the lab he transmitted a radio message over half a mile and noted how radio waves 'go through walls'. J. J. persuaded him to join Trinity despite the expense and got him some teaching and some reviewing for *Nature*. When Röntgen discovered X-rays J. J. immediately saw their importance. He and Rutherford used X-rays to turn gas into a conductor of electricity. They saw that negative and positive ions were formed and this suggested that the rays were streams of negatively charged particles. The five papers Rutherford published over the next two years established him as an experimental scientist of international reputation. For Rutherford had the ability to *measure* reality, while J. J. and others speculated on its nature.

After three years in the Cavendish Rutherford left for a chair in physics at McGill in Montreal. Some, such as C. P. Snow, allege that it was characteristic of Cambridge snobbery and indifference to scientific research that J. J. made no effort to retain him; and Rutherford himself wrote letters complaining that his chance of a fellowship at Trinity seemed slight and he was up against 'the prejudice of the place'. In fact good judges thought he would have walked into a fellowship. But the dominant reason was that Rutherford was obsessed by his research. If he had got a post in Cambridge he would have had to teach long hours. At McGill a professor was paid only £100 less than J. J. at Cambridge; the physics department was sponsored by a Midas who bought any apparatus required so the professor did not have to fund-raise; and the post would enable Rutherford to marry his New Zealand sweetheart.

It was in Canada that Rutherford made his major discovery, with Frederick Soddy, on radioactive decay and the theory of disintegration. His reputation was now immense, and in 1906 Sir Arthur Schuster, professor of physics at Manchester, made a remarkable proposal. He would retire early and arrange for Rutherford to be appointed in his place with full authority over all parts of the department. There was, of course, some correspondence about salary. Manchester paid better than any other British university, recognising that distinction in research would give the university a unique cachet; and Rutherford did some hard bargaining. He could afford to: Yale, the Smithsonian and other North American universities were making him offers and McGill at once upped his salary. Rutherford hesitated but Schuster won the day. The post was never advertised and Rutherford was appointed. Very different from his transition to the Cavendish laboratory later, in 1919. Then it was clear that only one man could take J. J.'s place, but how was it to be done? The Vice-Chancellor was powerless and could not make an offer. Indeed since the salary was only £850 compared with Manchester's £1,250 and it was impossible to calculate exactly how much he would receive from fees, no one could name a figure, let alone negotiate. Nor could Cambridge assure Rutherford that his plan for expanding the Cavendish would be accepted. And, of course, it was impossible to by-pass the board of electors who were appointed to prevent a job being struck. Eventually the conscience of the electors was placated and, since Rutherford was the only candidate, he returned to the Cavendish.

He returned as the acknowledged master of the atom, the man who had disproved J. J.'s model of the atom as a plum pudding in which the negatively charged electrons were stuck like plums in the pudding of the atom. Rutherford declared, as the result of years of experiment, that the atom had a nucleus. Hans Geiger and Ernest Marsden had observed that when alpha particles (helium nuclei) hit gold foil most went through but one in 8,000 went backwards: as Rutherford said, 'it was as though you had fired a 15 inch shell at a piece of tissue paper and it had bounced back at you.' At first Rutherford's model of the structure of the atom was no more than an hypothesis.

However, it was not intuition but months of hard work and failed experiments that led him to conclude that the atom is like the solar system, a nucleus surrounded by electrons. Between 1910 and 1914 the evidence accumulated and the model became accepted by both physicists and chemists. David Wilson, Rutherford's biographer, tells the story of Rutherford insisting loudly that ions existed – 'jolly little beggars so real that I can almost see them' – as evidence that Rutherford 'lived in a world in which he was himself a part of the process he was observing and measuring'. Peter Medawar* was to say of him that his discoveries were 'the invention of a fragment of a possible world' and his experiments were measurements to prove that the imagined world really existed.

Rutherford came to the Cavendish as the leader of a great lab at Manchester. Geiger, Marsden, Moseley and the great Danish theoretician Niels Bohr had worked with him there. He brought his former student at Manchester, James Chadwick, with him; Mark Oliphant and Harrie Massey came from Australia, and Francis Aston and Charles Ellis flourished under him. In 1932 Chadwick discovered the neutron, Patrick Blackett the positron and John Cockcroft and Ernest Walton split the lithium atom. It was an epic year in the history of physics.

Rutherford could not get the funds he believed he had been promised from the government. Everyone had to make their own equipment or borrow or steal it. Despite Chadwick's urging Rutherford would not raise funds from industry even when the Vice-Chancellor told him of a benefactor willing to help him. But if his team were deprived of resources, and the horde of graduate students whom Rutherford thought it was his duty to accept ate into what few pieces of equipment there were left, on a crucial count they were fortunate; Rutherford was an unselfish

---

* Sir Peter Medawar (1915–1987) won the Nobel Prize for his work in the immunology of transplantation. He considered science as a deductive creative art from which came ideas that experiment verified or disproved.

leader. Charles Darwin (grandson of the great Darwin) made a suggestion to him about the collision of an alpha particle with a hydrogen nucleus and was told to write a paper about it. 'One has heard tales of great men who had had suggestions given to them by their juniors and have incorporated them into their train of thought to such an extent that they forget their original source.' Indeed there were. Rutherford's biographer refers to J. J.'s propensity to be 'not, unfortunately, famous for giving others credit where it was their due'. One day Aston, who had for long worked with Thomson, rushed up to Rutherford to tell him that he thought he had identified yet another isotope but J. J. refused to believe him. Rutherford said, 'Gow down on yer knees, me boy, and thank yer Miker that the Old Man hasn't swiped it.'

The most fascinating of all those who worked with Rutherford was the Russian physicist Peter Kapitza. Kapitza said that his thirteen years at the Cavendish were the happiest of his life. He shamelessly flattered Rutherford, called him the Crocodile, and after his death wrote that you forgot the few imperfections – the hot temper, the tactlessness – and saw 'only a great man with an astounding brain'; you remembered the cordiality, the jokes, the loud laughter, and the willingness to go to any lengths to help foreign scientists after 1918 and again after Hitler. Rutherford liked teasing and liked Kapitza teasing him. Chemists were always good for a tease: their research, he said, was so dull. But when he came up against that ornery Yorkshireman, the chemist Fred Dainton, he lent him some of the Cavendish's apparatus. Rutherford was not erudite: his forte was to come up with daring hypotheses based on hours of experiments, often leading to blind alleys, but always returning full of hope and ingenuity.

He took no interest in technical detail and he would not argue with colleagues or other scientists. Many scientists work through discussion. Rutherford believed in work on the bench.

High flown theoretical ideas were taboo. To this there was one exception: Niels Bohr, who would expound his ideas very slowly for an hour or two. But Rutherford was adamant: 'Don't let me catch anyone talking about the universe in my laboratory.' This led him to commit an injustice. Rutherford loathed J. D. Bernal. Bernal threw out ideas and left others to pick them up. He was a communist, a technocrat who preached that inefficient capitalism must be replaced by a new mode of production directed by scientists. He laid down the law about politics and he laid women. Only Lawrence Bragg stopped Rutherford from throwing Bernal out of the lab. Yet Bernal was applying physics to living molecules such as proteins and viruses: he was a pioneer in X-ray crystallography and in molecular biology. One of Bernal's research students was Max Perutz, later a Nobel Prizeman and head of the famous MRC molecular biology laboratory. Perutz recalled that when Bragg was head of the Cavendish after the Second World War he was irritated by Francis Crick and James Watson, who 'lounged around, arguing about problems for which there existed as yet no firm experimental data instead of getting down to the bench and doing experiments. I thought they were wasting their time.' So did Bragg. But remembering, perhaps, the case of Bernal, he did not throw them out or starve them of resources, and they became the famous discoverers of the structure of DNA. With typical generosity Perutz said he learnt that 'there is more than one way of doing good science'.

Rutherford gave his young colleagues a hard time: 'When are you going to give me results, results, not your chatter?' But they learnt that these remarks were a subconscious outflow addressed impartially to colleagues, graduate students, lab assistants and workmen. He had the contempt of the colonial for the leisurely approach to work in the mother country. He would question his students about their experiments: he did not supply answers – they must learn through his questions how to ask questions

themselves. Kapitza summed it up: 'The Crocodile values so
highly that a person should express himself that he not only
allows them to work on their own themes, but also encourages
them to put sense into their futile plans.' That was still true,
added Perutz, when he himself left the Cavendish forty-one
years later.

He read a vast amount of history, knew his English classic
novelists, and some modern novelists too; and was taken by a
Chekhov play performed in Cambridge. He enjoyed crowing
over archbishops and dignitaries when they discovered how well
read he was. He pitied those who studied the humanities, 'the
poor chaps who haven't got labs to work in', but he was only too
aware that 'the literary fraternity' was opposing science getting a
greater share of resources. F. M. Cornford had the Cavendish in
mind when, in his satire on university politics, *Microcosmographia
Academica*, he referred to scientists as the Adullamites who are
dangerous 'because they know what they want; and that is, all
the money there is going . . . They are not refined like classical
men, that is why they succeed in getting all the money that is
going.'

His house would have made an aesthete shudder, but it was
homely and filled with the bric-à-brac of his life and memories
of New Zealand. His wife, who never took to Cambridge, had
the spartan common sense of her upbringing; he had his lab,
she her garden. If Lady Thomson could sometimes be a tartar,
Lady Rutherford was a gorgon, ordering colleagues and graduate students who came to lunch to get to work mowing and
hoeing. Rutherford revelled in his fame and the decorations
and citations he won. No scruples deflected *him* from accepting
a peerage. Yet when he died he 'cut up', as he would have said,
for a pittance. He never made a penny out of his discoveries
and despised those who took out patents. Science was knowledge and knowledge should be free for all. He continued to
ignore his colleagues' requests that he should raise money from

industry. At last, in the year before he died, he was induced to accept – provided it was given to the university and not to him personally – a quarter of a million pounds from the car manufacturer Herbert Austin, who in return got a peerage. This was engineered by John Cockcroft and Ernest Walton, who were now building their first accelerator. They wanted to build a cyclotron. But Rutherford's parsimony had already damaged his team at the Cavendish. Pope's lovely line proved all too true: 'The sick'ning stars fade off th'ethereal plain.' When in 1933 Rutherford refused to build the cyclotron Chadwick left for Liverpool, taking Feather with him; Blackett went to London; Ellis left and Oliphant threatened to go to Birmingham. Still wedded to experiments with simple hand-made equipment, Rutherford recoiled from vast expenditure on new machines. It was said of J. J. that he opened the door to new physics but never went though it himself. It could be said of Rutherford that he never went through the door to Big Science.

The First World War brought Rutherford into the political world. When he came to the Cavendish few knew of his work on detecting submarines by sound waves. What did become known was the story of Rutherford sending a message to the anti-submarine warfare committee to say he could not attend the meeting because he had split the atomic nucleus which, if true, was of greater importance than the war. He was furious at the way the army and navy treated the scientists who were attached to them, but he learnt how to work in Whitehall. He loathed Lindemann (Lord Cherwell, Churchill's 'the Prof')* even more than he hated Bernal because Lindemann attached himself to Churchill and enjoyed political intrigue. Rutherford worked though channels. He was no committee man. Not for him those happy afternoon hours at Cambridge spent in self-

---

* Frederick Lindemann, Lord Cherwell (1886–1957), the only professor to compete in tennis at Wimbledon; professor of experimental philosophy (i.e. physics) at Oxford (1919), student of Christ Church (1922–57); became friend and adviser to Churchill (1921–56).

satisfying arguments for defeating proposals for change. He was a fixer: a word here, an understanding there and the agenda for the next meeting was settled and its conclusions agreed in advance. Civil servants knew that he would not go behind their backs and, even if decisions went against him, would not leak to the press. During the 1920s he pv'.lished (for him) little and spent much time on promoting science in government. Henry Tizard* and Solly Zuckerman†, both Oxford scientists, were his successors.

In the twentieth century Trinity could boast that in nearly every branch of science, including the most recent such as radio astronomy, it could number fellows of the Royal Society. Littlewood and Hardy transformed pure mathematics (in which Cambridge, despite all the pother about Wranglers in Victorian times, had fallen behind the mathematicians of France and Germany). In physiology Adrian, Hodgkin and Huxley (who used as an undergraduate as to read Milton antiphonally with his kinsman George Trevelyan) each won a Nobel Prize, all were awarded the Order of Merit, and all became Masters of Trinity. To win a scholarship to Trinity was the goal of bright scientists in the sixth form. At the end of the century Trinity used its wealth to set up a science park in the city and to found Newton studentships for post-doctoral scholars. Of course eminent scientists flourished in other colleges, notably St John's and Caius; but the pre-eminence of Cambridge in science and mathematics among British universities – the nearest challengers being Imperial College, London and University College, London – owed most to Trinity's example.

---

* Sir Henry Tizard (1885–1959) was a Whitehall scientist who clashed with Lindemann over the development of radar. He was the most important link between the armed services and scientists during the Second World War and its aftermath.
† 'Solly', Lord Zuckerman (1904–93), professor of anatomy, University of Birmingham (1943–68), scientific adviser to Supreme HQ Middle East and Allied Expeditionary Forces (1943–46); chief scientific adviser to Secretary of State for Defence (1960–66) and to Her Majesty's Government (1964–71).

CHAPTER EIGHT

The Don as Wit – Maurice Bowra

The Oxford of the first sixty-five years of the twentieth century was almost as far removed from Oxford today as was the Oxford of Jowett's day. After the First World War the heads of colleges still held sway, and most colleges numbered barely 200 students. It was an Oxford where three-quarters of the undergraduates came from the public schools and the swagger direct grant schools like Manchester and Bristol. Only 19 per cent came from maintained grammar schools. The academic leaders were Balliol, Merton, New College, Queen's and Corpus, with Somerville first among the women's colleges. The social leaders were Christ Church and Magdalen. No one could read for a degree in economics, political science, geography or anthropology, and it was not until 1920 that Ernest Barker* won support to set up a new and later famous school in philosophy, politics and economics (Modern Greats). The classics – Mods after five terms, Greats after seven terms – was the school with the highest prestige. History was not far behind, weighted towards English history and the study of documents such as *Stubbs's Charters*. To study English you had to master Old and Middle English and other philological and classificatory hurdles. Modern languages followed suit, and a proposal to establish a 'European Greats'

---

* Sir Ernest Barker (1874–1940) was a Balliol man and fellow of several Oxford colleges. He became the first professor of political science at Cambridge (1928–39) and was one of the earliest explorers of pluralism and the ideas of Gierke and Figgis about the State.

was turned down. Lindemann and Hinshelwood shut the gate on engineering. The university imposed a quota on the numbers the women's colleges could admit.

It was at Oxford where, until 1970, 62 per cent of the students studied the humanities and 73 per cent of them were undergraduates. Very few bothered to take a PhD. Fellowships were sometimes awarded immediately on the result of performance in finals but were often obtained by hanging around for a year or two hoping to impress in meetings of academic societies and by picking up some teaching. No one boasted of 'breakthroughs' in research. 'Show me a researcher and I will show you a fool,' said a provost of Oriel in pre-1914 days. A don would be known to be engaged on a particular line of enquiry but his scholarship was a by-product of his main duty – which was to teach. The tutors, not the professors, were the gatekeepers to the academic pastures: very few of them were scientists.

The years 1900–1940 were the golden age for Oxford undergraduates. To get a first was a hall-mark for life. The average and the stupid could also get a passport to life through a Blue or by making a name for themselves at the Union. Undergraduates reflected the public school ethos, grammar school boys assimilated to it. Loyalty to the college and to the well-known dons in it was a sign of good form. This was the time when you made friends who might be important to you later in life. There was more to the mystique than that. Oxford dons may not have been bound by political allegiances as strictly as in the days when Peel or Granville or Eldon lobbied for support: by now the ties were to the far wider circle of the new governing classes. They approved of the Oxford ethos and would do battle for it. Whereas the Victorian Royal Commissions swept away archaic statutes and customs, the Asquith Commission of 1919–21 endorsed Oxford's collegiate tutorial system, made no special provision for science (except to reserve the Parks for laboratories); and they opposed proposals to add lay members to governing bodies. Such radical reformers as existed retreated. No one asked the subjects studied to be relevant or of practical use. Quite enough if those who worked at them could teach undergraduates to recognise when a charlatan was talking. The alliance between Oxford and the governing class grew even stronger.

The golden age of the don came a little later – in the years 1945–75. The don had risen in public esteem. The wartime boffins had won renown and began to be called to Whitehall to advise ministers. They had security of tenure and, though less well-off than civil servants, they were their own master. They could lecture on what they liked and take long holidays. Some could supplement their income by writing for the weekly reviews, and by giving talks on the BBC. More academic staff were needed as the movement for the expansion of higher education gained ground and culminated in the Robbins Report. So their salaries, paid mainly by the State, shot up. Between 1958 and 1968 salaries rose by over 28 per cent, vastly in excess of inflation. Even as stimulating for the dons was the admission of four times as many graduate students after 1945. Some dons became public political figures. A. D. Lindsay as Master of Balliol was well-known as a Labour supporter who gave sermons in chapel and lay sermons in hall; and G. D. H. Cole and A. J. P. Taylor were similarly open left-wing supporters. Conservative dons such as Lindemann were too numerous to mention. After 1919 more dons were prepared to give their time to undergraduates. Urquhart found a willing colleague in Kenneth Bell. Bell took Balliol men for a walk round Oxford. At Christ Church J. C. Masterman, Keith Feiling, Robin Dundas and Robert Longden became guides, philosophers and friends to generations of undergraduates. So did Dacre Balsdon at Exeter, Bruce McFarlane at Magdalen, H. W. Garrod at Merton, and Christopher Cox at New College. Nevill Coghill, C. E. 'Tom

Brown' Stevens and Harry Welldon made friends with undergraduates outside their own colleges. Some were towering
scholars like C. S. Lewis; others like Hugo Dyson hardly wrote
a word. There were salons that defied college boundaries. One
flourished at Wadham under Maurice Bowra, another under
Tom Boase at Magdalen and a third in his own apartments
under the improbable 'Colonel' Kolkhorst, much lauded by
John Betjeman.

In the fifties Oxford was at the height of its reputation. Its
scientific status had begun at last to rise. Before 1939 – with
the exception of Howard Florey and Ernst Chain, the true pro-
genitors of penicillin – Oxford biology developed only in the
clinical departments of the Radcliffe, aided by Nuffield's
munificence. Even so Oxford had in the twenties lost an offer
from the Rockefeller Foundation for clinical medicine because
the trustees could find no one to negotiate with. There were,
however, two show pieces – Lindemann's resuscitation of the
Clarendon laboratory, in physics; and Cyril Hinshelwood's
superb achievements in physical chemistry, which persuaded
Nuffield to build a laboratory for him – his previous labs being
in the cellars of Balliol and Trinity. Perhaps Hinshelwood's gift
for foreign languages, the elegance of his English and his love
of literature persuaded Oxford to ask the University Grants
Committee for funds to build laboratories in the parks. By 1990
Oxford had won six Nobel Prizes and ninety-six fellowships in
the Royal Society.

A few clouds floated high in the sky. Oxford had moulded the
sixth-form syllabus in the schools but mass secondary education
began to create problems. Guy Chilver persuaded the university
to abolish Latin as a compulsory entry subject for scientists;
rumbles were heard about the narrowness and parochialism of
Oxford's students. Must each college have its own requirements
for an entry exam – how could schools memorise their variety?
Was the history school too preoccupied with English history

und did it not ignore European and American history, social, economic and demographic history, cultural history and any interpretation of history that did not see history as the story of liberal institutions? Should not those who study literature discuss why they think a poem or a novel or a play is good, and why should all Victorian and twentieth-century literature be eliminated? Why were so many reputable academic subjects not to be found in the examination syllabuses?

But there were more disturbing problems than these. The Robbins Report of 1964 roundly criticised the Oxbridge administrative systems and their lack of consideration of national needs and those of other universities. Oxford responded at once and set up a commission under Oliver Franks, a former head of house and renowned public servant, to examine matters. Most of his recommendations were accepted but those concerning the colleges were shelved or fudged. But there was one statistic in the report that did Oxford enormous credit, astounding as it was to those who believed that Oxford dons idled in the vacations and that the university was simply a teaching seminary for gentlemen and future statesmen. Oxford scholars produced more books and articles in the humanities than any other university. One of those scholars – he wrote seventeen books during his forty-nine years as a don – was Maurice Bowra, the Warden of Wadham.

Bowra's life was influenced by two experiences when he was young. At seventeen, on his way back from China during the war via the trans-Siberian railway, he stayed in Petrograd and was overcome by the profundity and beauty of Russian literature and the contradictions in the Russian character. The second experience was the slaughter, the filth and the incompetence displayed in the war itself. He was born on the Yangtze, where his father was in the Chinese customs service, and sent to Cheltenham College, which he disliked as a philistine school –

though from it he won the top scholarship to New College. The army was all too like school, impervious to common sense, and run by ageing regular officers whose notion of training cadets and subalterns was to be as bloody-minded as possible. In a sense matters improved when he joined his unit in the artillery but he saw action in Passchendaele, in the retreat of the British armies in the spring of 1918, and in their final victorious advance. Years later I saw him at a dinner party in Cambridge during the Second World War turn on some gallant RAF officers, who were contrasting the luxury of the evening they were enjoying to the terror that lay ahead next night, when they would be bombing Germany and could well expect to be shot down by night-fighters. Bowra delivered a furious rebuke, asking them if they knew what it had been like to live in mud, shit and decomposing corpses. Had they ever watched an enemy shell destroy the headquarters one had left a few minutes previously, and then dig out the bodies of one's regimental companions?

The war also left Bowra fuming at a society that was class-conscious and worshipped good form; and in which you played games not to win so much as to be loyal to the club and to slight outsiders. Anyone competitive, like the Olympic athlete Harold Abrahams who actually trained to improve his performance, was ostracised. At Lords the amateurs in county cricket walked onto the field from one gate, the working-class professionals from another. This sexually repressed, anti-American society, contemptuous of women and proud that it had defeated the General Strike (Bowra took the side of the strikers), was not for him. He astonished Oxford by his brash, noisy repudiation of the public school ethos. Not that he was an aesthete. He was as much a patron of the Boat Club as of the scholarship boys. He became the leader of the libertarians, the enemy of soft-spoken conformity.

When he was demobilised and came to New College to read

Greats he found himself being taught philosophy by H W B Joseph. Horace Joseph was famous for the string of successes achieved by his pupils in Greats and was a passionate teacher of the school of Cook Wilson,* and a man who convinced many that his own philosophical method was the key to the discovery of truth. He died in 1943 and after the war his reputation dissolved as the new analytic school of Oxford philosophers derided him as a logic-chopper – the man who had tried to discredit Einstein by asking quibbling questions about relativity. One of his pupils in the twenties while waiting for his tutorial heard Joseph upbraiding the man ahead of him, 'Mr Robinson, this won't do, this won't do at all.' Robinson, an Australian, was not to be put down. 'Well, Mr Joseph, if wishes were horses, beggars would ride.' 'No, Mr Robinson, because the wish to ride would then be a horse.' Bowra could not make head or tail of this way of reasoning. He did not see that he was playing a game that he had to learn and master. So he decided to take the classical curriculum and began with Greek and Latin literature. Gilbert Murray took to him and in the end Bowra conquered his fear of philosophy. But those who knew him in those days believed that Joseph cast a blight upon him and permanently destroyed his self-confidence in discussing abstract ideas.

He began by translating Pindar's *Pythian Odes* with his friend Wade-Gery, the first of many collections of excellent translations. Gilbert Murray had composed Swinburnian translations of Greek plays; Bowra chose a modern idiom. He then made his name with *Tradition and Design in The Iliad*. He believed that Homer existed as a man and that the *Iliad* was a poem with a plot, a design and a unity, but that the poet intended it to be recited. But his next major work, an edition of Pindar, was a

---

* John Cook Wilson (1849–1915), who started the reaction at Oxford against Idealism, later developed by Prichard and Ryle.

disaster. Pindar is a lyric poet requiring exacting qualities of interpretation and textual analysis. His forty-five odes celebrate the victors in the games at Olympia, Pythia, the Isthmus of Corinth and at Nemea. The losers in the games are humiliated for failing, whereas the victors in their moment of triumph are transfigured: a divine spirit has taken over their mortal frame; the victor almost becomes a god – and in that moment we understand what is the meaning of life and the justification of being born. Bowra responded to the poetry and from it formed his own belief that poets are inspired by some force that comes from outside them. Bowra was not a textual critic. He loved poems too much to take them to pieces and provide variant readings of obscure passages. He read too fast and his hostility to pedantry undid him. After 1945 a new generation of classicists took over in Oxford, influenced by the example of Edward Fraenkel, a refugee and a classical scholar of European reputation, who made classical studies more professional when he was appointed to the chair. Fraenkel's contempt hurt Bowra, and when in 1964 he wrote another critical study of Pindar his enemies mocked him. 'Have you seen the Pindar?' said Denys Page, by now professor of Greek at Cambridge. 'It will make you weep – with laughter.'

When Gilbert Murray retired he would not support the man Bowra thought should be appointed. J. D. Denniston had written the definitive work on Greek participles, and that did not appeal to Murray, an excellent scholar but also one who had devoted part of his life to popularising Greek literature. Murray liked Bowra but disapproved of him, and in the end E. R. Dodds was appointed. Dodds was unwise enough to publish the proverbial slim volume of his own verse and Bowra, much cast down, did not spare him. He used to quote from the slim volume at parties.

As a friend pointed out, his rejection was a blessing. He had been tempted to stay at Harvard on a visit there but in 1938 he was elected Warden of Wadham: Lindemann supported Bowra for the vacancy because he was so outspoken an opponent of Nazi Germany. Bowra did not desert the classics. A book on Sophoclean tragedy appeared in 1944 and five more books on Greek poetry and culture followed. But the war released his passion for European poetry. In a series of books he analysed the greatest poets of modernism in France, Germany, Italy, Greece, Russia, Spain, Ireland and England. And for good measure he published two books on epic poetry. George Seferis, the Greek poet, spoke of him as 'one of the few Europeans still left in Europe ... with an intimate knowledge of poets from Pasternak to Lorca'. No one could rival his command of languages and his mastery of what the poets who had followed the symbolists were saying. He ranged from Blok to Cavafy. One should never forget the debts contracted when one is young. I read the first of these volumes, *The Heritage of Symbolism*, when I was in my twenties. I had never read Valéry or Stefan George, and Bowra gave me some notion of what Rilke was about; and his volume of translations from Russian poetry was another book of utmost importance to me. The only precursor of what he was doing was Edmund Wilson in *Axel's Castle*.

To mention Wilson, however, makes one realise Bowra's limitations as a critic. Wilson was quirky, erratic and, when for instance writing on the Dead Sea scrolls, no more than a journalist. But if we ask which of the two explored the literature and culture of his times to greater effect there can be but one answer. There was a heroic cast to Wilson's thoroughness: he went at his material with greater intensity, he would go to all lengths and pains to master his sources and to distinguish reality from appearance. The struggle lay only partially concealed beneath the readable, persuasive prose. What is more Wilson, as a fine critic must, dug into himself to find the answers. You can sense the granite of his sensibility splintering as he drilled it to discover how far the strata had shifted under the impact of the work of art. Little of this prodigious energy emerges in Bowra's criticism. John Sparrow once wickedly said that it was a pity that Maurice had cut himself off from posterity: his prose was unreadable and his verse was unprintable. It is true that his prose was flat. It is true that he was an interpreter, rather than a critic, of poetry. It is true that he ignored the revolution in criticism during the twenties at Cambridge which was, perhaps, that university's most striking contribution to the study of the humanities between the wars. But when the customary reservations about his workaday methods have been made, his achievement was considerable and recognised when he became President of the British Academy. If he was not among the great creative scholars of his times – and only a handful at any one time can be so described – he was an immensely learned man, and he made you feel ashamed of your ignorance and slovenliness. The range of his reading challenged your own provinciality and sloth. In the post-war years he was always suggesting that one should read poets whom the new orthodoxy had dismissed as negligible or harmful – Tennyson, Swinburne, Kipling. He did not exaggerate their achievement: much of Swinburne, he would say, was meaningless. But he determined to show what they had achieved. He was a traveller forever suggesting that if only you would journey further you would be transfixed by some new and life-enhancing experience.

Deep-seated as was his hatred of injustice and cruelty, the rule of life by which he set most store, so it seemed to me, was to read poetry, to live by it and with it, to turn to it for wisdom and to pray that it would continue to replenish the springs of feeling which flow ever more sluggishly the older one gets. Above all to *reverence* the poets as men, like Pushkin's prophet, on whose tongue a burning coal had been laid. Not only dead poets, but the living exponents of the European heritage. You realised that beneath the noise and the laughter was the conviction that unless you refreshed yourself by re-reading the poets and letting them, if only for an hour or so, take command, you would inevitably become a castrated pedant or a dehumanised bureaucrat – and beyond redemption.

The dead can speak only through their own writings, and, as is often said, Bowra's published works give no inkling of what his conversation and tone of voice were like. That voice . . . Echoes of its intonations and inflexions reverberated through Oxford and London. People who had never met him used his phrases; Evelyn Waugh's undergraduate diaries are full of them, though at that time he was not one of Maurice's friends; and Osbert Lancaster acquired his voice and manner lock, stock and barrel, as if it had been auctioned. His speech came in bursts like a machine gun, using army slang satirically. His voice had the carrying power of the Last Trump; but when he lowered it and spoke as if imparting a confidence the affection within his nature rose to the surface until, as if alarmed that there was something the matter with him, he reasserted himself as the archangel and blew a tremendous blast. Using the notation of *Hymns Ancient and Modern* you could score an utterance as follows: 'They are a particularly agreeable pair. (*dim.*) I enjoyed my visit with them (*pp.*) enormously (*ff.*) ENORMOUSLY' His conversation resembled a naval battle of old. Like the *Royal Sovereign* breaking the line at Trafalgar, all cannon double-shotted, he fired deafening broadsides. Spars ignited, mizzen top-masts crashed to the decks, studding sails were blown over board, splinters ricocheted, inflicting fearful wounds on friend and foe alike. But when the smoke cleared you found that you had all the time been sitting in the stalls witnessing a splendid transformation scene in a pantomime. What he said, or what he wrote in his letters, expressed the world which he had invented and which was subject to all the complexities of appearance and reality, *Sein und Schein*, that he knew so well in literature; he never suffered from the delusion that the world which his wit created was a mirrored actuality. You realised that you yourself, like everyone else, including those most devoted, would be impaled upon his scandalous, reckless comments. Although one friend might shake with laughter when gouged, another might suffer and feel diminished by his quips. Yet it did not matter: they were his contribution to what he called the Higher Truth, not be confined by the shackles of scholarly accuracy from which, in the life that he shared with his friends, he was glad to be relieved.

At any gathering or institution with which he was connected spirits shot up when he was in action. He had the extraordinary gift of making people feel that life was more exciting, more full of possibility, adventure, depth, comedy and poignancy than they had dreamt possible. His disillusioned friends felt this. So, more astonishingly, did his enemies and detractors. The very fact that he was full of frailties (never absurdities) – that he was impulsive and governed by passionate emotions – put heart into his colleagues. The occupational hazard of being a don is to become pedantic, and an hour with Bowra was like being given a blood transfusion. It sounds a brutal voice. But the brutality was often assumed. When his old tutor Alick Smith was elected Warden of New College he expressed his conviction that it was for the best in alarming terms:

> The omens were excellent. Now, when I was elected Warden of Wadham there was a clap of thunder and Milne's wife committed suicide in the gardener's shed with a large saw. Took her five minutes. When Smith was elected, Bolt – a Fellow of the College – died. Next day his wife committed suicide in the gas-oven of the Warden's lodgings. Discovered by Mrs Fisher. Yes, I should say the omens were tip-top.

His wit resembled that of another Oxford Smith. In invention, rapidity and fantasy he was the heir to Sydney Smith. Like Sydney Smith's long conceit about the fat lady which ended by him declaring that she was so large that there was nothing to do but to read the Riot Act and disperse her, Bowra would start, for instance, by arguing that love and sex were incompatible and declare that sex was inescapably in the head. He then expounded the extreme view that appurtenances were more seductive than the beloved. Whereas others maintained that a look, a twist in the hair, the set of the eyes, the expression of the mouth, the walk, the tilt of the hips, created the obsessions which were the snares, Bowra put forward fetishism as the animator and argued that the object was more important than the subject: white shorts, bloomers, plimsolls, gaslight – these were examples of the objects which elicited lust. He maintained that at one time his friend Philip Ritchie's grey flannel trousers occupied his mind far more than Philip Ritchie. Why did one fall in love with people whose morality was repulsive? Why should cards, crooks and bad hats exert such stunning erotic force? Did vitality, good looks and panache compensate for loutish sensibilities and low habits? How could one ward off the curse of intellectuals in love – guilt? Or he might read poetry in a deliberately non-poetic voice – he hated *une voix dorée* – but in a style which emphasised the metre and rhythms. Like other dons of those times – like Isaiah Berlin – he enjoyed inventing games, like classing poets as in the finals. Goethe notably failed to get a first: 'No: the Higher Bogus.' 'Maurice, we've forgotten Eliot.' 'Aegrotat.' Suddenly he would be off on a conceit. What was the quintessence of the Wykehamist? Who could be said to be 'Very Wok of very Wok'? Minute charting of the channels through which the Winchester conscience drains. Was there sufficient evidence to establish the emergence in the evolution of the species of a Wykehamist thigh characterised by its massive girth (examples cited: R. H. S. Crossman and John Sparrow). You found that in playing such games his wit illuminated not only the conceit which took his fancy but human nature. Faced in a museum in Italy with a row of busts of later Roman emperors, he paused in front of each and identified them, 'Last, Gow, Adcock, Page . . .' and mysteriously the marble statues began to assume in one's mind the features of these eminent classicists. There might be a bust whose face, except for the beard, had been completely weathered away into total anonymity, but that would not defeat him: 'Senior Fellow under the old Statutes.'

He was not a connoisseur. Italian primitives did not awaken his finer powers of discrimination. ('Too many Gaddis and Daddis.') He stalked when sightseeing. He was not a man to linger over his aesthetic experiences. He would approach the Michelangelo *Holy Family*, pause, regard it as if it were a recalcitrant colleague, deliver judgement, 'Greatest work of man,' and plod along to the next. But mention a painting later in the day and he would nearly always make some comment about its spiritual or literary qualities. He must have visited some churches and galleries twenty or thirty times.

Anthony Quinton noticed how his talk was peppered with figures of speech, puns and inversions: 'The sort of man who would give you a stab in the front'; 'He gave me the warm shoulder.' And contradictions: 'Awful shit, never met him'; 'Queer as a coot, nobody minds.' 'Might it be possible,' a friend put to him about a willowy critic, 'that he had dyed his hair?' 'It never crossed my mind that he didn't.' The young are often troubled by conscience. Maurice reassured them. It was 'a loud thing which struck twelve o'clock and said don't'.

Loyalty was not a virtue which he measured out by drops into a glass. His loyalty to his friends was unquenchable and he expected them to be loyal too. Intellectuals are often not. They are disliked by other men because they vacillate and move gingerly to judgements about people, slide away at the first hint of trouble, see the merits of the other side so clearly, and then decamp when their friend is in trouble, or worse, when he is in disgrace. They ridicule the notion that a man has any *a priori* duty to be loyal to his family; and if not to his family, why then to an institution or to colleagues? Intellectuals give their first allegiance to ideas, and (so they believe) to the truth; and if a friend has made what to them seems to be an error of judgement or taste, still more to have betrayed an ideal, they do not hesitate to round on him. To them personal and family loyalty leads at worst to the Mafia and at the least to that closing of the ranks by which the Establishment wards off menace and excludes anyone who might upset its value system. Splendid as dedication to ideas can be, intellectuals sometimes forget that it can lead to that humiliating perversion of the intellect, the defence of the party line.

Bowra was fierce in loyalty to his ideals. But he differed from other intellectuals in being even fiercer in loyalty to his friends. If a choice had to be made between friends and truth, friends won. His loyalty to people and to institutions was passionate and uncompromising; and if a friend failed, for instance, to get a post he concealed the blunt truth in comforting him afterwards and took it out on his opponents. Such tenderness did not extend to them: he pursued his enemies relentlessly. When he gave the oration at the memorial service for his old tutor Alec Smith the air was so dark with the arrows he despatched, like Apollo spreading the plague among the Grecian host before Troy, that you half-expected groans to arise from the congregation and the guilty to totter forth from St Mary's and expire stricken on the steps of the Radcliffe. Loyalty for him was not a simple matter. If anyone outside the circle made a feint at any of his friends, or at any fellow or undergraduate of Wadham, good, bad or indifferent, thunderbolts were hurled. Within the circle, however, anything could be said about anybody. He could hector, but so long as no mortal sin had been committed he remained unshakeable. Towards the end of his life he disapproved of the views on universities, students, literature and the law which John Sparrow was expressing, but he remained obsessed by Sparrow's personality; was, as ever, amused when they met; and he would speak of him between denunciations with ironical affection. Three friends of his youth were particularly unassailable. With Robert Boothby and Cyril Connolly he felt entirely happy; and the third, Dadie Rylands, for whom in his undergraduate days long ago he had bought silk shirts in the High, could do nothing wrong. He had other friends in Cambridge but none was held in such esteem as Rylands, of whose delicate perception into the motives of human beings he stood somewhat in awe and to whose judgements on poetry he deferred. Maurice used to regard him in wonder as one who had fought with beasts at Ephesus; and Dadie was indeed the only person whom I ever saw, when Maurice was demolishing someone's character unscrupulously, pull him up sharply like a preservationist halting a bulldozer in the act of levelling a silly but loveable old building.

Bowra belonged to a generation who put enormous weight on friendship. Friendship was something far more than casual geniality: it made demands, it imposed duties and much should be sacrificed for it. It was not to be confused with party-going, still less with *Mitdabeisein*. Friendship implied unreserved affection and support, but it was a dry fierce heat, not humid; he was vehement, and he rebuked. He wanted his friends to do well. Like Jowett he expected them to make the most of their gifts. Whatever they produced was not enough: they must push on and do better still; and he could awaken self-confidence and dispel what he used to call a 'sad state of Minko'.*

Once given, his friendship was hard to lose. Goronwy Rees lost it when Maurice judged that he had joined a witch-hunt, and since cruelty to human beings and injustice to individuals were cardinal sins, a terrible anathema, asking him whether he

* 'Minko' is the German colloquialism for *Minderwertigkeitskomplex*, or inferiority complex.

was planting a Judas tree, followed.* Non-speak was a condition anyone might find himself in with Maurice: in this he was not unique among the iconoclasts of the twenties of which he was a leader. But normally he was indulgent to younger friends because he was intrigued if he found that they held to some notion of value that was new to him provided it was not ideological. The loss of any friend, old or young, was not a sorrow, but a blow between the eyes which made him stagger, only to march on, the blood trickling down his face. When Marcus Dick died I remembered Maurice describing him twenty years before as 'the new kind of don; they give tutorials with a bottle of whisky by the armchair and a girl in the bedroom', and being so pleased at his marriage. His friends' affairs and intentions, honourable or otherwise, won his absorbed attention. He was ready with advice (if asked) and unoffended when it was not taken. Early on in my time as a don, in which I was settling in but not perhaps settling down, I got a letter from him: 'We are all much worried about you – these goings on – most unsuitable in a young don. Hard work, my boy, that is what we expect from you. A good book – it is much needed – no one is writing and our civilisation is going to pot with books on "Planning for God", etc.' All he asked was to be kept informed. 'Rosamond dining here last night assures me that you are to be married at any moment. I do not pay much attention to this but a word of news either way would be interesting.' And at another time when I did not know whether I was in love or infatuated he sent the only message of any use: 'Don't forget that your old friends are devoted to you and will stand by you no matter what you do.'

As an undergraduate he intrigued the pre-war dons. 'Heard

* In fact the articles that Rees wrote for a popular Sunday newspaper correctly hinted that Anthony Blunt had been a spy: but at that time there was no evidence that this was so and Bowra, with memories of the havoc Senator McCarthy created in American universities by spurious denunciations, was outraged.

a lot about you, both for and against. Come to dinner next Friday . . .' ran a postcard from Robin Dundas, the curious Christ Church don who embarrassed, or more often amused, the young by cross-questioning them about their sex life. As a young don he was the great liberator and became the leader of what he called the Immoral Front, composed of those of whom the Establishment disapproved – Jews, homosexuals, people with odd views or ways of life. Cyril Connolly, Rex Warner, Cecil Day Lewis, John Betjeman, Osbert Lancaster, Isaiah Berlin and A. J. Ayer were his special friends. Where Maurice was concerned there were no barriers between senior and junior common rooms, and his comments about other dons made what he called Bad Blood. When he was elected Warden of Wadham and some young friends at Merton gave him a gargantuan lunch, matters got a little out of hand and a verger, hearing a disturbance in chapel, found Maurice preaching a sermon and his friends prostrate with laughter in the aisles. (The story that it was Betjeman preaching and Maurice sitting on the altar smoking a cigar can be discounted.)

Throughout the years he entertained undergraduates to lunch and dinner. I first met him before the war at his Sunday morning salon, to which I was taken by a friend. He sympathised with and civilised the young, and he was unexcelled in getting a tipsy bore out of the room before the boy knew what had happened. He taught them not to be pretentious and encouraged them to be themselves, not to conform. He was also in his day a fine tutor, exacting but encouraging. He talked to them about his work – what he had been reading, and when he left they wanted him to go on talking. His comments on meeting some undergraduates at King's were flattering: 'I liked the boys very much and felt that they are nicer and cleverer than ours, which I did not feel two years or so ago. I fear that Mr Murray*

---

* Ian Murray was a scholar at King's after the war. Bowra's prognosis proved to be accurate.

will come to a bad end but I expect much of the others. Tell them I have discovered fragments of a new Canaanite epic – no talking horses, alas, but a good goddess who makes infamous propositions to a handsome young man.'

He did not lose his head in the mild disturbances at Oxford at the end of his days as Warden. One of his undergraduates libelled a don, who demanded his expulsion. Maurice made him apologise, but refused to expel him. One did not send young men down for indiscretions. His obituarist recorded that when some undergraduates wanted to send their objections to the proctorial system to the Privy Council, Maurice met the objection 'Why should they?' with the simple retort: 'Because they are entitled to and because they want to.'

In Proust's final volume the enchanting youthful creatures of the *belle époque* become in their middle and old age monsters unrecognisable as what they once were. So for a few of those whom Maurice created in the twenties – he created part of almost all his closest Oxford friends – he lost his lustre. They heard only the malice and forgot the generosity. They were offended by the coarseness and were no longer impressed by his enthusiasm for literature and scholarship. They contrasted the Maurice of their youth with the post-war Warden of Wadham. In becoming Warden and Vice-Chancellor some qualities atrophy, such as the delight in ideas for their own sake and the energy to pursue them. The energy had now been diverted into other channels and with it went something that his older friends had believed was inalienably his. The attributes of the intellectual are as jealous as the Muses of the arts: at first sight of a rival – in this case leadership, which a Warden or Vice-Chancellor should exercise – they take flight in disgust.

Among his early companions who rose to high positions within the Establishment were some who considered that he never grew up. Cyril Radcliffe became a law lord and chairman of numerous advisory committees – though not one of his judgements came to be cited as an important point of law and the recommendations of his committees appear in retrospect to have been anodyne. He despised Bowra's public advocacy of liberal causes as an indiscretion of his youth and donnish ignorance of how the world works. Maurice would have replied that he knew only too well how the world works and how to recognise a time-server or a tyrant. His conception of liberty was not utilitarian. It was Byronic.

Nevertheless once Bowra became head of his college he had no choice. The only free intellectual is he who evades all responsibilities and executive duties and remains as uncommitted in the world of action as he is committed in the world of ideas. Bowra was by nature a poacher and he disliked having to draw on the velveteen breeches of the gamekeeper. He mourned his youth. He once pulled out his wallet to show me a photograph of himself when he was young, and I noticed the quizzical, amused, sensual mouth. The bull-dog had once been an engaging bull-terrier.

Of the Seven Deadly Sins the one he was most prone to commit was envy. He used to criticise Evelyn Waugh for denigrating the worth of any other writer or the success of his friends, but at times envy was the clue to his utterances. He wanted what other people had got and wanted them not to have it. Out of his letters peered the green-eyed monster when he mentioned Isaiah Berlin. Here was an old disciple, famous in America and wooed by the organisers of international gatherings, the foremost historian of ideas in this country. He wrote in a powerful idiosyncratic style, the living embodiment of his personality and mind, a vehicle which was a reproach to Maurice's own inability to let himself go in prose; a man with the entrée to any society yet willing to give time to humble and obscure scholars whom Maurice would have dismissed as bores; more able than he, when the warm breezes of adulation from the world fanned him, to preserve the kernel, the ice-cube of his integrity. When

one invited the other to dinner Isaiah would propitiate his
mentor and allow Maurice to dominate the stage by joining the
auditors. It cost Maurice much to write his letter of congratulation when Isaiah received the OM. The bile rose; but to give
in to such a base emotion would be despicable; so he choked
it down. He told his friends how much Isaiah deserved it. But
he could not suppress his joke. The OM, he said, was the rich
man's CH. He was furious with Isaiah for defending Suez and
Vietnam, and was unsympathetic when Isaiah considered he
had been misrepresented in an interview at which, Maurice said,
he was at his worst, 'pompous and pious and a total coward'.
But outbursts like this against even his closest friends were
common in his letters. He once said of John Maud* that one
must learn to take the smooth with the smooth: where Maurice
was concerned you learnt to take the rough with the rough.
Both Berlin and Roy Harrod (to whom Maurice was bound by
long, deep friendship) wrote noble eulogies of him; and such
was his power to create people and make them catch a glimpse
of promise in themselves they had not known was there, that
gratitude effaced resentment.

Friendship means comfort: for grief, unhappiness and fear.
Those at Oxford who knew Maurice best believed him to be
secretly unhappy in the years after 1945. Great talkers use talk
as an opiate. An opiate for what? For the returning pain of
failure to achieve what could or ought to be achieved; for the
ruses used to deceive and cover up the failure; for the fear of
exposure, shame, blackmail, death. He met the death of friends
with bluster: 'Heard of any amusing deaths lately?' But when
he wrote, after the Dickens scholar Humphry House died, 'It
has been a bloody time. Humphry's death robs me of my most

---

* John, Lord Redcliffe Maud (1906–82), life peer (1967), fellow of University College,
Oxford (1929), Master (1963–76), permanent secretary, Ministry of Education (1945),
later of fuel and power; high commissioner and later ambassador to South Africa (1959–
63).

distinguished and most interesting colleague. Tom Dunbabin, a heroic archaeologist, is dying of cancer which the doctors diagnosed for seven weeks as lumbago,' the words do not begin to express his grief and hatred of death. His manner was Johnsonian, and like Dr Johnson he teemed with inner doubts. Johnson, muttering, grimacing, touching every post along a street, breaking off a conversation to repeat a phrase in the Lord's Prayer, was eccentric to the verge of madness. Maurice was not, but he had his manias. He had money-dick: constantly referred to the expense of existence, and once told A. L. Rowse, whose earnings from academic activities were to that historian a source of pride, that he could not afford to become Warden of All Souls. Blackmail haunted him: one of his oldest friends was ruined by blackmailers. Some ridiculous incident would convince him that at any moment he might be exposed. In 1940 a German friend was arrested and he was convinced that he too would be arrested, exposed to shame and driven to suicide. I remember once hearing him and Dadie Rylands each assess how great his failure in life had been and I wondered at all the misery which these two, who meant so much to others, endured.

Bowra became a renowned university administrator after 1950. After his three years as Vice-Chancellor he was re-elected to the Hebdomadal Council by a record number of votes and continued to serve on the central bodies for years. He saw university politics as a ceaseless struggle against the enemies of freedom, vitality and the intellect: they were the *bien-pensants*, the trimmers, the advocates of the sound and safe, not to mention clerics, technocrats and progressives. When you were with him the large Johnsonian face was forever mobile, responding to your remarks, amused, dominating. But one feature in his face never smiled: his eyes. They were pig's eyes, fierce, unforgiving, unblinking, vigilant. They were inspecting the enemy's dispositions. Lucid as his prose was, his universe was Heraclitan and Dionysiac.

To anyone outside a university the recriminations that follow elections and appointments inside it seem petty and absurd. But to Bowra appointments were by far the most important issue in the university, and in this he was right. Appointments matter more than anything else – more than syllabuses, cost effectiveness, plot ratios, student load, and all the other terms of art with which scholars, if they are to continue to run their affairs, have to concern themselves. The right men – outstanding and productive scholars, devoted and stimulating teachers, men of originality and imagination, open-hearted and magnanimous – are the life-blood of a university. But where are the paragons to be found? At the moment of choice the scrupulous quaver. Original, yes – but is he *sound?* Full of vitality, but a trifle too vulgar? Draws an audience, does he? – are we sure he is not a charlatan? A difficult man – hardly likely to be acceptable to our colleagues? And so the inoffensive and second-rate slip in. It is easier in the natural sciences to detect quality than in the humanities. At Harvard Harry Levin, the doyen of literary studies, put forward Vladimir Nabokov for a vacant chair, but found his proposal countered by the famous linguist Roman Jacobson, who said, 'The elephant is a splendid animal. I admire it greatly but I would not appoint an elephant to a chair in Russian literature.' Bowra cared deeply for scholarship. Whatever holes could be picked by experts in his own writings, he was a professional, hard-working and disciplined, who brought order and light to any subject he touched, quick to spot a dilettante or the bogus. He did not want lightweights. But still less was he prepared to put up with stolid and unimaginative pedants, the worthy men who unquestionably had made contributions to the subject but in doing so were helping to kill it. On one occasion he burst out in anger, 'The board of electors have made a disgraceful election of a young queen. He may refuse, in which case he will be replaced by a thin old queen. Anthony Blunt behaved abominably and killed the only good candidate. I have always said he was a back-stabber, from the highest motives of course. Bryson was the Queen-maker throughout. The Bugger's Opera.'

There were bad appointments as well as good in his day – as indeed there must always be when future achievement is impossible to forecast and the choice so often lies between settling for a limited but tangible output and gambling on the sample in a small core, which may well prove deceptive, as evidence of a hidden gold-mine. But able though he was in marshalling support for his man, he put scholarship before personal friendship. He was fond of Enid Starkie, but he rightly judged that as a scholar she was not in the same league as Jean Seznec: in the election to the professorship of French she lost by one vote and Maurice's letter of comfort to her was sensitive and truthful. Where he excelled was as a tireless spotter of talent in fields far from his own. Many young scholars owed much to his encouragement and promotion – among them some of the most able and gifted. He used to tell me that he always looked for vitality and strength of character and that it was as easy to be dazzled by signs of brilliance as it was to be over-impressed by quantity of published work. Where appointments were concerned, confidentiality was a convention to be dismissed from the mind. Even if he were not on the board of electors he could be guaranteed to be relaying without compunction the story of the proceedings within forty-eight hours and details of all the manoeuvres, intrigues and votes cast attributed personally. Those who maintained that the proceedings of all appointments committees should be open had nothing to complain of if Maurice was involved.

He was a powerful Vice-Chancellor, but different from other strong Vice-Chancellors. Oxford was served by a redoubtable registrar (chief administrative officer), Douglas Veale – who wrote the minutes of Council meetings *before* the meeting, leaving gaps to record dissenting views; and when A. D. Lindsay was Vice-Chancellor he and Veale rail-roaded business through, diverting funds to build laboratories, stopping opposition to Nuffield's donations to clinical research and hoodwinking Nuffield, who wanted to finance a college for engineering, into building a college for the social sciences. Lindsay bludgeoned Council. Bowra's methods of winning support were different. He delegated; he spoke admirably on great occasions; and his entertainment was princely.

Everyone at Oxford knew who was Vice-Chancellor when Bowra held the office. 'Bowra, Champagne and strawberries. Three glasses' was Enid Starkie's* grateful memory of one of his garden parties at which she appeared, in Maurice's phrase, 'in all the colours of the Rimbaud'. He knew what he wanted and set out to get it by keeping the committees amused. He hated deviousness. Open opposition won his respect. Of Bill Williams, Montgomery's intelligence officer during the war and Warden of Rhodes House,† he wrote:

> He is a hard-boiled customer who is not afraid of making highly wounding remarks. I rather like him, as at least he is not cagey. He is against Guy‡ as he thinks him pernickety. In fact Guy is very good indeed in the Chair. He is less good on some other committees as he is hopelessly honest – not really a fault. But I can see that he won't go down very well with the Tory clique.

He was not indulgent to his successors: 'The Vice-Chancellor bumbles on, splitting infinitives until the floor is covered with them.' Or of another: 'As Vice-Chancellor he has one great

---

* Enid Starkie (1897–1970), fellow of Somerville College, Oxford, reader in French literature.
† Sir E. T. 'Bill' Williams (1912–95), fellow of Merton College, Oxford (1937–9), senior intelligence officer to Eighth Army, 21 Army Group (1944–5), fellow of Balliol (1945–80), Warden of Rhodes House (1951–80).
‡ Guy Chilver, fellow of Queen's College, Oxford (1934–65), later Dean of the University of Kent.

virtue. He does not in the least care what conclusions are reached on any matter.' Or again: 'He does not now even read the papers for Council and gets them all wrong. Just when we seem to be in sight of a decision he goes into reverse and it all starts again.'

When he was in the chair his object was to get matters through on the nod, and to do so he set his tank on course directly towards the objective and opened the throttle. He did not have much patience with those who could not keep up with the pace at which he conducted business. Nor with those who came to the meeting expecting to discuss matters until teatime: they found themselves a few minutes after three o'clock outside the room hissing and muttering, uncertain how to fill in the time. They accused him of wanting to get decisions rather than to get them right. Indeed he resembled a fine infantry commander. You knew that using every stratagem he would fight for his men and be prepared to evade or even disobey orders from above; you might disapprove of him but you could not deny that he would scrounge, hi-jack and brow-beat so that his show could have every advantage. Ultimately his loyalty embraced them all, the devoted and doubters alike. He could be unscrupulous and twist the rules. If votes were needed he set himself to collect them. 'Had all the votes lined up, everybody perfectly all right; took particular trouble with the mathematicians; mathematicians voted the wrong way.' His eyebrows shot up when one of them excused himself by saying that he had been convinced by the arguments. Maurice rarely allowed himself to be convinced by arguments. He had heard them all before and recognised the apparently artless comment as a well-worn trick of the trade. He mastered the arguments before he went into committee, made his judgement and expected his allies, if they had not the energy or wit to do so themselves, to trust him. But on occasions they stumbled away sore and saddened. For if it became clear that he would lose – and he was lightening-quick to sense how the votes would fall – he would switch to avoid defeat and loss of prestige, leaving his allies in disarray. He would hurtle along the down-line, crushing a reputation on the way, and then, aware of silent disapproval among his auditors, switch into a siding, change tracks and career back on the up-line flashing praise. It seemed not to cross his mind that someone might think this cowardly or dishonest. Veale found him the most difficult of all Vice-Chancellors.

He was no university reformer. When he heard that Cambridge intended to abolish the system of admissions whereby each college had its own separate policy and procedures, the despair of schoolmasters, he declared that it was a splendid reform in that it would enable Wadham to get an even better entry. But when change was forced on the ancient universities by the emergence of an admissions system under UCCA he threw his weight behind it. He once made a speech in which he said: 'The undergraduate suicide rate is higher than it ought to be.' What then happened confirmed him in his view that public pronouncements were an error: all the progressives in Oxford were on his doorstep demanding instant action and a university psychiatric service He shied violently. Yet he kept things moving. Oliver Franks* was not the sort of man who could have become his intimate friend: but he respected him as honourable and dispassionate, voted for him to become Chancellor against Macmillan, and threw his weight behind the Franks Report for reforming Oxford's administration when it was published. He did so because he thought most of its recommendations were wise, but he got additional satisfaction in doing so because some of his enemies and perverse friends did not fail to appear in their true colours.

* Oliver, Lord Franks, fellow of Queen's College, Oxford (1927–37), Provost of Queen's (1946–8), ambassador in Washington (1948–52), Provost of Worcester (1962–76).

Like numbers of people Bowra could not bear to renounce the gifts and places which the Establishment had to bestow. No call came in the Second World War, and even after his successful Vice-Chancellorship his name did not feature on those lists which circulate in Whitehall of possible chairmen of government committees. What kept him out of national affairs as much as anything was the fear inspired by his unbridled tongue. If he suspected that someone was oiling, that person was 'winning golden opinions all round': one don, who was winging his way to Vice-Chancellorships, was described as a 'go-getting slug'.

As he grew older he yearned for praise. Sitting next to Queen Frederica of Greece at lunch in the embassy when his friend, the poet George Seferis, was ambassador, he was told by the Queen how odious royalty found flattery. 'Really, ma'am?' replied Maurice. 'I can't get enough of it.' His craving for honours was voracious. It was not simple snobbery, nor his resentment at the decoration of the undeserving, nor mean-mindedness. It came in part from a natural desire to show his seniors, the Old Gang, who thought he smelt of brimstone, that they could not keep him out. Was the great stodge of able, complacent people going to exclude him and, while pretending to shuffle the pack, turn up all the familiar face-cards? Isaiah Berlin believed his obsession with honours a sign that his self-confidence had been fatally impaired by Joseph. If he could only pile up honours and set them beside the ever-lengthening line of his books, if he could construct out of them a palisade, a barricade, then surely, then at last, his reputation would be beyond challenge. Both greater and lesser men have become a prey to such fantasies: and indeed the hunger to acquire medals and hoods on acquiring honorary degrees is not as rare as all that in academic life.

In fact he did not do all that badly. His honorary doctorates multiplied. His peers elected him President of the British Academy. The fact that he was made a knight before he was Vice-

Chancellor, showing that he had been honoured for his scholarship and not for his skill as an administrator, gave him particular pleasure; and when other vice-chancellors or high academic administrators were similarly rewarded he enjoyed analysing their scholarly achievements – 'They say he once had something to do with agriculture.' He set store on the letters of congratulation he received – and did not receive. When he was elected professor of poetry at Oxford he wrote:

> I am only too pleased to sit in the chair of Arnold, Bradley, Ker, Mackail, etc., and hope to raise the level from that of my predecessor, a deplorable clergyman. The campaign was very enjoyable and C. S. Lewis was outmanoeuvred so completely that he even failed in the end to be nominated and I walked over without opposition. Very gratifying to a vain man like myself.

When his name appeared in the New Year's Honours as a knight he replied:

> It was all very gratifying and I make no attempt to hide my pleasure. As you know, I have had my full share of persecution mania and this has dealt it quite a blow. I am much enjoying the obvious discomfiture of enemies. Poor Cross, who is a martyr to envy, tried to be nice in his letter but did not really succeed. Page has not written and nor has Fraenkel – all is as it should be.

He ended loaded with honours. Oxford gave him an honorary doctorate of law and Wadham not only prolonged him for two years but invited him to stay in college after retirement. The high German decoration, *Pour le Mérite*, given in the past to Thomas Carlyle and Bernard Shaw, comforted him in old age. He stood there in the embassy, surrounded by guests. As an eminent German scholar made a speech in his praise, he looked as if he were facing a firing squad while the sentence of death was being read to him. In the event he was not shot but nearly garrotted, as it was only after a struggle that the ribbon could be got over his massive head and round the stalwart neck. But after Frau Dr Lohmeyer had run round him several times, heaving first from this angle and then from that, the medal eventually ended up under his left ear. One final pleasure awaited him. When, in the last year of his life, he was made a Companion of Honour he wrote: 'Any sane man likes to see his work recognised and Aristotle was right when he said that honour was the greatest of external goods.'

He enjoyed visits to the *beau monde*. Lunches and dinners at Ann Fleming's and Pamela Hartwell's* gave him pleasure, but the fashionable world, still less the world of fashion, was not a place he was tempted to inhabit. The secrets of *haute couture* remained mysterious to him even when, in his old age, Anthony Quinton's American wife Marcelle expounded the art of buying day clothes at Hartnell's precisely because it was renowned for evening dresses. In his youth he had courted Bloomsbury and aristocrats. Both had repulsed him, and he neither forgot nor forgave (he once referred to E. M. Forster's work as a wedding-cake left out in the rain). Aristocratic bewilderment at his conversational gambits made him ill at ease and he could lose his nerve and appear to suck up. In fact he had no desire to get in with them. More to the point he was contemptuous of anyone in his circle who courted the rich in café society. For him they represented a special Gehenna of boredom and falsity, and it seemed unthinkable that anyone would voluntarily expose themselves to such vapid conversation and mindless company. Eccentrics were more to his taste. He loved John Betjeman for delighting in their company: they were to him a proof that

---

* Ann Fleming, née Charteris, was married first to Lord O'Neill, then to Lord Rothermere and finally to Ian Fleming. Pamela Hartwell was the daughter of F. E. Smith and married Lord Hartwell. Both were notable London hostesses.

human nature was unpredictable and untameable by the law-givers and the technocrats.

He was homosexual in his younger days, very much the fashion in Oxford of the twenties. It was he who coined the phrase 'the Homintern' and knew, with his friend Adrian Bishop, the pleasures and the horrors, humiliation and hysteria, of cruising. He spoke his mind if some priest was done out of preferment by *bien-pensant* opinion, but someone as robust as he had little patience with sissies. He lampooned Raymond Mortimer in verse:

> When the dusk descends
> He wanders afar;
> And enjoys a gay tussle
> With Jolly Jack Tar.

> Or expounds to stout guardsmen
> The claims of Cézanne;
> He knows all the ways
> Of a man with a man.

> Where else in the world
> Can such graces be seen?
> Our greatest, our only
> Philosopher-queen!

Not to have married brought bitter regrets. When Anthony Powell's wife called him a 'carefree bachelor', he hit back: 'Never, *never*, use that term of me again.'

Exasperated by her adopted country, Lydia Keynes once said that Englishmen were either boys or old boys. Maurice was both. He was an immensely masculine bisexual, but no exponent of the art of chatting up girls: when with them he had not much instinct for what they were thinking or feeling. Nevertheless he proposed to the greatly admired beauty of Lady Margaret Hall,

Elizabeth Harman (who was later to marry Frank Pakenham, then a student of Christ Church);* and also to Sally Graves, also much courted. He actually became engaged to Audrey Beecham, who joined the Republican cause in the Spanish Civil War. But she suddenly took fright: 'What shall I do?' she asked Bob Boothby – a man of some experience in such matters. 'I feel as if I am being whirled dizzy on a merry-go-round revolving at eighty miles an hour.' 'Jump off,' said Bob. Perhaps most of all he loved Joan Eyres-Monsell.† During the post-war years Barbara Warner, Elizabeth Bowen, Penelope Betjeman, Iris Murdoch, Baroness von Wangenheim (whom he rescued from Germany) and Elsie Butler, professor of German at Cambridge, had a special relationship with him. He liked women to join his weekend parties for lunch or dinner: they were often good-looking but generosity and audacity were the qualities he particularly admired. Feminine vagaries, wiles, stratagems and bad behaviour intrigued him: one of his favourite characters in literature, whom he said he was always recognising in real life, was Cleopatra. 'A pi tart' he would say. The most reckless girls sexually, he would declare, were also gifted with the greatest power of self-deception and, as mothers, ferocious in the protection of their children. His analysis could be deadly. He described Lys Lubbock (Cyril Connolly's mistress) as a 'mouse at bay' and Rosamond Lehmann, full blown by now, as a 'meringue-outang'.

Zwei Seelen wohnen, ach! in meiner Brust.' Like Reynolds's portrait of Garrick, the spirit of Comedy pulled him by the arm,

---

* Frank Pakenham succeeded his brother as Earl of Longford in 1961. Student (i.e. fellow) of Christ Church and lecturer in politics (1932); Labour minister (1946–51), Leader of the House of Lords (1964–8). Lady Longford was the biographer of Queen Victoria, Wellington and Byron and the author of other historical works. Sally Graves married R. C. Chilver, journalist, civil servant; Principal of Bedford College, London, and subsequently of Lady Margaret Hall, Oxford (1971–9).

† Joan Eyres-Monsell was the daughter of Lord Monsell. After the war she married Patrick Leigh Fermor, who with Greek guerrillas captured General Kreipe in Crete and smuggled him in a submarine to Cairo in 1941.

while Romantic Tragedy summoned imperiously. The comedy
of encounters in bed inspired his finest flights but his vision of
love was romantic. One of his conceits consisted of drawing a
line across the northern hemisphere, everywhere south of which
was the sex zone, everything north of which the drink zone.
The line ran north of Provence, Italy, Greece and Persia, thence
to the Himalayas, north of China, south of Japan, and dived
south to the Mexican border. ('America? Drink zone pretending
to be sex.') The people in the sex zone might well live in
countries where wine was grown, and might even have strict
sexual conventions; but for them sex was associated with happiness, gratification, enjoyment – a necessity in life to be luxuri-
antly indulged with either boys or girls, a delight associated with
gaiety and never with remorse. In all Cupid's pageant there was
no monster – except one, Death, feared and detested as the
great annihilator. Conversely the people in the drink zone could
not come to terms with sex. Sex was acknowledged as a force
of overwhelming power – what people produced more talented
and ingenious practitioners than the Germans? But in the drink
zone sex was cursed with guilt, darkness, despair, complexity.
So, far from men fearing death, the death-wish lay heavy upon
them. When Siegfried spoke of *'leuchtende Liebe, lachender Tod'*
he was asserting that redemption after the disasters brought
about by passion could be achieved only through death after
love.

Bowra saw as many connections as divisions between Greek
drama and the Romantic Movement. Men and women in love
were possessed by a *daimon*. Infatuation led to self-deception;
self-deception to delusion; and delusion to misfortune and
calamity. When the tempest stove in the life-boats and smashed
the vessel against the rocks, what was the point in apportioning
blame? Cataclysmic forces beyond human control tossed men
and women about. To fail to recognise the existence of these
forces was to turn your back on the insights of the Romantic

Movement and to ignore the sombre utterances of the poets of antiquity. His sense of ridicule was too acute for him to subscribe to any inflated Romantic theory about passion, but equally his sense of the grand style and his warm-bloodedness made him hostile to cold-hearted sex. Much of his verse was a satirical commentary on the sexual morality of his world.

What did he believe? 'Looking forward to meeting God. Got six questions to put to Him. UNANSWERABLE.' But then, belief was not to him the substance of religion, it was a mere attribute. Just as he held the old-fashioned notion that poets were inspired, so people's beliefs seemed to him to be a poor guide to their spiritual state. This scepticism about propositions had two consequences. Dogmatic Christianity with all the meaning that it had for John Betjeman or Evelyn Waugh was beyond him. But so was a rationalist interpretation of being: atheism or earnest agnosticism seemed to him to be mechanistic, brittle, superficial, cold, and to exclude so much of experience as to be unworthy of a serious man's attention. As a classical scholar he drew his religion, so it seemed to me, from ancient Greece and Rome. If he could hardly claim much of a reputation for *gravitas*, he had his full share of *pietas*. The gods must be given their due, and by humble rituals he showed that he did not forget them. When he entered a Roman Catholic church he would march to the stoup and cross himself. In this he certainly surpassed Dr Johnson's friend Campbell, who had not been in a church for many years but always pulled his hat off when he passed one: indeed he scarcely ever missed chapel at Wadham. In his Oxford, so dominated by philosophy, so dedicated to the discovery of the truthfulness of propositions and the niceties of belief, his conception of religion appeared strange. But it would not have seemed strange to a modern Greek who lives in a country where a child cannot go to school unless he has been baptised, where Easter is celebrated with gusto in the churches, and where intelligent and cultivated people, whose views on the eternities are not to be supposed to be all that different from other Europeans, cheerfully accept the rituals of the Orthodox Church and will burn a candle in front of an icon like the humblest.

Maurice used to explain his actions by saying that he wanted only to be polite: but there was in him a desire to propitiate and placate, almost a plea for forgiveness. It was as if, like a conquering Roman general of old mounted in the chariot during his Triumph, he heard the slave behind him whispering in his ear that he was mortal. The congregation at his funeral found themselves singing 'Lead Kindly Light', and the line, 'I loved the garish day and, spite of fears, Pride ruled my will', was not the kind of penitential self-humiliation which he inflicted upon himself. But *hubris* and *nemesis* were often in his thoughts. His splendid exuberance, his irrepressible vehemence, his razor-sharp sense of the ridiculous and his overwhelming drive could have made him degenerate into a dictatorial, overbearing bully. The memory of what the gods do to the great and powerful, however well-intentioned they may be, kept him in check. The poet he revered most was Homer; and he did not forget the passage where Achilles is reminded by his old tutor that prayers are the daughters of Zeus. If a man rejects them, they send Infatuation to harm him and make him pay the penalty. Unlike Achilles Maurice gave the daughters of Zeus the honour due to them. 'Dear Dawkins died very nicely in front of the college. He fell down in the street and was off to eternity. As he lay there he looked like a schoolboy, with all the wrinkles gone and a beatific smile on his face, the crutch flung aside. A nice end and may I have one like it.'

The gods heard his prayer.

CHAPTER NINE

The Don as Performer – George Rylands

A university is – among other things – a community in which people teach. There are some who intend to hand out what they believe to be true, a set of conclusions; others put before their students the present state of research in their subject. Others try to convey what they themselves are learning, they give their audience a sense of participating in the birth of ideas – as Wittgenstein did, stammering, falling silent, beginning again, once more faltering until he could express *exactly* the thought he was pursuing. A few gifted students may prefer to listen to the drone of a renowned don, head in his script, indifferent to the fidelity of his audience, indeed sometimes proud if they melt away; and his loyal supporters contrast the content of his lectures with those of the flashy charlatan holding forth at the other end of the building to a horde of students thunder-struck by his performance.

And yet dons have to perform. At any rate they have to communicate with their students, and it is common knowledge that some of them are very bad at it. There was, however, a don in the newly founded English faculty at Cambridge who was an outstanding performer, both in the lecture room and in tutorials. This was George Rylands – known always as 'Dadie', his own mispronunciation in infancy of 'baby'. A performer, not only as a teacher, but a performer in the theatre, which he considered an extension of teaching Shakespeare. And not merely a performer, a celebrity.

Dadie Rylands was the son of a land agent who had married the daughter of a parson. His parents moved from Gloucester to Dorset, members of the middle class of the county who managed the business of the gentry for them. He was a product of the charmed educational system of prep school and public school in the early years of this century. His uncle ran a prep school in Dorset, where he was drilled in Greek and Latin and devoured Victorian novels with his cousin Hester, the elder daughter of the headmaster. English poetry seemed to have been imbibed with his mother's milk. In college at Eton he was the contemporary of the prolific writer Christopher Hollis, and a year senior to Steven Runciman and Cyril Connolly. He was the first boy to produce a play in College Hall: he played Viola and won the Shakespeare Gold Medal (later sold to meet undergraduate debts). From Eton he won an open scholarship to King's. After reading classics he switched to English and was the first pupil of F. L. (Peter) Lucas, a Trinity man who had absconded from the classics to join the English faculty. Lucas found that his pupil was far better read in George Eliot and the Victorian novel than he himself. A starred first was followed by a fellowship at King's on the strength of a thesis that later became his first book, *Words and Poetry*. There were also the traditional two slim volumes of verse. He and Peter Lucas taught English at King's. They were the reverse of empire-builders as both preferred undergraduates to have read classics or some other subject first. Dadie took less pride in the number of pupils who got firsts than in those whom he had roused from laziness and a certain third class to get a good second.

The English faculty at Cambridge was then unlike any in the country. It did not compel students to study philology and Anglo-Saxon. It related English poetry not to Anglo-Saxon but to Greek and Latin literature. The first dons in the faculty were determined to meet the jibes of Bloomsbury and other writers that the last thing professors of literature ever asked themselves

was why poems and novels touched the heart. The founding
fathers also took another notion from Bloomsbury. Why not
examine what a writer is doing, what makes him tick, rather than
pontificating about him, as the Victorian critics did? Matthew
Arnold said poetry was a criticism of life and praised Dante and
Milton for criticising it. But what about Sappho or Catullus or
Pope, who certainly criticised life? Arnold ignored them. Why
not respect and honour the artist and celebrate his achievements for a change?

Why not, indeed, pay attention to what a poem actually
meant? That was the question asked by the most original mind
in the English faculty, I. A. Richards. He handed those attending
his lectures a sheet of a dozen or so poems and asked them to
say who, they thought, wrote them and what they meant. His
audience, which included dons, gave astonishing replies. A
greeting to Meredith on his birthday was said to be a Cavalier
drinking song, Longfellow was preferred to Hardy, and 'Wood-
bine Willie', a First World War sentimental poet for 'our men
in the trenches', was hailed as superior to Gerard Manley Hopkins and Christina Rossetti. Most of us, Richards concluded,
were so full of preconceptions about words – what he called
'stock responses' – that we could not construe our own language
in verse. He insisted that we should read the text closely; and
this exercise – dating a poem and saying what it meant – became
a standard practice in scholarship exams and the tripos.

Rylands had no quarrel with the practice of dating and analysing the meaning of the text. He admired Richards and took his
pupils through Donne and the metaphysicals with gusto. But
he was on a different tack. In 1928 he published *Words and
Poetry*, a disquisition on Mallarmé's reply to Degas. Degas had
complained that his sonnets would not come out right, yet he
was full of excellent ideas. 'My dear Degas, poetry is not written
with ideas, it is written with words.' Rylands believed it was the
exact choice of words, with their echoes, ambiguities, associ-

ations, harmonies, cadences, and sometimes their magic, that distinguished the poetic from the banal. For if not – if the moral content was the criterion – how was it that poets still moved our hearts when they repeated the platitudes about life and death uttered by poets in ancient Greece or Rome? In poetry, so he argued, everything depends on the words and the music, the interplay of rhythm and metre. Why did Dr Johnson condemn *Lycidas?* The cause was simple. Johnson had no ear. *Lycidas* is music. When Victor Rothschild invited Rylands to compile a brief anthology of his own writings he chose pieces on Spenser, Donne and the unfashionable A. E. Housman, who told us that poetry is a secretion and comes and goes at its own will: the poet cannot command it. What is more, poetry sometimes is mere music – the music of the spheres – and means nothing.

But there was another critic as influential as Richards. This was T. S. Eliot. The high tone, the arcane references, the immediate judgement offered as a truth beyond question, the new concepts of 'objective correlative' and 'dissociation of sensibility', the seriousness of his discourse by the finest modernist in poetry had great effect. A don in Downing, F. R. Leavis, still hoping for a permanent post in the faculty, accepted Eliot's challenge to 'revalue' English literature. Milton, he thought, had been displaced with little difficulty. Fielding was 'important not because he leads to Mr J. B. Priestley, but because he leads to Jane Austen, to appreciate whose distinction is to feel that life isn't long enough to permit of one's giving much time to Fielding or any to Mr Priestley.'

No one, Rylands thought, did more harm to literature than Leavis. Leavis encouraged the young to despise vast areas of literature. The obsession with ranking works of art, he thought, encouraged priggishness in the young. A few years his senior, Leavis had in fact praised *Words and Poetry* in the *Cambridge Review,* and for a short while Rylands supervised Queenie Leavis before her marriage. But when later she jumped to the wrong conclusion that a hostile review signed G.R. was by him and wrote him an insulting letter, relations were severed. In common with the rest of the English faculty he found Leavis an intolerable colleague; but if a pupil said he wanted to be supervised by Leavis he would always try to arrange the transfer. He did not shirk his duties on the Faculty Board or as an examiner, but university politics were not for him. He lectured on Shakespeare, and Donne and Pope, and the social and spiritual background to nineteenth-century literature. Another course was entitled 'Translation: Imitation: Inspiration'. Another on the influence of Greek and Latin on style. He held his audience not merely to the end of the lecture but to the end of the course. But although he published essays on Shakespeare and gave the British Academy Lecture in 1951 on Shakespeare's poetic language, by far his most influential book was the anthology of Shakespeare, compiled at the suggestion of Somerset Maugham. During the war it was in many soldiers' knapsacks and remains the only anthology which concentrates on the poet rather than the drama. John Gielgud gave memorable performances reciting passages from Rylands's *The Ages of Man*.

Dadie's debt to Shakespeare the dramatist was paid in the most direct way. He was well known as an undergraduate actor and as a young don appeared in numbers of productions. The sight of the lay Dean of King's as a Bright Seraph in *Samson*, 'spotlit high up on the organ in the Guildhall and wearing little but the canonical six wings naturally raised eyebrows in circles in which eyebrows were habitually raised,' wrote Patrick Wilkinson. In 1928 he began a series of productions that made the Marlowe Society renowned as the nursery where those who were to become famous in the theatre learnt to speak Shakespeare's verse. In the 1920s the actor-managers like Frank Benson subordinated everything to the star performers. Plays were cut, lines decimated, and small parts told to get off the stage as quickly as possible. Actors gabbled, the text was massacred and lines were rarely 'pointed' to get the important poetic image stamped on the audience's mind. The art of speaking blank verse had disappeared in Victorian times – unlike in France, where the Comédie Française maintained the tradition of speaking Racine's alexandrines.

Justin Brooke had founded the Marlowe Society to stage Jacobean drama as well as Shakespeare. A King's don, Frank Birch, and after him for thirty years Dadie Rylands, trained undergraduates to speak blank verse. In 1928 Rylands directed *King Lear* (Michael Redgrave as Edgar); and during the war, when experienced undergraduate actors were scarce, he played Lear, Claudius, Othello, Macbeth, Caliban and Leontes in his own productions. In 1948, when Stalin ordered the blockade of Berlin and sent a 400-strong Cossack choir to sing in the Alexanderplatz, the British Council found themselves in a dilemma. Every professional company was under contract and could not represent Britain to counter Soviet culture. So they invited Rylands to bring the Cambridge Marlowe Society (aided by the Madrigal Society) to perform in Berlin. They played *Measure for Measure* and Webster's *The White Devil*. After the war Peter Hall, John Barton, Trevor Nunn, Derek Jacobi, Corin Redgrave, Clive Swift, Richard Cotterell, Toby Robertson, Simon Gray, Daniel Massey, David Brierley, Peter Woodthorpe and Ian McKellen were among the most gifted actors and directors who learnt from him.

It was not until Peter Hall became director of the Royal Shakespeare Company and formed a permanent company with a theatre in London as well as at Stratford-upon-Avon that the full effect of Rylands's work began to be seen. John Barton, who had won a fellowship at King's by work on Shakespeare's text, joined Hall and learnt to direct professional actors. He also trained them to speak verse. For the next twenty years splendid productions emerged from Stratford. In the eighties, when Hall and Trevor Nunn were no longer there, the standard declined. Not only did naturalism return – speaking the verse as if it was prose because poetry is embarrassing. Silly ideas also distorted productions – Goneril and Regan became the feminist heroines in *King Lear*, Prospero portrayed as a patriarchial, colonial governor, the Venetians played as ruthless capitalists abetted by the detestable Portia, whereas Shakespeare with his marvellous moral sense asks us to condemn Shylock's avarice and vengefulness and also to pity the monstrous way he is treated and finally condemned by the unpleasant Venetians.

Dadie did not confine himself to Shakespeare. Among his productions in Cambridge were Shaw's *Heartbreak House* and *Captain Brassbound's Conversion* (in which Michael Redgrave was acted off the stage by Arthur Marshall as Lady Cicely); Maxwell Anderson's *Key Largo*; Goldoni's *The Servant of Two Masters*; Schnitzler's *Dr Bernhardi*; Pinero's *The Second Mrs Tanqueray*, and *Treasure Island*, in which he played old Pew. T. S. Eliot came to see his production of *The Family Reunion* and was delighted to hear the audience rock with laughter, whereas in London the comedy had been played by professionals as a solemn religious verse drama. After the war Dadie directed four Greek plays and played Oedipus opposite Joyce Carey in Sheppard's translation.

He was soon well known in the theatre outside Cambridge. For thirty-four years he was a director of the Old Vic. His connection with the professional stage began when he was asked in 1930 to devise a programme of ballet poetry in London with Lydia Lopokova. But it was his Marlowe Society productions that induced John Gielgud to ask Dadie to direct him and his company, in which Leon Quartermaine and Leslie Banks were the other male stars, in *Hamlet* and *The Duchess of Malfi*. It was Gielgud's greatest performance of Hamlet and Edmund Wilson was bowled over by Peggy Ashcroft's Duchess. It was 'The most fascinating show in London ... in fact one of the best productions I have ever seen anywhere ... Directed by the poet

George Rylands it is so immensely imaginative and skilful and
the acting so dynamic and disciplined that it holds you from
beginning to end.'

His next assignment was to be asked by Robert Helpmann to
devise the scenario for his first venture as a choreographer,
Hamlet, to be danced to Tchaikovsky's Fantasy Overture. For
this he got no acknowledgement, Helpmann professing uncon-
vincing amazement that such an omission from the programme
could have been made. But Sir Thomas Beecham invited him
to speak Byron's poetry in a production of Schumann's *Manfred*
on the BBC's Third Programme and was so pleased that
he asked him to appear in performances at Glyndebourne,
the Festival Hall and Aldeburgh. Elisabeth Bergner implored
him to direct her in America in *The Duchess of Malfi.* Everything
that could go wrong did. Bergner was fascinating and very
funny but temperamental and maddening; the original Bosola
could not remember the words; his replacement could not learn
them; so Dadie had to play the part for the dress rehearsal
and several performances until he had to return for term in
Cambridge.

Dadie used to say that he had learnt to direct by acting in
productions by Frank Birch and by Sheppard. Birch plotted
every move and worked out the timing of every speech before
the production began; Sheppard changed everything in every
rehearsal. Dadie took as his model in directing Shakespeare
Granville-Barker and the pioneer William Poel, who used no
scenery, never cut the text and attended to the words. He was
at his best with undergraduate actors. He did not waste time
trying to get them to move like professionals or 'act'. Those who
had natural gifts he welcomed, but he stopped gesticulation,
mouthing and mannerisms. Shakespeare towered over his contemporaries because, as an actor, he understood how the
theatre worked, but it is his poetry that moves us. And if we
are to be moved we must hear the words. Since Shakespeare

experimented with the blank verse line throughout his career, a play of 1595 will be spoken differently from one in 1610; and above all the lines must be spoken intelligently. Imposing these principles he was to obtain a unique sincerity in performance.

He was never tempted like Birch to turn professional director. He had a clear notion of the mood of each production, but was short-sighted and never learnt more than the elements of lighting. He was also uninterested in movement or 'business'. Nor had he much patience with professional actors who wanted to discuss what might have been in Macbeth's mind before he met the witches. Gielgud, the best speaker of blank verse on the English stage, admired him but was somewhat taken aback when he asked Dadie to take him though a soliloquy and was interrupted: 'John, have you *any* idea of the meaning of what you've been saying?' Just as Sheppard was always willing to speak about Greek poetry and drama at any school or gathering, however obscure, Rylands dedicated himself to bring poetry to a wider audience. For twenty-five years he was chairman of the Apollo Society. He arranged and took part in recitals all over the country and inveigled stars in the profession such as Peggy Ashcroft or Jill Day Lewis to take part. He was a great deviser of programmes and his instant recall of passages that chimed or contrasted with each other was invaluable. The British Council asked him to record the entire Shakespeare canon. Begun in 1957 it was completed in Shakespeare's quatercentenary year, 1964. Dadie wrote the sleeve notes, Thurston Dart arranged the music and 137 discs in all were cut. Most of the cast were old members of the Marlowe Society but Gielgud, Ashcroft, Irene Worth and Patrick Wymark all took part; and William Devlin spoke Lear. He followed this up by cutting fifty-five discs recording poems of some 122 English poets. He was indeed a performer: lecturing for the British Council across the globe from Australia to Lisbon; giving sermons in Westminster Abbey on Johnson and at King's on Shakespeare; and arranging or appearing in many recitals and programmes.

He differed from other performers in a singular respect. He did not like the sound of his own voice and sometimes did not recognise it – though he had only to speak a few words on the telephone and he was recognised immediately. He had a light, resonant voice; he never dramatised or used elocutionary tricks and was always intelligible, taking care never to drop the voice at the end of a sentence. He was an exquisite reader. His lectures, though packed with material, were original in their effect, their delivery and their arrangement rather than in the argument itself or the method of analysis. In later years he professed to be astonished that at a college meeting fellows, part of whose duties he imagined was to communicate their knowledge, mumbled and dithered and used the occasion for clearing their minds and massaging their egos. He was not a great actor: he did not move well; but he had a stage presence and he could hold an audience by his voice alone.

His fame as a lecturer and teacher spread far beyond the university. Not only did undergraduates from other colleges as well as King's ask him to give them tutorials. Few men, including professional scholars, can have had more books dedicated to them: scholars and novelists of all ages went to him for advice and stimulus. No one could riddle a manuscript with holes more devastatingly yet at the same time place his finger so unerringly on the weak points so that the writer, instead of despairing, at once saw how to recast the book chapter by chapter.

Dadie became a Cambridge celebrity almost as soon as he arrived. Sheppard was so taken with him when he took the scholarship exam in December that he insisted that he should leave Eton and come up to play Electra in his production in Greek of the *Oresteia*. His good looks were remarkable: fair wavy hair, slim, feline in manner, he bewitched the old and was taken up by A. C. Benson, then Master of Magdalene, by Denys Winstanley and Dennis Robertson in Trinity, and in London by Lytton Strachey – it was Strachey who taught him that to compare Shakespeare with Racine to the detriment of either was idiotic. It was through Keynes that he met Virginia and Leonard Woolf, she so iridescent, such a tease and flatterer, he so slow, arctic, the soul of justice. Needing money when writing his thesis, he became an assistant at the Hogarth Press. The first things he printed were labels to stick on the remaining copies of T. S. Eliot's *The Waste Land.* Covered in printer's ink by day, he set out by night, from the top flat in Vanessa Bell's house in Gordon Square, hoping that no ink sullied his white tie and waistcoat, to go to myriad parties: to the Navy party (to which Strachey went in the full-dress uniform of an admiral); to Norman Hartnell's Circus party; and to the White party given by the extravagant and attractive Sandy Baird. It was in those days that he made friends with Eddy Gathorne Hardy, traveller and for long Logan Pearsall Smith's amanuensis, the publisher Roger Senhouse, and the painter Peter Morris, with whom he first visited Venice. Soon he acquired the reputation of being tricky, ill-behaved and demanding – but the complaints came from those who insisted on seeing more of him than he was prepared to allow. He was in fact a familiar figure in memoirs of the past: one of those young men who are violently admired in their generation and combine a volatile temperament with physical beauty.

He often caused havoc. An important influence in his intellectual development was Topsy Lucas, married to Peter. She was the novelist E. B. C. Jones, the youngest of Robbie Ross's nieces, and her admiration for him became so intense that, despite the fact that he was unable to give her what she desired, she separated from her husband. He was also to be found at the salon of her sister, who was married to the professor of Greek. Weekends in vacation were spent at Ham Spray with Strachey and later with Frances Partridge; and after the war at Long Crichel with the long-time literary editor of the *New Statesman* Raymond Mortimer and its music critic Desmond Shawe-Taylor. All his life he travelled in vacations, principally in Italy but also in Egypt and Palestine. In each generation a new set of undergraduates streamed through his rooms, among them John Lehmann whose sister Rosamond was looking for a publisher for her first novel. Dadie found one and she dedicated *Dusty Answer* to him.

There were in fact two parts to his life: before and after his mother's death. His father had died when Dadie was still young and his mother possessed his soul. In one sense she disciplined him strictly, in another she spoilt him by encouraging his waywardness. Between them there arose strong emotions of love and hate. Furious quarrels were followed by intense reconciliations. On being elected a fellow he had been allotted a set of rooms in the Old Lodge (which at that time was expected to be pulled down). Carrington and Douglas Davidson decorated them:* Carrington was dissatisfied with her work, which she said resembled that of a diseased mouse, and attributed her failure to too many cocktails. These were the rooms in which he gave Virginia Woolf luncheon and set before her 'wreathed in napkins, a confection which rose all sugar from the waves. To call it a pudding and so relate it to rice and tapioca would be an insult.' These were the rooms in which undergraduates were invited to meet scholars from Oxford, the stars of the London and New York theatre, producers, critics, savants, writers and critics who had been charmed by him and came of their own accord. Before the war he was an indefatigable entertainer of the young. That was when I got to know him and became platonically devoted to him for the rest of his life.

---

* Dora Carrington was married to Ralph Partridge, beloved by Lytton Strachey: she adored Strachey and killed herself when he died. Douglas Davidson was a painter and friend of Rylands.

They were also the rooms that became synonymous with gaiety, with parties where the gramophone blared ballet music or schmaltz, the drink flowed and couples revolved or reclined. When the Vic Wells Ballet (as it was then) made its annual visit to Cambridge, Robert Helpmann would perform at the end of the evening his Dance of the Seven Veils clad only in a sheet; and a wicked caricature in the college magazine hailed Dadie as Victor Indoor Ludorum.

But it would be wrong to picture him as a child of Pan or Priapus extracting honey at his ease from whatever flower took his fancy. Between him and his desires came the curse of his mother. Dark and hideous neuroses pursued him and, like the Harpies, snatched the food from his mouth before he could eat. His life was tragic. Guilt denied him any happiness or love that he might have found in his sexual encounters. Drink alone released him from this sense of guilt, but when it operated it released other evil potencies which ran like rats among his guests. He became quarrelsome, pettish and jealous; he would declare himself deserted and betrayed by his friends. Defenceless himself before any attack, so thin-skinned and vulnerable that his friends never dreamt of turning his own weapons against him, he used his tongue as his mother had taught him, to sting those about him. When his sexual passions were aroused he became a travesty of himself and behaved so outrageously that his friends would cap each other's stories of the devastating evenings that they had endured with him. The squalor of his rows in Nice or his escapades in Cannes were relieved only by the comicality of the predicaments in which he found himself and his good-humoured sense of his own ridiculousness – the next morning.

He did not believe that sex and love were compatible. He would deny that affectionate, trusting, adoring married couples really experienced sexual love. Like Proust he considered love a delusion in which the lover becomes infatuated with the beloved, is obsessed by jealous fantasies and makes demands which the beloved cannot possibly fulfil. He fell in love only three times and suffered much; and he was so racked by guilt and a sense of physical shame he sometimes became impotent. He identified sex with lust, not love, with danger and with frenzy. Someone who went to bed with him described it as like being in a rugger scrum.

The misery of his sexual relations was paralleled by embarrassment in worldly society. On occasions the sparkling guest or the indefatigable host at Cambridge could lose his nerve when in London faced with strangers: his manner became strained, he forced the pace and took to the bottle. When nervous a couple of cocktails transformed him into a staggering sot. After the first night of Gielgud's *Hamlet* he failed to appear at the supper party which Binkie Beaumont of H. M. Tennent's had arranged at the Ritz: on returning to the theatre Beaumont found him dead drunk in his box. After his lecture to the British Academy in 1951 he was prostrated by drink within half an hour, and after disporting himself deplorably at White's, was violently sick in Bob Boothby's car and had to be sponged down by the Warden of Wadham in the Athenaeum. After twenty years as a university lecturer he still needed brandy before giving a normal lecture. At heart he remained a country boy, astonished by the luxury of Somerset Maugham's villa at Antibes. He liked to contrast dry, austere, high-minded Cambridge with worldly Oxford, where success was the currency and brilliance your credit. He was satirical about old friends like Cyril Connolly who were captivated by London life. Ready though he was to plunge into the Great World, he swam as fast as he could to climb out the other side and rejoin his intimate friends. People who were puzzled why he did not cut more of a figure in the literary life of London did not understand that in the vacations from Cambridge he hurried into retreat, pruning and gardening by his mother's side, vexing her because he refused to introduce his smart friends to her and in return submitting with ill grace to her needling and teasing. They spent the holidays in taking tiny revenges on each other.

When war was declared he already held the post of steward in the college. Before that he had been Dean, and those who wondered whether he could deal with cases of discipline were startled to hear that he had reduced a beefy member of the Boat Club to tears by his cutting remarks condemning some act of boorish behaviour. He now became in addition Domus bursar, praelector and sole director of studies. His conscientiousness and mastery of detail astonished Clapham, who had regarded him hitherto as a *flâneur*, and his terror lest Keynes, whom he idolised, should catch him out contributed to his zeal. (He did catch him out once and rebuked Rylands for allowing defective plumbing in a poor widow's home to be mended at college expense when she was on a full-repairing lease.) But it was not for nothing that his father had been an estate agent, and despite the hours of work – he had taken over from Keynes the management of the Arts Theatre and not only directed but played the major roles in the Marlowe Society productions – he enjoyed perhaps more than any others the years when he ran the college with Sheppard and Donald Beves, the senior tutor (another indefatigable amateur actor).

As an administrator he surpassed all in improvisation and meeting the unexpected and impossible in wartime. He was loyal to those who were loyal to him. Anyone he had appointed should stay: even when after the war he or she was not right for permanent employment. People always worked their fingers to the bone for him – his manners towards servants were perfect – he could not see that others might take a different view. He was a dictatorial administrator. Committees, debate, or consideration of the views of colleagues he knew to be misinformed or misguided, irritated him beyond endurance. At the end of the war a new burden fell on him. His mother moved from

Dorset to Grantchester and he would bicycle out there and back every day.

This account omits one factor – his power. As a moral influence he was formidable. Just as his temperament was the product of his relationship with his mother, his views he inherited from those who formed him in youth – from Sheppard, Keynes and Strachey and his other mentors. He had a pious reverence for the grand old men of the academic world like G. M. Trevelyan, and he used to recall his awe when he was elected to the Apostles and had to speak before G. E. Moore, Russell and other senior members of that society. The vigour with which he expressed his views in a college meeting was matched by the courage and clarity with which he took his stand on an issue. He was the only man who could (occasionally) restrain Sheppard with whom he had several blazing rows. Like Keynes he was not above an unscrupulous argument but it was always fairly, and never deviously, expressed. Time and again at meetings of the governing body he would intervene with an argument that cut through scruples and hesitations and convinced the fellows that there was a right course of action and any other was wrong.

When Sheppard was about to retire his friends put Rylands's name forward to succeed him as Provost. But understandably there was opposition. No one in the college, indeed no one except his most intimate friends, knew of his life away from Cambridge; but unlike the discreet behaviour of other homosexual dons Dadie had not concealed his orientation. Yet in fact a great change came over him. At the beginning of Plato's *Republic* Cephalus tells Socrates how the other day he met Sophocles, then an old man, and asked him whether he was still stirred sexually. Sophocles tells him he has at last found peace. 'I feel as if I had escaped from a mad and furious monster.' When Dadie's mother died in 1954 the monster left him: he haunted London no more and his holidays were spent with old friends, revisiting old and discovering new sights. In the discussions within the college Stephen Glanville, the professor of Egyptology, a fellow-resident in college and separated from his wife, emerged as the front runner to succeed Sheppard. He was some fellows' first choice and the second of many; and Dadie at once withdrew. Two years later, after Glanville's sudden death from a coronary, Dadie won an overwhelming number of votes at the first meeting of the fellows. He pondered for a week and withdrew, asking his supporters to transfer their votes to Noel Annan. He had decided that he could not endure a life in the chair at meetings and of entertaining in the Lodge. But for years to come he continued to be elected to all the major college committees. He also decided to retire from his university lectureship. A new generation of literary critics had been appointed in the faculty, such as A. P. Rossiter, Graham Hough and Matthew Hodgart, and the techniques used by the old stalwarts such as himself, Eustace Tillyard and Tom Henn were dated. He did not have an analytic mind and the theory of criticism did not interest him.

For thirty-four years he was chairman of the Cambridge Arts Theatre Trust, succeeding Keynes on his death. This was the heaviest cross he had to bear. The audience which before and during the war had packed the theatre began to evaporate. Television and bus journeys direct to London theatres diminished audiences; and costs of production rose. Keynes's policy had been for the theatre to provide opportunities for Town and Gown to mount productions of ballet and opera and for theatrical touring companies to come to Cambridge. Part of the trouble was that the theatre held too little money since Corpus had – at that time – refused, when it was built, to sell land in the Eagle courtyard on which four or five fellows' cars were parked. His friends in the theatre such as Binkie Beaumont responded to his appeals for help; and so did King's. Not so the City and the Arts Council. For years both refused to make any contribution, the City because it considered that the theatre was run for the benefit of dons and students, the Arts Council because the drama director and panel considered Cambridge should be like other provincial towns and employ a repertory company.

By 1959 the theatre's finances were parlous. So Rylands appealed for an Endowment Fund, wrote to 4,000 old Kingsmen and achieved his target of £75,000, to which the college added £25,000. In 1965 the City at last gave an annual grant of £2,500; in 1968 it was reduced to £1,000. The Arts Council next gave an annual grant of £3,000, but the policy of regional devolution later ate into it. Nor had the rich Cambridge colleges been much better. So in 1982, when he was eighty, Dadie launched yet another appeal. Where else in the provinces, he asked, would you be able to see in the course of a year a play by Shakespeare, a Feydeau farce, an Agatha Christie thriller and plays from Shaw to Brecht, operas from Mozart to Britten, Gilbert and Sullivan, revues and two children's shows? Where would you see a succession of West End stars and notable premières of plays by Kopit, Pinter and Orton?

His prodigious activity won public recognition. For his services to Shakespearean studies he had been made CBE in 1961. In 1975 the university paid him the rare tribute of awarding him the honorary degree of Doctor of Letters. So did Durham, where the Chancellor, Margot Fonteyn, bestowed it with a kiss. In 1987 he was made a Companion of Honour. Yet a question forms in the mind. When, in his extreme old age, the government imposed upon Oxford and Cambridge demands for evidence that dons were 'productive', what would the Quality Assessment Committee have made of Rylands's pursuits when they were considering the standard of work in the English faculty? Where were the books, the controversial articles that showed he was 'pushing back the frontiers of knowledge'? What had he been doing? Play-acting? Surely we want stout volumes on the shelves and not a succession of ephemeral activities.

Would the idea that he had enhanced the culture of the country have crossed their minds?

Perhaps the government's inquisitors would have spared him because he became a benefactor. When he was young he had nothing except what he earned as a don. His grandfather had been a Liberal MP, one of three brothers who carried on the family business of making wire in Warrington. When his uncle died Dadie inherited a considerable fortune. Throughout his life he spent little on himself: even at the tables in Monte Carlo before the war he disciplined himself and broke even – unlike Sheppard, who returned penniless. So far from indulging himself now that he was rich he became ever more austere and gave most of his fortune away to the college, the university, the Arts Theatre, the Fitzwilliam Museum – and to a children's ballet. He belonged to a generation of intellectuals that considered taking a taxi to be an act of gross indulgence, and in old age he expected his friends, to their chagrin, to drive him home after dinner rather than he should commit mortal sin. Like many of his generation he could not get used to inflation. To entertain as he had in pre-war days seemed to be exorbitantly expensive; and after his mother's death his zest for social life waned. By this time the expectations and demands of his legion of friends had become almost insupportable. But you had only to appear and his interest in you and his affection at once lit up.

His vitality and stamina seemed inexhaustible. It was this vitality that made any party, any dinner, any gathering where he was not present, seem devitalised. He revelled in your gossip, was ready to cap it with his own, was even readier to slide from an account of the latest production he had seen in London, into an analysis of dramatic method in Ibsen and Chekhov, thence into reflections about the distinction between envy and jealousy, or between beauty and allure, and the difference between coarseness and vulgarity (coarseness reveals something, vulgarity conceals something). He enchanted his friends when he read aloud: sometimes on a long holiday abroad a novel – *The Way We Live Now* or Le Fanu's *Uncle Silas*. Go to Sunday breakfast with him and he would read hilarious passages from Dickens or pursue the concept that English poetry excels when it combines the abstract and the concrete, the abstractions performing concrete actions, as when Keats moves from the world of abstraction to the world of vision, 'My sleep hath been embroidered with dim dreams'. On another Sunday in the summer of 1943 he lay in a punt with friends on the river reading deplorable Victorian poetry like Locker-Lampson's 'I'm in love with Neighbour Nellie, Though I know she's only ten', followed by Tennyson's *Lady Clara Vere de Vere* and *The Vision of Sin*, which he said was an accurate description of a party in King's. And then he switched – to *The Lady of Shallot* and *Maud*. As he read other boats drew up to listen until the river was nearly blocked.

But he was not only a talker. He could listen. None surpassed him as a confidant, grave, utterly engrossed in a friend's troubles, unravelling truth from delusion without a reproach, intent on setting an affair of the heart in perspective after which he could advise what the next move should be. In the workings of the heart, as in the revelations of life in literature, he was unrivalled. All novels about love, he used to say, hang on a few states of mind, for instance: 'I love you dearly, therefore you should give up everything and love me'; 'You ought to love me because I suffer'; 'I want to be loved for what I am and not for what I do for you'; 'You treat me kindly but you treat others equally kindly and therefore your kindness does not count at all' – and so on. He did not accept the platitude that one learnt more from one's contemporaries than from one's teachers. He said he had learnt immensely from his seniors and again from his juniors, who put new ideas to him. He believed in the King's ideal of dons and undergraduates treating each other as equals and learning from each other.

Dadie was a man of the strongest emotions. He would break down at the death of an intimate friend and was distraught at his mother's funeral. His passionate nature enabled him to empathise with the delinquencies and sufferings of poets and with the wayward lives of writers and friends. In character he was a remarkable combination of sophistication and simplicity. He had a quick eye for signs of *déformation professionelle* among those who became barristers or media men. Self-importance he detested and he suspected those who were ready to lay down the law about politics or make judgements about other people. Friends under attack were defended vociferously. That did not mean his friends could do no wrong. He was an exacting friend: if you made a remark he considered silly, insensitive or devoid of moral insight you would be devastated by a satirical or wounding remark. That was how he had been brought up at home and by Strachey.

He would take someone up and fascinate him by his sympathy and generosity. Then suddenly all would change. He found the new friend mean or stupid, or he was hurt by some act that he called ungrateful. A coolness supervened; or a quarrel was picked and an apology demanded. Such was his power for good and his fascination that the breach would usually be healed; but understandably that particular friendship was never quite the same.

That was true of his friendship with Arthur Marshall.* He was inseparable from Arthur since 1928. He used to say that no one had ever made him laugh more. But Dadie liked to tease, and his remorseless teasing – and perhaps Arthur's devotion to the trivialities of the professional theatre – led to coolness in the fifties. Arthur said he could endure it no longer. He once

* Arthur Marshall was a schoolmaster at Oundle (1931–54), private secretary to Lord Rothschild (1954–8), worked for H. M. Tennent (1958–64), wrote for the *New Statesman* (1935–81); noted reviewer and performer of monologues purporting to be schoolgirl stories.

said that friendship with Dadie was like being on an ocean liner from which one was hurled into the sea for a misdemeanour; as one surfaced one saw the heads of a dozen old friends bobbing in the waves.

Rylands was a moralist but of a rare kind: he often condemned those who judged others and would say that he lacked the experience or knowledge to make a judgement. He wept when an old friend of his younger days, Anthony Blunt, was exposed as a spy; and when asked what he made of it, replied he knew nothing of such matters. He might make judgements, very severe judgements, on what people said or did. He thought ill of Goronwy Rees for getting married without telling Rosamond Lehmann (Dadie's old friend), with whom he was having an affair, excusing himself by saying that that was the least painful way to break it off. Dadie conceded that that might be so, but he was outraged when Goronwy said that he hoped after three months of marriage to take up with Rosamond again.

Most of us at some time behave badly or foolishly in love, and where the individual was concerned you felt that the prayer of the founder of his college, Henry VI, was never far from his mind: 'Lord Jesus, who created me, redeemed me and preordained me to be what I am . . .' We are what we are – preordained by God. As Hazlitt said, 'An irritable man who puts a check on himself only grows dull and loses spirit to be anything.' That is why Dadie took his text from what he called 'Shakespeare's Gospel', an address he gave in the chapel. The first of all Shakespeare's virtues was mercy, and forgiveness should follow. Judge not that ye be not judged.

As he grew older, more and more his close friends were women. He always had women devoted to him, some helpless and hopeless in love such as Anne Barnes, the wife of the BBC mandarin George Barnes, some hoping to marry him like the actress Joyce Carey, others old allies like his cousin Hester Chapman, who wrote a novel about their childhood, *Ever Thine*. He became an icon, forever being visited by the media, who wanted to hear his memories of Bloomsbury and life in the twenties; or to ask him to perform in some programme or talk about Shakespeare and the modern theatre.

Life in college became difficult for him in his eighties. Deafness imprisoned him and dinner at high table was bewildering since he was more likely to find himself next to strangers with dining rights and their guests rather than fellows. His friends were dying about him, but he was not lonely. The widows of Cambridge colleagues and a procession of friends, often from abroad, made appointments to see him. In his nineties he rarely left his rooms: deaf and nearly blind he was attended by a posse of carers whom he charmed. A few months before he died one of them took him by train and taxi to London to see another survivor of Bloomsbury days – at ninety-eight two years his senior – Frances, the widow of Ralph Partridge, beloved by Strachey. But he was miserable and longed to die. He was no stranger to misery, the misery of his sexuality and of evil thoughts that his life had been a failure. Yet every day he would sit in the window seat of his room overlooking the Great Lawn and find a moment of happiness in holding the hand of an old friend and radiating affection. He was ninety-six when he died.

He was not Socratic, yet in those last years his friends thought of him as Plato did of Socrates: 'a man of whom we may say that of all whom we met at that time, he was the wisest, justest and best'.

CHAPTER TEN

The Don as Dilettante – John Sparrow

John Sparrow came to Oxford already with a reputation as a scholar. As a schoolboy at Winchester he discovered at the age of sixteen a copy of John Donne's *Devotions upon Emergent Occasions*, which he bought for three shillings, and published before he left. He also had a reputation as a footballer and, at a time when few of his kind followed the professional clubs, was a fan of Wolverhampton Wanderers. (A. J. Ayer backed Tottenham Hotspur.) He had a genius for friendship: not only was he a charmer, he was a fascinator. Saturnine and handsome, with thick dark-brown hair, he had a roguish smile and you could see the mischief in his eyes. He fascinated in the way a fine actor fascinates us. Francis Haskell* considered him superior as a raconteur to Bowra or even to Berlin. The timing in his stories was exact, the telling pause here, the speed-up there, the lifting of the eyebrows, the varieties in tone as well as pace and, just when you thought the end was coming, an unexpected diversion. A little too well rehearsed? Perhaps: but that too engrossed the listener. He was a tease and he was to spend his days devising ploys to tease the earnest and high-minded. He learnt from Bowra to detect humbug, pretension and obscurity masquerading as profundity. He owed much to him and saluted him with a memorable epitaph:

---

* Francis Haskell was a fellow of King's (1954–67) and professor of art history at Oxford (1967–95).

Which of the two, when God and Maurice meet,
Will occupy – you ask – the judgement seat?
Sure, our old friend – each one of us replies –
Will justly dominate the Grand Assize:
He'll seize the sceptre and ascend the throne,
Claim the Almighty's thunder for his own,
Trump the Last Trump, and the Last Post postpone.
Then, if his strong prerogative extends
To passing sentence on his sinful friends,
Thus shall we supplicate at Heaven's high bar:
'Be merciful! you made us what we are;
Our jokes, our joys, our hopes, our hatreds too,
The outrageous things we do, or want to do –
How much of all of them we owe to you!
Send us to Hell or Heaven or where you will,
Promise us only, you'll be with us still:
Heaven, without you, would be too dull to bear,
And Hell will not be Hell if you are there.'

He was a near contemporary of the novelists Anthony Powell and Henry Yorke (Henry Green) and of the critic Peter Quennell; the exact contemporary of John Betjeman; Christopher Sykes was one year and Osbert Lancaster two years younger. His friends were all in Bowra's circle: Cyril Radcliffe, Bob Boothby, Sylvester Gates, Roy Harrod and, in Cambridge, Dadie Rylands. His charmed career proceeded apparently without effort when he was elected to a fellowship at All Souls and entered the chambers of Cyril Radcliffe and Wilfred Greene, both fellows, to practise law at the Chancery Bar.

He was soon being given important cases and penetrated the mysteries of wills, trusts and corporate law. Mr Tulkinghorn would not have hesitated to brief him on the affairs of Sir Leicester Dedlock. He was every inch a Wykehamist. It was Winchester's role to educate the pro-consuls, generals, judges, officials – the regulators of the wheels of State. Wykehamists learn precision and are taught the art of drawing distinctions like the young seminarist who, when asked by a cardinal on a visit, 'Monsieur l'Abbé, your superiors are full of praise for your promise in casuistry: tell me, is it canonical to baptize an infant on point of death in soup?' 'In your soup, Your Eminence, no: in the seminary's soup, yes.' This training was reinforced by Horace Joseph's tuition at New College. Throughout his life he stalked inaccuracy and folly with merciless ferocity. When he reviewed Marcuse's *Essay on Liberation,* which he described as the nastiest book he had ever read, you can hear the knife go in again and again and, as he leaves the twitching body, he jeers like a Homeric hero at Marcuse's sentimentalism with which he tried to hide his contempt for people by quoting from a young black girl: 'unfortunately the young black girl – whose existence one may be permitted to doubt – turns out to be no more worth listening to than the old white man.'

He cared very much for people. When the war came he joined up as a private and revelled in barrack-room life. He was commissioned in the Coldstream and won the hearts of the men in his platoon by his smile when he returned their salute and the care he took over their worries and grievances. He became devoted to his servant, guardsman Boynton, who was attached to Headquarter Company. 'I wonder what I am attached to the War Office?' 'You? *You're* attached to me.' With his legal training it was inevitable that he would be posted from regimental duty to the Adjutant-General's office, where he did three tours of the armies overseas reporting on morale. He knew how to talk to the men – as a footballer he could play kick-about when inspecting a depot. His reports told the truth, so it was not surprising that the Secretary of State demanded they should be toned down: the passages on conditions in troopships, relations with American troops, pay and allowances contained political dynamite.

Oxford had differed from Cambridge in late Victorian and Edwardian times in that the cult of homoeroticism was not encouraged by the dons. Jowett would have been horrified by Lowes Dickinson's book *The Greek View of Life*. Had women been honoured in Athens, Jowett protested, as they were in England now, Plato would have rewritten the *Symposium*. W. L. Courtney, tutor of New College for fifteen years from the mid-1870s, was perturbed that, if a tutor took an 'intense interest in the boys themselves', he might get too interested in them and the relationship would be 'apt to grow morbid'. Arthur Sidgwick at Corpus was a generous host but he would never have encouraged the same degree of intimacy as Lowes Dickinson. Sparrow revered Pater and collected Pater manuscripts as well as his books. But at the turn of the century there was to be no successor to Pater among the Oxford dons. The aesthetes were undergraduates not their teachers.

Sparrow was an active homosexual. He made numbers of friends among the young at Oxford, nearly always to their advantage. He educated and teased them. He also cruised in London. Nor did he fail to seize an opportunity with unscrupulous effrontery. Visiting a friend Sparrow found him expecting a young man called Robin to stay. His friend was elated because Robin had sent him red carnations. Over dinner Sparrow managed to entrance Robin and cajoled his friend into agreeing that Sparrow might supplant him with Robin. Next morning Sparrow left a note: 'Slight headache, bad conscience – but not really a bad conscience. My only words are words of apology and just one of self-justification viz. that I would never have acted in this way if I hadn't had your express permission. It is your reproaches I dread.' He sent his friend white carnations. Next day he discovered why there had been no reproaches. His friend and Robin had gone to bed together after Sparrow had retired for the night. Sparrow sent a postcard: 'In view of the facts ascertained during the past twenty-four hours I am released of any compunction whatsoever of apologising further. Old humbug! I now know you better, like you better and have – if possible – even less respect for you than ever before.'

His views on homosexuality were characteristically perverse. He opposed the bill that was to make homosexual relations between consenting adults legal. Bad enough to be told that one was mad or sick but could be cured; worse still, he thought, to remove the two things essential to homosexual pleasure – the sense of guilt and the dangers of disgrace and imprisonment. He amazed some of his friends by surrendering in middle age to a buxom young married woman whose vitality, reckless humour and uncloying adoration broke down the barriers. He was somewhat put out when she had an affair with his own lover in Oxford. Late in life he left a clue behind him about his own sexuality. He published the diary of an elderly Victorian expatriate, Edward Leeves, who in 1849 had been driven out of Venice by the Austrian bombardment of the city, where republicans had risen against their Germanic rulers. Leeves returned to old haunts, the barracks in Albany Street, occupied by the Horse Guards, and met trooper Paxton (nephew of the Chatsworth gardener) who was 'a bold audacious Blackguard such as I like'. Leeves nicknamed him Screw and could deny him nothing. Paxton milked him of several hundreds of pounds. And then Leeves met Jack Brand, who had enlisted under an assumed name. Jack's goodness melted him. 'He used to answer me when I told him how I loved him, "*I believe* you". He never asked me for a farthing. It was there for the first time I heard him sing. And then he laid his head with his beautiful hair on my shoulder. Gentle boy! Who and what were you?' He was never to find out. Leeves went for a week to Scotland and fixed a date to meet him on his return but Jack never turned up. He had died of cholera. Leeves was shattered. The thought of that beautiful body rotting in the ground made him shudder. 'Strong thunder and lightning. Poor Boy! I trust that he sleeps well.' As

Housman wrote, when the night was freezing fast, 'And chiefly I remember how Dick would hate the cold.' In the anguish of grief the image of the beloved takes corporeal shape. 'The sense of leaving Miss Brawne,' wrote Keats, 'is beyond everything horrible – the sense of darkness coming over me – I see her figure eternally vanishing.' 'At this moment last year I was talking to you, Jack, and you were telling me your name,' wrote Leeves, 'I see you now, Boy! Would you could see me!'

Why did Sparrow publish this curious fragment of a diary? He despised Leeves as a fussy, twittering sissy whereas he was masterful and masculine. But Sparrow was possessed by the very strongest emotions, whether in controversy or in love, and he had a fellow feeling for Leeves's suffering. He was a romantic. He left behind an unpublished poem that he had sent to John Betjeman expressing in horticultural metaphor the vigour of his sexual drive, which he found overpowering. Romantic love was what he craved. (He was revolted by the act of sodomy.) He could not endure to see how the new generation, the young of the seventies, loved. 'Love for them means a diffused benevolence which finds expression in altruistic concern for the alienated and the oppressed, the love of the love-in. The one thing love does not mean to them is the mysterious, possessive, devastating, personal passion . . . the intense preoccupation of one individual with another.' That is the spell that Benjamin Constant understood when he described Adolphe's subjection to Ellénore.

In April 1951 the Warden of All Souls, Humphrey Sumner, died. As is well known, All Souls was an anomaly in Oxford. The college had no undergraduate or graduate students. There were the 'London fellows' who had left Oxford to follow a career in law, politics or public life, some of them elderly and eminent, others like Sparrow young and making their way in life. There were a few who held professorships tenable at All Souls and a few scholars whose tenure had been prolonged as a reward for their achievement. Then there were the young prize fellows who had chosen to stay in Oxford, work on an academic subject and tutor undergraduates in other colleges in the hope of being offered a teaching fellowship in a college. The fellows were rarely united on anything and certainly not on a successor to Sumner. Many names surfaced, like apples in a cask of brandy, only to be hit sharply on the head to sink to the bottom. A majority could always be found to keep someone out. Very soon such a caucus formed to defeat A. L. Rowse, a historian of promise and a gallant opponent of appeasement at the time of Munich, but whose vanity, touchiness and growing pretentiousness were notorious. (He was later to declare that he had identified beyond shadow of doubt Shakespeare's dark lady in the sonnets, in the course of which he dwelt on the blindness and stupidity of all other Shakespeare literary scholars who, lacking Rowse's historical training, should be dismissed as worthless. None of them unsurprisingly was convinced by his arguments.) Another possibility among the younger academic fellows was Isaiah Berlin, who had just returned to the college after an extended wartime career as a diplomat.

From the start Sparrow's name was mentioned, and as usual he wrote to all his friends for advice although he had already made up his mind. He wanted the wardenship. He did not want a future in the law. To be a judge? Unthinkable. To slave on writing opinions on cases depending on construction? Too tedious. For the whole of the summer term he and Berlin lived in each other's pockets, counting votes, exchanging intelligence and writing each other voluminous letters. They said what they thought of each other – 'One sparrow,' said Isaiah, 'does not make a Sumner' – but they were friends who shared apprehensions about the intentions of their elders. They were appalled to hear that such a dry stick as Edward Bridges was being considered, and unconvinced when a much-loved historian, Ernest Jacob, entered the lists. Then another nonentity, Sir Eric

Beckett, began to be mentioned. Before the final election meeting Berlin withdrew his name. He was known to favour reform and he knew that the elderly London fellows would never vote for him: a few may have blanched at a Jew and agnostic presiding in chapel. After a term of delectable intrigue the fellows in June elected Sir Hubert Henderson, a Cambridge man who had been a fellow of All Souls since 1934.

It was all to do again. Ten days later Henderson suffered a stroke and at the turn of the year resigned. By that time Berlin was in America and took no part in the election, pursued however by sheaves of letters from Sparrow, fighting the battle, as his biographer said, after it had been won, preferring the debate to the decision. This time Sparrow succeeded and became Warden for twenty-five years.

What would he do? Gradually it dawned on those who had voted for him that he was not in the smallest degree interested in doing anything. Academic life bored him. He advanced no subject, intervened in no faculty, sat on none of the central university committees and declined the Vice-Chancellorship when it came his way by rote. He was a supremely selfish man. What did not interest him he did not do. Like numbers of eccentrics he was not exactly a scholar, but a man of scholarly taste and beyond question learned. Some thought he would now pursue his study of Donne or follow up his leanings towards literary criticism: he had published in 1934 an essay entitled *Sense and Poetry*. But no; he was a bibliophile and built up the second or third best private library in England and was chosen to give the Sandars lectures on bibliography at Cambridge. He loved the concision and ellipsis of Latin lapidary inscriptions and later in life published eight handsomely printed volumes of examples of this art. He had gathered these, wrote Richard Wilberforce, his generation's most distinguished judge, 'in the walks and excursions to churches, monuments, libraries and archives, the distillation of years of patient devotion'. There followed a collection of Renaissance Latin verse. A projected life of Mark Pattison came to nothing, but in 1965 a short account of that melancholy man and his unhappy marriage appeared. To Hugh Trevor-Roper, the Regius professor of history – a man of the centre right, even more elegant than Sparrow in his transfixion of pomposity and progressive gobbledegook – such scholarship was purely decorative: Sparrow had no interest in ideas. Presented with any problem, his acute mind would unerringly light on the outer periphery, there to play with some marginal triviality. Historians distinguish between a historian and an antiquarian. Antiquarians are scholars, often men of immense learning, but they draw no conclusions from their work or relate it to wider questions. John E. B. Mayor, professor of Latin in Cambridge in mid-Victorian times, spent his life collecting instances of where every word appeared in Latin literature in order to confound Lewis and Short, the authors of the standard work on lexicography. But he never made anything of it; he spent his life compiling lists. John Sparrow did more than that. His contribution to learning did not resemble that of a scholar who in choosing his problems enlarges our understanding of his period and our life. But it is a contribution none the less.

What then did he do at All Souls? He used every art to defeat attempts by others to change the college. He did not need to study Cornford's *Microcosmographia Academica*: the principles of obstruction that it analysed were ingrained in his nature. If a proposal was put to the Governing Body that he disliked he would argue that to accept it would set 'a dangerous precedent'. If that argument failed to convince, he might change his tack and plead that the time for such a move was 'not yet ripe, or that admirable as it was to pass such a motion now would hinder a yet more admirable change in the future'. Nor was he above declaring that the proposal had sounded reasonable enough until he heard the speech supporting it of the Gladstone professor of government (Max Beloff).

On one matter he was fortunate. The college was not plagued at the time of the Suez debacle with the divisions of the days of Munich. Sparrow described the mood of the fellows in 1956 as 'a hot-bed of cold feet'. He was wrongly accused of racial prejudice when he voted against the admission to a fellowship of a Ghanaian; and his judgement was vindicated when the man supported Nkrumah in his attempt to make the University of Ghana his creature (unlike another professor, Alex Kwapong, who had won a first in classics at Cambridge). Indeed the second black fellow, Hugh Springer, won his enthusiastic support. Inevitably he opposed the election of women fellows, and when Bernard Williams's name was mentioned as his possible successor he exclaimed, 'There will be women in the college before you can say Joan Robinson.' The spectacle of this redoubtable Keynesian, a supporter of Chairman Mao and clad in trousers or kimono, may have been one reason why Williams's candidature did not prosper; he later became Provost of King's.

Meanwhile the clouds that were gathering about Oxford's future and the future of British universities – which Bowra had encountered – gathered above his head. The Franks Commission began to ask what was the purpose of All Souls. Was it to remain a club or should it help Oxford by creating fellowships for those who held university posts in new branches of science and the humanities and who had no fellowships? Or should it become a college for graduate students? Had Sparrow had a scheme of his own that would placate the commission but preserve the college as a club, he could have united All Souls behind him. But he was – and these were his worst sins – too lazy and too selfish to take the trouble to devise one. The university wanted All Souls to take graduate students who were flocking to Oxford, particularly from America, and for whom the colleges, dedicated to teaching undergraduates, made little provision. Sparrow's tactics were to allow the debate to drag on, confident that every scheme for change would reveal insuperable obstacles. Graduate students? But where to house them? Erect a new building in the Warden's garden? Well, he would not dream of opposing such a scheme on selfish grounds. But had its supporters realised that the money needed to endow the studentships would then have been mopped up by the building? Finally, after all, it was decided to admit graduate students, the Franks Commission were so informed and proceeded to draft their report. And then a whisper was heard, a rumour gained currency, incredulity turned to suspicion and suspicion to something worse. Could it be true? But it was ... in January 1966 the college changed its mind. A young fellow, the conservative sociologist Bryan Wilson, an ally of the Warden, came up with a new proposal. Why not use the surplus funds to finance visiting fellows? True, it would not help the university with its problems, but no matter. Sparrow shrewdly allowed the new proposal to be discussed and, as he guessed, the majority in favour of graduate students dissolved. The young fellows had always disliked it. They backed Wilson, and Professors Beloff and Berlin were confounded. Lord Franks made a spine-chilling judgement: 'We are compelled to infer infirmity of purpose.' One of the junior fellows, David Caute, resigned and wrote in *Encounter* a bitter account of the Warden's manoeuvres. 'Turn-Caute' was the Warden's feeble riposte.

That jet of criticism trickled off the duck's back. Edward Bridges, former secretary to the Cabinet, peer, conductor of an enquiry into the non-fellows problem at Cambridge, called on the Warden. Should he not consider his position? Not reconsider it (i.e. resign), the Warden noted – and did nothing. Fifteen visiting fellowships were established but not until he retired was a woman fellow allowed to sit for the All Souls examination for young prize fellows. Gallant as always, Sparrow found her 'faultless and delightful'.

Sparrow was not as much at fault as it may appear. All Souls was better fitted to be a post-doctoral institute than a graduate school: the natural habitat of the graduate student should be the lab or the faculty. He was not unique among heads of colleges in wanting to keep things as they were. Few concerned themselves with the wider issues of higher education and the anomalies that Oxford and Cambridge caused in what was becoming a national system of higher education. Each college set its own conditions of entry, each group of colleges set its own requirements for the scholarship exam, and the public schools and grammar schools, recognising the Oxford and Cambridge scholarship awards as the blue riband of sixth-form education, chose as best they could between the bewildering options and variants. Yet when the tutors of Trinity and King's at Cambridge proposed a uniform set of entry requirements they were met with dogged opposition, led at Cambridge by such respected figures as Arthur Armitage of Queens', who was to become in time Vice-Chancellor of both Manchester and Cambridge. Nevertheless Sparrow irritated the younger academic fellows in the last years of his wardenship, not so much by his refusal to consider fairly proposals for change as by his delight in parading his defence of the war in Vietnam and the frivolity of his solution to Oxford's traffic problems – which was to divert the Thames down the High.

He had become the most notorious reactionary in Oxford. He liked to expose the inconsistencies in the plans of reformers and mock their gullibility for being taken in by clichés. In the aftermath of the *Lady Chatterley* trial he denounced the witnesses for the defence as humbugs. However, it was not simply humbug that he was out to expose but humbuggery; and in a fascinating analysis he established that Lawrence had portrayed Mellors as having anal intercourse with Connie. Were the expert witnesses so inexpert that they had failed to notice this passage and why had they concealed this indecency when prosecuting counsel, having toyed with the passage, said, 'I don't know what it means'?

But it was Sparrow who laid himself open to the charge of humbug. He knew well enough that a criminal trial in England is not concerned primarily with the truth. It is concerned with guilt or innocence. There was no obligation on Gerald Gardiner, who led for the defence, to draw the jury's attention to an episode unfavourable to his cause when prosecuting counsel missed the point. Nor was it true that all the expert witnesses were so inexpert as to miss it too. In conference before the trial it is true that the Oxford don Helen Gardner did not understand the passage, but the Cambridge don Joan Bennett, the first to write a critical study of Virginia Woolf, did. So did Graham Hough,* and both raised the matter. Gardiner's junior, the wily Jeremy Hutchinson, did not conduct a university seminar on the point. He asked: was it not possible for the passage to be interpreted in other ways – could it not be argued that Lawrence was describing normal sexual intercourse from behind? Sparrow should have acknowledged that the book that was on trial was really John Stuart Mill's *Essay on Liberty*. He was pilloried, possibly not in the best of taste, as the Warden of All Holes.

The delight in controversy grew on him as he aged, particularly since the excesses of the student revolutionaries enraged him. He was libelled in *Cherwell*, and All Souls was plastered with graffiti: CHAIRMAN MAO ON SPARROW: MAKE HIM INTO BIRD'S NEST SOUP. He waged war against them, captured a student banner, spent hours reworking the slogan so that it read OXFORD REVOLUTIONARY STUDENTS *SILLIES*, surreptitiously returning it to them confident that they would not notice the emendation. Silly? John had already found new evidence of the decline of civility. Young men now wore beards and side-burns: they resembled Victorian curates. The clean-shaven,

---

* Graham Hough was a fellow of Christ's and later of Darwin (1964–75), reader in English at Cambridge (1966–75).

well-groomed English youth had disappeared: today he wore an
anorak and jeans. The unisex movement, he thought, was as
dangerous. 'Raise. The clarion call again, Beards for women,
Breasts for men.' He hated beards as much as he hated dogs.*
Surely the two great G men of our culture, Gillette and Guillotin
should be celebrated, not consigned to oblivion. Chicago University heard him asking if we did not have too much humani-
tarianism, equality and liberty. Are we to abolish examinations
because they deny equality? Or punishment in schools and
prisons if we are to preserve nobility, genius and imagination?
The spirit of the Latinist stirred within him when he made a
defence of syntax and begged us not to use words like 'viable',
'syndrome' or 'dynamic' as nouns; or to fall into academic jargon. 'I was recently invited,' he said, 'to a symposium called
"Perimeters of Social Repair". I suppose we should be grateful
for not having said "Parameters".' When one professor told
him that a young scholar was 'capable of forming insightful
associations between the elements of his knowledge'; and when
another professor added of the same young man that he was
'sophisticated in interpersonal relationships', Sparrow asked
why they could not have said the young man was shrewd.

Had the Bowra tradition of wit run into the sands? Across
high table at dinner Leslie Rowse reproached him: 'You don't
read my books, John. Do you know *Tudor Cornwall?*' Pointing
to the philosopher on his left Sparrow replied, 'Do you know
Stuart Hampshire?' An impromptu? Perhaps. Funny? Fairly
funny. When he published *Words on the Air*, his talks on the
BBC, you heard the shade of his old tutor Joseph speaking.
'What *is* a word? It's not just a sound. Is it a sound that stands

---

* This was not the view of T. G. Bonney, a Victorian fellow of St John's, Cambridge, who
noted that beards came in after the Crimean War. 'How anyone,' he wrote, deploring the
trend back towards shaving, 'who has once known the comfort of a beard . . . can return
to a daily scraping of the skin, possibly of the whole that is "shavable", passes my compre-
hension.'

for a thing? But not all words stand for a thing – lots of them don't . . .' He could still summon up his barrister's skill in cross-examination to make a fine critique of the conspiracy theorists of Kennedy's assassination. But as old age gripped him he became crotchety and tiresome.

Cambridge is more merciful to her bachelor dons than Oxford. Some colleges there allow them to continue to live in their rooms when they retire until they die or are forced to move to a sanatorium. An abuse? Possibly: but humane. At Oxford they must leave college and find somewhere to live. Sparrow made no attempt to make arrangements for retirement and with ill-grace accepted a college-owned flat a long way out on the Iffley road. His memory began to fail and he took to the bottle. Only too well-known as a reckless driver, he was stopped by the police one night accompanied by his friend John Gere. While he was being tested for being over the alcoholic limit he turned to Gere and said, 'Tell me, John, did we hit that baby as we turned into the High?' He lost his driving licence and his loneliness was intensified. He was so often drunk at dinner that he was banned from dining in All Souls. One talent still remained his: his talent for friendship, even if he mortgaged it too often. Sometimes the old gaiety returned. He wrote a verse, 'Growing Old', which was often quoted and misquoted and rarely acknowledged.

> I'm accustomed to my deafness
> To my dentures I'm resigned
> I can cope with my bifocals,
> But – oh dear! – I miss my mind.

John Sparrow's failings were not unique. There are always a handful of dons who have lost heart with their subject, have been battered by hostile reviews of their work and can no longer get a warm glow by voting in a minority of one in college meetings or university boards. They shrink into their shells or retire into domesticity. His letters, said his biographer, showed his gift for procrastination, circumlocution, contradiction, self-deprecation and every other twist and turn. He would take three pages to argue himself out of one position and into another, and the next three returning to where he had started . . . The golden rule, in nearly every case, was to avoid reaching a decision. He knew himself only too well.

> Here, with his talents in a napkin hid,
> Lies one who much designed, and nothing did;
> Postponing and deferring, day by day,
> He quite procrastinated life away . . .

CHAPTER ELEVEN

The Don as Magus – Isaiah Berlin

When John Sparrow was learning Greek and Latin, another boy three years younger was also mastering languages. His first language was Russian because he was born in Riga in the days of the Tsar; his second language was Hebrew because he was a Jew. He had to learn German and then, when the family managed during the Revolution to escape from Petrograd and reach London, he had to learn English. Isaiah Berlin's father was a timber merchant and had for long had business connections in England and, still more important, a bank balance there – profits from his wartime plywood trade. He continued his business and he and his wife doted on their son. Nothing was too good for him. They sent him to St Paul's, a London public school that admitted Jews, and there he continued the process of assimilation and learning to please. He remembered a senior boy, Richard Kahn, later to become Keynes's adjutant and invent the 'multiplier' when Keynes was working out the principles of the *General Theory*, telling him not to bow to masters and prefects. There he found Leonard Shapiro, who had spent summers with him at a dacha outside Petrograd where they discussed Bakst and Benois and Russian painting. Not topics for English schoolboys. There was something odd about him. He strolled about the school talking, talking, talking . . .

Isaiah Berlin was one of the clever undergraduates that Maurice Bowra brought out. He always acknowledged Bowra as

a liberator who encouraged him to be himself and not to conform to the staid ethos of college common rooms. So far from
restraining Berlin's torrent of talk he stimulated it and indeed
gave his talk a resonance and a form – the rapid association of
ideas that was specifically Bowra. He wrote as he talked, and he
was the most dazzling talker of his generation. It was for Berlin's
conversation, his lectures, as much as for his published works
that so many honours – among them twenty-five honorary doctorates – rained upon him. Strangers sometimes could not follow him because his tongue had to sprint to keep pace with his
thoughts: ideas, similes, metaphors cascaded over each other,
and in his efforts to depict every facet of his subject he would
never use one word when two should do. Someone once timed
him: he scored 400 words a minute. His memory for names,
events and the behaviour of the protagonists in his stories was
fabulous. It was like watching a pageant.

He was not part of the gilded society of wits in the twenties.
His contemporaries were more serious: Freddie Ayer, Stephen
Spender, Goronwy Rees and Humphry House, and they had far
more in common with the generation that immediately succeeded his than with the wits – Stuart Hampshire, Ben Nicolson,
Jeremy Hutchinson and Herbert Hart. They were not worldly
or obsessed with social success like the wits, not as brilliant nor
dandyish and snobbish. They prided themselves on being a
critical intelligentsia and most of them had heterosexual and
not homosexual tastes. But Berlin saw the point of the aesthetes.
They had been idle but 'created an atmosphere which had a
certain excitement. Which is completely lacking now.'

At Corpus he duly collected firsts in both Greats and Modern
Greats and, like others in the inter-war years, hung around
uncertain what to do. Richard Crossman thought him an ami-
able rattle, the sort of man who would do to teach philosophy
at New College even though he had published nothing and had
no experience of teaching. According to Berlin Crossman got

him appointed by telling lies to the fellows. 'He said I had been offered a fellowship at Exeter. I never was. That I had been offered a job at Brasenose. I never had.' Crossman's plot succeeded and Berlin was dejected to find how dull – with the exception of the Warden, H. A. L. Fisher – the senior common room was. From this he was rescued by being elected – to his astonishment – a fellow of All Souls. At the age of twenty-three he became a public figure. He was the first Jew ever to be elected to All Souls. The Chief Rabbi wrote to congratulate him, he was invited to the Rothschild splendours at Waddesdon. He continued in fact to teach for New College until the war. But Crossman was livid.

In those days at All Souls he talked philosophy with John Austin and later invited Ayer, Stuart Hampshire, Donald Mackinnon and others to join Austin's seminar (held in Berlin's room), where they discussed each week the minutiae of analytic philosophy – to the horror of the older generation of Oxford philosophers, Prichard and Joseph, who heard that everything they had taught for a generation was being demolished and overthrown. Not that Ayer and Austin were in agreement; after Ayer published in 1936 his memorable book *Language, Truth and Logic*, they were always in contention. Berlin distrusted logical positivism: to him the verification principle dismissed as meaningless whole chunks of human experience – art, music and the numinous. Berlin's account of the discussions in this seminar express unforgettably what it was like to be a young don in those days. Publish their ideas? Ludicrous. Their ideas were provisional steps towards establishing the truth about certain particulars – *a priori* statements, *qualia*, other minds and the like. Sometimes it seemed as if truth – a minute part of it – had been caught and pinned down. 'Those who have never been under the spell of this kind of illusion even for a short while,' wrote Berlin, 'have never known true intellectual happiness.'

He became above all a don. He immersed himself in the

affairs of the college, indefatigably sociable. As Dr Johnson said of Richard Savage, 'at no time in his life was it any part of his character to be the first of the company that desired to separate'. At New College and All Souls he talked until his exhausted guest tottered to bed, only to find Berlin sitting on the end of it, unwilling to bring the evening to an end. (On the historic occasion when he called on Anna Akhmatova they talked straight through the night.) He was at his happiest in a small group of intimate friends at All Souls or, years later, sitting in a corner of the Russian Tea Room on 57th Street a few blocks down from the offices of the *New York Review of Books* with Robert Silvers, Stuart Hampshire and the Lowells. As a bachelor – in the days before the war he was always called Shaya – he was renowned as the most amusing young don in Oxford, fat, roly-poly and irrepressible. People noticed that he enjoyed meeting celebrities: Virginia Woolf, Elizabeth Bowen (who became a friend) and the London men of public affairs whom he met on weekends at All Souls. He defended worldliness and thought dons and intellectuals drew a curtain between themselves and reality in avoiding upper-class society.

His door was always open. Colleagues, friends from London, pupils dropped in to gossip. He loved gossip. An election to a chair would inspire him to give a dramatic performance of the proceedings. He could make himself into David Cecil, Henry Price or Maurice Bowra and convey the tone of voice and the structure of the sentences of the other participants. The treachery of Bloggs, the craven behaviour of Stiggins, the twitterings of the outside electors and, when it came to the vote, the *volte-face*, the defection of those you had imagined were your closest allies. Brought up to imagine that such proceedings were sacred and secret, Cambridge friends reeled. 'I practise,' he once told the Chief Rabbi, 'the Oxford way of keeping a secret. You only tell one person at a time.' He was the prisoner of his sense of humour. It was not English humour. It came from the Russian part of his make-up; from Gogol, from Chekhov. He loved jokes. He loved games. Who was a hedgehog, who was a fox? What is the difference between a cad and a bounder? When others were maddened by the perverse, egoistic, self-satisfied speeches in a college meeting, Isaiah revelled in them – to him they revealed the perennial eccentricity of human beings. But the jokes masked the seriousness with which he considered academic appointments. He would telephone remote American universities where he knew a former don was teaching, urging him to put in for a post in Oxford for which Isaiah thought him fitted; and he would telephone those he did not know personally. Conversely he would consult scholars in disciplines outside his own, asking whether an applicant for a post was up to it – what was special about his or her contribution to the subject? Tutorials with his graduate students were exacting. Aileen Kelly* remembered him not so much for making inspired connections between ideas as for his insistence on accuracy: 'Not 1848, it was 1846. You must check your facts.' On the other hand when, after the war, the colleges were flooded with undergraduates demobilised from the armed services and he found himself teaching eighteen hours a week at New College in one-to-one tutorials, he found the routine intolerable. Too many seemed to him 'dull and polite and spiritless'. The truth, perhaps, was that they bored him because he was bored with analytic philosophy and was looking for a path to escape.

It was very different when obscure visitors came to consult him. The composer Nicholas Nabokov accused him of liking bores too much. But then Isaiah was meticulous in obeying the obligations of a scholar. No one was ever turned away who came to him genuinely wishing to discuss a problem. To watch him in the days of his fame at Mishkenot Sha'ananim in Jerusalem, spending hours with those who queued to seek his advice, was

---

* Aileen Kelly, fellow of King's (1995) and lecturer in Russian.

to realise that he honoured anyone in search of truth. His oldest, dearest friend of sixty-two years, Stuart Hampshire, thought it was 'his deep-seated unvarying patience' that was the clue to the affection and reverence in which he was held, 'patience in attending to people, in constantly thinking about them, and about their needs ... This generous quality of his in giving time to people was connected with a complete absence of self-importance. He always refused to divide his time into measured bits and then to allocate it appropriately.'

When war came no post was offered to him. He was exempt from military service – the doctor's forceps at his birth had damaged his left arm – and as a foreign-born subject many channels were blocked. Guy Burgess concocted a mad scheme whereby he and Isaiah should be sent to Moscow via Vladivostok. Burgess was recalled and left him stranded in America. (Burgess's quick mind amused Isaiah; and when later he was exposed as a spy Berlin always referred to him as 'my friend Guy Burgess', although he drew the line at corresponding with him in Moscow as Harold Nicolson did.)

He remained for the rest of the war in America and did not in fact return to Oxford for good until the summer of 1946. He had reported from the embassy in Washington on the American political scene and on the personalities in the administration, in Congress and in the trade union movement, with such élan that his despatches became compulsory reading in the War Cabinet Offices, culminating in the comical *faux pas* of Irving Berlin instead of Isaiah being invited to lunch with Churchill. After the war he accepted part-time posts in American universities but refused offers of permanent appointments. He always enjoyed America and in 1949 in a BBC broadcast declared that the future of Britain lay neither with the empire nor with Europe but with America.

During the war he faced another predicament. He had always been a Zionist and in Washington became an admirer of Weiz-

Oliver Franks, 1947, provost of Queen's, Oxford.

George 'Dadie'
Rylands, 1938.

Steven Runciman
in his rooms at
Trinity, 1937.

Dadie Rylands and Edward Bates, 1937.

Ian Scott-Kilvert and Dadie Rylands in the archway of Gibbs' building, King's College, 1939.

Raymond Mortimer, Dadie Rylands, Maurice Bowra in the Gate of Honour, Caius College, 1943.

John Sparrow,
*c.*1954.

Yehudi
Menuhin,
Nicholas
Nabukov,
Isaiah Berlin at
the Bath
Festival, 1959.

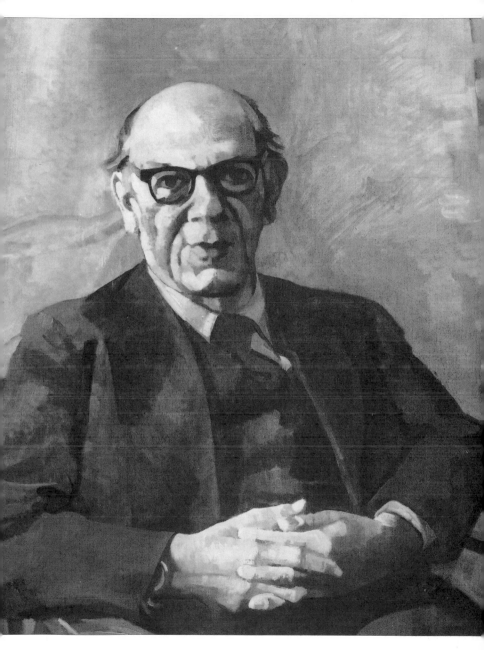

Isaiah Berlin (portrait by Lawrence Gowing, 1982).

Jane Harrison
(by Augustus John,
1909).

Betty Behrens,
*c.*1950.

mann, who put his trust in the British to honour the Balfour Declaration and establish a state of Israel. In the embassy Berlin found himself in a dilemma. He advised Halifax as ambassador how to deal with the Jewish lobby, and Weizmann how to approach Halifax. He once tipped off the Jewish lobby about a proposed Anglo-American declaration against recognition of a Jewish state until after the war. Henry Morgenthau went straight to Roosevelt. The State Department (which was almost as anti-Zionist as the Foreign Office) caved in and the declaration was withdrawn. Isaiah was ashamed of the part he had played and concealed it until he spoke in old age to his biographer: he had failed to reconcile two conflicting duties. But he did not hesitate to condemn Jewish terrorism when the King David Hotel was blown up. Years later when he met the instigator of the outrage he refused to shake Prime Minister Begin's hand.

When Israel became a state he was besieged by Weizmann, Ben Gurion and others to emigrate there and offered post after post. He refused. An article by Arthur Koestler wrung a declaration of his own faith from him. Koestler argued that Jews had a choice: go to Israel and live like Jews or assimilate with the people of the country in which they lived. Berlin disagreed. In *Jewish Slavery and Emancipation* he analysed what it meant to assimilate. It meant becoming too eager for Gentile approval, too ready to detect and explain the tribal customs of their hosts. He used an unforgettable metaphor. It was as if Jews were hunchbacks. Some, the assimilationists, denied that they had a hump. Others claimed the hump was diminishing and if soothing ointments were applied it would disappear. And then there were the Zionists who were proud of their hump, who knew that however well Jews were treated by the country they lived in they would feel uneasy and insecure. But Jews should not be bullied by the Koestlers of this world. Jews are entitled to choose. Indeed there was no one sole way in which Jews should live. He himself was unable to believe in God, but he remained orthodox and never failed to observe Yom Kippur or celebrate Seder at home. Why should he leave England, a country he idealised for its tolerance and civility?

He left no one in doubt on the public issue. He never forgave those who forgot to conceal their anti-Semitism, the nastier ways of snubs, pinpricks, acts of exclusion which Gentiles inflict upon Jews. When he was learning the Hebrew letters as a child the old rabbi said, 'Dear children, when you are older you will realise how in every one of these letters there is Jewish blood and Jewish tears.' He once asked Avishai Margalit whether, if he possessed a magical Aladdin's lamp that if rubbed would turn all the Jews into Scandinavians, dull perhaps but happy, free from the history of their martyrdom, he would use it. Certainly not, Margalit at once replied. To Berlin the answer came a little too pat. 'He took this,' said Margalit, 'as an unbearable lightness to Jewish suffering.' Yes, the creation of the state of Israel created an injustice to Palestinians. But after the Holocaust? As he lay dying he dictated his conviction that partition of the Holy Land was the only solution to give Palestinians rights to their land and give Israel Jerusalem as its capital city, with the Muslim holy places under a Muslim authority and an Arab quarter under UN protection. 'He made me proud to be a Jew,' said the Chief Rabbi at his funeral. 'He enlarged our mental and moral world.'

But what was he to do if he returned to Oxford for good? He knew what he would not do. On a visit to Harvard he met a logician, Harry Sheffer, who told him that in philosophy the same old questions kept on being raised. One had no hope of increasing permanent knowledge. All night long, sleepless on the flight back to England, Berlin considered what Sheffer had said and concluded that he was right. He wanted to study something which might change people's understanding of life, to know more at the end of his life than he did at the beginning;

but what should it be? One incident stirred his mind. He had accepted an invitation from the British ambassador in Moscow to visit Russia. He found the intelligentsia there cowed: Pasternak spoke to him of his guilt at having to collaborate with the regime and his shame at being a Jew. When he went to Leningrad he asked after the poet Anna Akhmatova. 'She lives near here on the Fontanka. Would you like to meet her?'

The story of that historic meeting has often been told. Its interruption by the boorish Randolph Churchill bawling Isaiah's name, and its resumption that evening when they sat all through the night at opposite ends of the room talking until, at ten in the morning, Berlin staggered home, threw himself on his bed and said, 'I am in love, I am in love.' She had read her poems to him and told of the days when her husband had been executed, her son arrested, and of the misery, humiliation and anguish of life for a writer in Stalin's day. When, years later, Pasternak phoned her to tell her Isaiah was married, the line went dead. She was stunned. 'Guest from the future, that he will really come to me. Turning left from the bridge?'

That visit gave him direct experience of the horror of life under Stalin. He would not join the militant anti-communist front headed by Nicholas Nabokov and Irving Kristol. He had too many friends in Oxford who, at the time of the Spanish Civil War and the rise of Hitler, had sympathised with the aims of Soviet Russia and had shut their eyes in the 1930s to the absurdities of the show trials. At the end of his life he welcomed opportunities to talk with Eric Hobsbawm, Britain's most distinguished Marxist historian, a cosmopolitan of international fame like himself. But one thing above all revolted him: violence. As a child he had seen in Petrograd a policeman dragged to his death by the mob and the sight remained engraved on his mind. With all his love of opera he disliked *Tosca* and *Turandot, Wozzeck* and *Peter Grimes*: they were too cruel. He heard that as a result of his visit Akhmatova had suffered further persecution. 'So our

nun is now consorting with British spies,' said Stalin, and his
minister for culture, Zhdanov, denounced her as half-harlot,
half-spy. None of them could believe that she had not seduced
Berlin. Though Berlin did not know it, worse had happened.
He had unwisely visited his uncle, Dr L. B. Berlin. Two years
later, his uncle died and after the collapse of communism, Isaiah
learnt of the consequences of the visit. He was sent an extract
from a book that had just appeared in Russia on Stalin's persecution of the Jews. It related how his uncle had been accused
of being part of a spy ring consisting of four other savants,
linked to the well-known spy Isaiah Berlin. Professor Berlin was
tortured not once but twice, the second time in so excruciating
a fashion that he 'confessed'. He was later set free but one day
in Moscow he saw his torturer across the street and fell down
dead. Isaiah commented, 'So I enter Soviet history at last. This
must be one falsification out of millions. – nothing they say can
be believed. So much for E. H.* and Eric.' Asked once whether
Hitler or Stalin was worse, Isaiah replied, 'My answer will sur-
prise you. I am a Jew and I should answer that Hitler was worse.
Yet not only did Stalin destroy tens of millions of human lives
... he also instilled slavish fear into people's souls, brought
the intelligentsia to their knees, extolled lackeys, mediocrities.
Apart from that he had a wonderful gift for playing on the lowly
instincts of mobs.'

He had already written before the war – because no one else
at Oxford would – a short book on Marx. He agreed Marx was
a genius: his contention that changes in technology changed
culture; that capitalism was international, affecting production,
manufacture and exchange; and that the class war was inevitable
– all this seemed to Berlin to be original, even if the ferocity
of the class war was exaggerated. He read the works of the

* E. H. Carr, professor of international politics, University of Wales, Aberystwyth (1936–
47), assistant editor of *The Times*, fellow of Trinity (1955); author of *The History of Soviet
Russia* in fourteen volumes (1950–78).

philosophers of the Enlightenment and found that they too exaggerated. He told American audiences that it was a modern illusion formed in the Enlightenment that all ills were curable. It is an illusion to believe that if only rulers were more rational they would discover how to cure these ills. On the contrary: men live by choosing their goals, 'not only by fighting evils'. Others, such as Popper and the Israeli political scientist Jacob Talmon, had argued that one could find the sources of totalitarianism in Condorcet and La Mettrie, but it was Berlin who settled down to read the German romantic philosophers Herder and Fichte. They had asked what it was that influenced men to act as they did. Was it not their language, their culture, their consciousness of belonging to a community, a nation? Long ago he had become devoted to two Russians, heroes to him, Herzen and Turgenev. Both remained indeterminates – liberals in the middle, abused alike by the young revolutionaries and the reactionary Slavophils. Herzen had led him to other Russian thinkers – Belinsky, Bakunin and Tolstoy – and in Tolstoy he observed the paradox of a man who understood how different and idiosyncratic human beings were yet who was obsessed with the determination to discover the one, sole rule of life under which all must live. As Berlin put it in his best-known book – Tolstoy was a fox who knows many things pretending to be a hedgehog who knows one big thing.

His first published essay on his return to Oxford was on historical inevitability in which he refuted one of the central tenets in Marxism. He refused to see human beings as flies struggling in the cobweb of historical causation. His lecture was a challenge to E. H. Carr, who in a succession of books had been suggesting that a wise statesman was he who understood the way history was moving and jumped on the moving staircase. Later, in 1961, Carr replied. How could Berlin believe that history explained anything unless he took social and economic factors into account? Were we really to waste time arguing

whether Hitler or Cromwell were good or bad men? What mattered were the impersonal forces that enabled them to seize
power. Berlin replied that Carr simply justified whatever happened. 'Whatever is, is right.' Are we to neglect ideas and the
motives of individuals, their intentions?

In 1957 there came a stroke of luck. G. D. H. Cole retired
from the chair of social and political theory and Berlin was
elected to it. His inaugural lecture answered those who thought
his publications inadequate. *Two Concepts of Liberty* went against
the grain just as his essay against historical determinism had
done. He took the unfashionable view that liberty meant not
being impeded by others. It was a negative quality. Its opposite,
positive freedom, was the child of Rousseau, to whom freedom
meant submitting to a higher will than one's own. What alcoholic in his senses would not willingly stop becoming a slave to
the bottle, what capitalist would oppose laws that stopped him
polluting the atmosphere and poisoning his fellow citizens?
Positive freedom was enshrined as the justification socialists and
welfare state liberals made for curtailing the individual freedom
of a few of their fellow-citizens so that the majority would be
free to do things that hitherto they had been unable to do.
'Freedom for an Oxford don,' it was said, 'is a very different
thing from freedom for an Egyptian peasant.' Berlin called this
claptrap. No doubt the peasant needs food and medicine, but
the freedom he needs today is 'identical with that of professors,
artists and millionaires'. It may often be necessary to sacrifice
freedom to prevent misery. But it *is* a sacrifice. If that gives pain,
well, pain must be given. Berlin asks that there should be no
double-talk. He later agreed that he might have minimised the
sufferings caused by laissez-faire government, but those sufferings were as nothing to the total despotism, and the crushing
of life and thought in totalitarian regimes that justified their
repression by appealing to positive freedom. No single contribution to political theory was more discussed when it appeared

in 1958, two years after the Soviet suppression of the rising in Hungary.

Berlin remained true to the tradition of British empiricism. Our own experience constitutes reality and history contains no message. Behind him strode Hume, Mill and Russell. But meanwhile he kept writing about the enemies of this tradition, who hacked at its very foundations: Vico, Herder, de Maistre, Hamann, Machiavelli. To him these too spoke truth. They told us that men and women do not obey the rational laws that economists and political scientists claim to have discovered. They are motivated by the laws, customs, speech of their native land. And from this sprang Berlin's defence of pluralism. There is no one moral code superior to all others that we should live by. Values are not absolute. Good ends conflict – you cannot exercise mercy without cheating justice. Freedom and equality are both good ends but if you want more of one you may well have to diminish the other. Some values are incompatible with others in your own culture and, of course, with the values of other cultures. You have to choose. And the values you choose determine your way of life. Sometimes, in extreme cases – shall I tell a Nazi the names of Jews in the locality if I have a promise that I can save seventy-two of them from the gas ovens – moral categories cannot apply. It is 'inexpressible arrogance' for those never to have been faced by so terrible a choice to condemn anyone in that predicament. He never forgave Hannah Arendt for having done so in her book on Eichmann's trial. But most of us are able in life to devise trade-offs – to sacrifice a bit of personal freedom for a slight extension of equality. You should try not to frustrate too many people. Do not, however, be optimistic. 'You cannot establish political government purely on the basis of what is rational. There are too many irrational drives in men . . . part of our basic human nature. If people didn't have deep irrational impulses, there would be no religion, no art, no love.' Berlin's favourite quotation, adapted from Kant, was: 'Out of the crooked timber of humanity nothing entirely straight was ever made.'

He was already a public figure. The amusing young don of the thirties had become a sage. Undergraduates flocked to his lectures, which he prepared and rehearsed for hours before walking rapidly onto the platform, depositing a thick script at which he never again glanced as he stood and poured out sentence after sentence, whole paragraphs, with scarcely a pause. His lectures reached an audience far beyond Oxford because he was a renowned speaker on BBC radio's Third Programme, often invited by its remarkable talks producer Anna Kallin, like him a Russian Jew. Those talks generated hundreds of letters and he soon became famous as a lecturer in America. He genuinely believed that he deserved few of the honours he was given. 'I have a pathological dislike of personal publicity,' he wrote me. 'It is like a terror of bats or spiders. I am not a public figure like A. J. P. Taylor, Graham Greene, Arthur Schlesinger, or Kenneth Clark. Nor an ideologue like Tawney, Cole, Oakeshott.' For years he had no entry in *Who's Who*, until he found that the entry form he had left lying around had been filled in by Maurice Bowra, with scandalous fictitious achievements. Then he gave in. 'I have been over-rated all my life,' he used to say. 'It is nicer to receive more than one's due, and I cannot deny it. All the same I cannot deceive myself.' When his old friend heard he was knighted, he murmured, 'I wonder why'; when he heard Berlin had been given the Order of Merit, his old friend (so Berlin liked to pretend) nearly fainted. Such astonishment was not all that odd. Maurice Bowra was under the illusion that Berlin had published little. But for his editor Henry Hardy we would never have had his collected works. It was not until the late seventies, when Hardy published his essays, that the range and seriousness of his *oeuvre* became plain.

Although he considered himself unworthy when he measured

himself against his heroes from the past, such as Herzen, he did not feel he had to apologise to his seniors or contemporaries in political theory – to Ernest Barker, John Plamenatz or Thomas Weldon, still less to Michael Oakeshott, whose defence of conservatism he regarded as Collingwood warmed-up. Oakeshott was sceptical of reason in politics: Berlin was not. He used to boast that he alone of his contemporaries of comparable intellectual standing had never made the faintest gesture of conciliation towards Soviet Russia even in the worst days of fascism in Europe. He admired genius, great men and women, and was not ashamed to worship heroes. He wrote tributes to Churchill and Roosevelt, but had no truck with Hegel, who taught that great men were beyond moral scrutiny. Weizmann, he said, 'despite his reputation as a master of *realpolitik*, forged no telegrams, massacred no minorities, executed and incarcerated no political opponents'. Isaiah was proud to have met such men and women as Pasternak and Akhmatova, Picasso and Virginia Woolf, Freud and Stravinsky, Russell and Einstein. But he also wrote about obscure friends or of an unpopular and eminent professor such as Namier. He moved at ease, unlike Bowra, among the *beau monde* but he was not seduced by it. About his friends he had no illusions. Even his oldest and most intimate friends were not sacrosanct, and he was quick to see the feet of clay among the rest of us. Sometimes he would nurse a grudge against someone who long ago had made some remark that distressed him. In his old age he would make disparaging remarks about Bowra, about his cowardice or lack of concern for truth or his sucking-up to the great – though he himself admitted that his own failing was the desire to be liked, to propitiate and not to offend. He had a puritan streak within him: he was not at ease in homosexual coteries and disliked sexual exhibitionism. Nor did he join even his closest friends when, with the rise of Hitler, they moved to the left and became active in politics. He never hesitated, however, to make incisive judgements about those he disliked. 'If Sir Oswald or Lady Mosley were in the room I should, I think, walk out without hesitation. I was acutely uncomfortable in the presence of Lords Beaverbrook, Cherwell, Radcliffe and – what peerage did Tom Driberg take? Them I thought genuinely evil, and Beaverbrook and Driberg sinister too . . . I did not think Lord Home or any of the Mitford and Foot families were in the least evil, but I would rather have not met them . . .'

He was criticised by both right and left for standing aloof from the politics of the day. He held mild liberal views, would sign a letter imploring the Soviet authorities to show mercy to some dissident, but he would not join the familiar list of letter-writers to *The Times*, headed by Ayer, protesting when some new issue of injustice appeared to have arisen.* He would not join the Campaign for Nuclear Disarmament and told Philip Toynbee that being a liberal meant risking one's survival in defence of one's principles. He would not endorse the Algerian liberation guerrillas because they used terrorism against civilians. As for Castro, he 'cared as little for civil liberties as Lenin or Trotsky'. To Berlin the very methods that economists and sociologists used prevented them from discovering what is at the heart of men and women. He distrusted technocrats in government and sapient reports with their self-confident proposals for restructuring institutions. That was why he did not pontificate on daily issues. Monetarism, social security schemes were not for him. He disappointed President Kennedy by not advancing views on the number of ICBMs needed.

He had discovered in Washington that he was attractive to women and fell in love with a giddy, upper-class cock-teaser, Patricia de Bendern, a relation of Oscar Wilde's Bosie Douglas. She was unreliable, desirable, a breaker of appointments and of

---

* He did once protest against the appearance at Oxford of a South African rugger team in the days of apartheid. Oxford's values should not be those of Twickenham.

hearts, and she threw her net over him again when he returned
to England. She played Nancy Cunard to his Aldous Huxley. He
dedicated to her his translation of Turgenev's *First Love*, the tale
of the agonies of a boy who falls in love on holiday with the leader
of his gang, a girl older than himself: only to discover that his own
father has been having an affair with her. The affair told him that
the fat young don – his old friend Stephen Spender called him 'a
baby elephant' – was not repulsive to women. Someone else might
care for him, and he had an affair with the wife of a friend, a
somewhat remote don. But this faded when he got to know the
beautiful Aline de Gunzbourg, who came from a famous French
Jewish family and was then married to the nuclear physicist, the
Austrian-born Hans Halban. Berlin was often criticised for being
timid, but he was not timid in love. The marriage was unhappy,
he won her heart and confronted Halban, admitting he was to
blame, but telling him that matters would only get worse if he
attempted to stop him seeing Aline. When Halban was offered a
prestigious post in Paris she refused to go and they divorced. She
and Isaiah married in 1956.

She transformed his life without changing it – if the paradox
be permitted. Now he had a fine house in Headington, a flat
in Albany, a summer retreat near Portofino. She brought him
much more than that: love and devotion. She caressed his exist
ence. But his routine as a don attending college meetings, as a
lecturer, a denizen of the Reading Room in the British Museum,
remained as it had been. She shared his love of music. Indeed
to have lived without music would have been a nightmare.
Unthinkable to live without Bach, unendurable without Beethoven and Schubert. He loved Rossini's tunes and Verdi for his
uninhibited choruses and his hatred of aristocratic brutality and
tyranny. But the late romantic composers, Brahms or Richard
Strauss, did not appeal; Puccini he despised, Stravinsky he liked.
No one, he thought, had ever played the Beethoven post-
humous quartets like the Busch ensemble. He admitted that

Toscanini was not the man for the thick brew of Wagner; but when one saw Toscanini as well as heard him the authority was such that, so he wrote me, 'this and this only was the truth – the intensity, the seriousness and the sublime *terribilità* totally subdued you'. Walter, Klemperer and Mahler and the luxuriant valleys of Furtwängler, yes – but Toscanini was Everest. 'The rest were not fit to tie his shoe-laces, mere Apennines covered with villas.' In his later years he found a friend, an intellectual as well as a profound musician, in the pianist Alfred Brendel, whom he thought the equal of Schnabel.

He continued to be a professorial fellow of All Souls and never resented Sparrow's success in being elected Warden, though he rarely agreed with him. 'Whenever,' he wrote me, 'John Sparrow and I during over half a century of friendship, found ourselves in a situation of some tension – over elections to the wardenship, women in All Souls, his treatment of gifted but to him unattractive junior fellows – the like, we used to begin our letter, "my dear old friend". This was a symptom of the need to draw on reserves of affection.' Berlin had wanted All Souls to become a graduate college but, though his proposal to amalgamate the college with the newly founded but ill-funded St Antony's was impracticable, he still felt that something should be done, in particular for the scholars and scientists who held university posts but no fellowships. So bitter had their sense of injustice become that they were threatening to obstruct the business of Congregation until their grievances had been redressed.

Berlin felt he owed a debt to Oxford that he could never repay, and in 1965 he agreed to become the first head of a new graduate college. His intimate friends joined in a chorus of lament. Why turn away from his true vocation, the life of the mind, towards administration, for which he had shown no talent? When Berlin was visiting Princeton a scheme took shape. Such was his reputation in America that the Ford Foundation made it known that they would endow a graduate college at

Oxford provided that Berlin would become its head. He said he would do so but only if he could raise substantial sums for building and endowment. Where could a suitable site be found and how could funds be raised to erect the buildings? Isaiah did not hesitate. He went to his own people, the Jewish community. Isaiah was well known and admired by Leonard Wolfson: he and his father Isaac agreed, provided the college bore their family name. Then the intrigues began. The Secretary of State for Education, Anthony Crosland, protested that the money should go not to Oxford but to one of the new universities. Solly Zuckerman, who was a board member of the Wolfson Foundation and chief scientific adviser to the government, hated Oxford: as a founding father of the University of East Anglia he had no doubt where the money should go. But Zuckerman had made an enemy of Mac Bundy, the head of the Ford Foundation and one-time adviser to President Kennedy. Bundy paid no attention to what he said and declared straight out that Ford would give four and a half million dollars towards endowment. The Wolfsons followed suit and their Foundation paid for the inevitable short-fall on the original estimate; Isaac contributed out of his own pocket Carrara marble to face the entrance to the dining hall and Leonard gave money to ensure that the trim everywhere was of unpainted hardwood.

Isaiah had to get his fellows to agree on the choice of an architect and then later to approve Powell and Moya's design. He remembered the melancholy history of the Nuffield College's foundation – of the fury of its founder, who found himself asked to approve a design with an Egyptian motif instead of the gothic which William Morris associated with his youth in Oxford. Wolfson was to be a new kind of college, with houses for families, and Isaiah was determined that it should be handsome as well as practical. He interviewed dozens of architects, determined to find one who put the claims of the client before his own ego. No one lasted long 'who thinks himself Michel-

angelo and would regard us as an inferior version of the Pope'
On only one of the three crucial votes did three fellows vote
against the proposal. While other colleges squandered money
commissioning an architect, rejecting his designs, commissioning another and then, after building had begun, altering
the architect's brief, Berlin brought the project home. He presided over the college until 1975. He was then re-elected to All
Souls and remained a fellow there, attending meetings until he
died.

Berlin's intimate friends, who grieved when at the height of
his powers he was diverted by the foundation of Wolfson College, had a point. Might he not have turned his attention to
the current wave of anti-Enlightenment, anti-rational philo-
sophies in Europe? Sartre he would have dismissed when he
became an apologist for Stalinism, and Heidegger as a Nazi who
had persecuted Jewish and liberal professors in the University of
Freiburg. But the influence of Heidegger and Husserl begot a
set of intellectuals in France every bit as challenging to the
Anglo-American empirical tradition as his nineteenth-century
romantics – Barthes, Lacan, Derrida, Foucault. But then, Berlin
had always insisted that we must set thinkers in their historical
context and for that reason the present was barred to him. He
had, after all, as his friend Bernard Williams said, 'discovered a
different kind of philosophy, one that makes use of real history'.

The neo-right and the extreme left both loathed him and on
his death let fly. The neo-right that emerged during the
Thatcher years accused him of liberal nostalgia blinding him
to the ubiquity of force, accident and the power of institutions.
Why did he praise England as a haven of tolerance, growled
Maurice Cowling in his lair at Peterhouse, when it was sustained
by respectability, moral conservatism, xenophobia and healthy
prejudice? Why did he condemn violence by the Israelis, when
violence alone could have created the state? (To which Berlin
might have replied that the violence he condemned was that

of the Stern gang, not of the Israeli army in 1948.) Were not his best-known ideas scraps of rhetoric and his work full of 'windy vapourings about liberal virtue'?

But it was the neo-Marxist left that were his most deadly enemies. Nurtured by the writings of Walter Benjamin, Althusser and Lacan, they were disgusted by his 'unbearable lightness'. The ideas of this 'people's intellectual . . . the personification of what the masses thought a philosopher ought to be' would not last. He failed 'to make the existential action which defines the solitude of the self', thought Linda Grant, herself a member of a Jewish family from Riga. She went on to make the astonishing statement that 'if his family had not left the Soviet Union, he might have had considerably less pleasure but more iron in the soul'. A bullet in the head more likely, or twenty years in a Gulag.

A far more publicised assault on Berlin was launched by that sizzling polemicist Christopher Hitchens. Hitchens remains faithful to the Simon Pure politics of the International Socialists of his student days in the sixties. Authority is sure to be morally corrupt and no government, western or communist, should 'scape whipping. He was indignant that Berlin prevented Isaac Deutscher being appointed to a chair. (Berlin considered his Trotskyism intellectually dishonest.) He was horrified that Berlin was willing to risk nuclear war – apparently Hitchens considered Kennedy should have given in to the Soviet Union over Cuba. He asked why Berlin was silent over Algeria. The reason was simple. Berlin disapproved of terrorism in establishing the state of Israel or of Algeria. And he was outraged that Berlin did not denounce Vietnam.

For Hitchens's generation Vietnam was the ultimate betrayal, as Munich had been for Berlin and his contemporaries. Berlin saw it as American liberals like Dean Acheson did: as yet another communist attempt to overpower a neighbour. When it became clear that the American military were prepared to lay waste

South, as well as North Vietnam, indifferent to the fate of civilians, without any certainty of victory, first Harriman and later Acheson spoke up. Should Berlin have done so? Should he have endangered the gift of the Ford Foundation in establishing Wolfson College on the grounds that if Mac Bundy was its chief the money was tainted? What effect would a Berlin pronouncement have had upon President Johnson and his entourage?

Berlin was not one of those intellectuals who feel obliged to 'take a stand' on public events; and he refused to be bullied on this matter any more than he allowed Koestler to bully him on Jewish assimilation. When he lectured on Turgenev's *Fathers and Sons* his sympathy in the end was with Nicholai Petrovich Kirsanov, who cannot understand his son's admiration for his fellow-student Bazarov's nihilism. And what is Hitchens if not a nihilist? That becomes clearer when he tangles with Berlin's notions of pluralism and liberalism and shows himself incompetent to handle either.

Perry Anderson, the most accomplished Marxist sociologist, was a more formidable critic. While Berlin was alive he took him to task for reading what he wanted into the minds of the thinkers he presented in such glowing terms. Kant, for instance, when he spoke of the crooked timber of humanity, was speaking of rulers, not the ruled. Good ends conflict, said Berlin, but that is surely true of every society that develops 'discourses justifying different roles within it'. What was his pluralism but the old platitude 'it takes all sorts to make a world'? Berlin, Anderson continued, tried to wriggle out of the charge that he was a relativist by admitting that there can be trade-offs between those who put, say, liberty above equality; but there can scarcely be trade-offs between nation-states, as the disasters of the twentieth century prove. Anderson with great skill displays a familiar argument. To declare that ideology is false – that any all-embracing explanation of human society is wrong – is to be as much enslaved by ideology as any ideologist.

Berlin refused to accept the bed-rock belief of the left: that goodness is indivisible, that the different aspects of truth and goodness can be reconciled. Religion and ideology answer the question 'How should I live?' People want to believe that there is one irrefutable answer to this question. Berlin says there is not.

He gave hostages to fortune. His lectures and essays were written after voluminous reading: but only occasionally, as in his judgement on Machiavelli, did he show how much he had read in secondary sources. He did not adorn his work with the apparatus of scholarship. There are few references to texts or footnotes to the work of other scholars, the generalisations flow majestically unimpeded by arguments with this authority or that interpretation. Some longed for him to settle down and write one 'big book' setting out his credo and defending it in classic academic style. But to do this would have been to betray his vision of life. He remained an unrepentant fox. There was no meaning to life, he declared. Impossible for him to believe in God in whom all mysteries are reconciled. Unacceptable even to live solely for freedom – freedom may have to give way on occasions to other good ends. Just as he stood for the right of Zionists devoted to Israel to decide not to go there but to live in the country of their choice, so he defended the right of those who opt out of politics. They should not be bullied into pronouncing on the major issues of the day.

More importantly Berlin told us that freedom is not logically part of self-government or democracy. A democratic government can as easily as a dictatorship impose severe limitations on individual freedom. Community values are a threat to individual freedom just as much as religious calls to accept some form of moral orthodoxy. He was not a relativist in values. Cruelty is always cruel, and even in a society which tolerated – even, perhaps, as in the *Iliad* gloried in – cruel acts, still the Greek and Trojan heroes agreed that some men went beyond the bounds of tolerated cruelty. No one can find a theory that reconciles one culture with another. It is an illusion to think that if all options were known to us reason could tell us which was the right option to choose.

He was a Magus, a magician when he spoke. He was loved by people with whom he had nothing in common: millionaires, world-famous musicians, unknown scholars, public figures. When he died the *Evening Standard* saluted him: 'The respectful sadness that met his death and the enormous regard in which he was held shows that intellectuals can still be prized as civilising influences in Britain.' The world of the don was a little less civilised when he left it.

CHAPTER TWELVE

Women Dons in Cambridge

On 4 July 1998 the University of Cambridge entertained over 400 women to celebrate the day, fifty years ago, when women were allowed to take their degrees: the eldest was ninety-seven years old. To its shame Cambridge was the last British university to admit women to degrees. Women had been allowed to sit the tripos exams and they were classed. But no degree. In 1897 it was proposed to give them degrees. The opposition was led by that inveterate leader of the non-placets, opposed to change of any kind, Professor William Ridgeway.* The country parsons came in train loads to veto the proposal. Swollen with free lunches in their colleges they flocked to the Senate House, elbowing their way through a rowdy horde of undergraduates as opposed to the proposal as their seniors. When the vote was lost the undergraduates set out for Newnham, but Eleanor Sidgwick, the Principal, had the good sense to close the college gates and prevented the mob sacking the place. In 1920 Oxford voted to admit women to the university. But not Cambridge. My father came up to vote for women – he took advice that the proper dress for a non-resident MA was gown and top hat – but the vote was again lost; and egged on by the vicar of Ixworth, undergraduates again marched on Newnham. This time they

---

* Sir William Ridgeway (1858–1926), fellow of Caius (1880), professor of Greek at the University of Cork (1883), Disney professor of archaeology, Cambridge (1892).

smashed the gates of the college. Eventually after the Second World War, in 1947, two fellows of King's moved that another syndicate be set up and its report was passed without a division. By that time the country parsons and non-resident MAs no longer had the right to vote.

A little before the fiftieth anniversary celebrations the sociologist Edward Shils, who moved between his home base of Chicago and Cambridge, determined to honour the early women dons, and he and Carmen Blacker assembled studies of twelve of them. Among them was Helen Cam, a formidable old battle-axe who bicycled the three miles from Girton three times a week to lecture at 9 a.m. on medieval constitutional history – she was a disciple of Maitland. She argued that laws were made not only by the King and the judiciary but by individuals who brought their grievances to the courts and demanded justice. She ended her career as a professor at Harvard, loaded with honorary degrees. Naturally Audrey Richards the anthropologist and Eileen Power* were included; as were Marjory Stephenson in Gowland Hopkins's department of biochemistry, the first woman biologist to become FRS, an expert on bacteria, and Honor Fell, who at the age of twenty-nine became director of the Strangeway Laboratory and won the support of the Medical Research Council. Elsie Duncan-Jones, Newnham College, lecturer in English, University of Birmingham chose Enid Welsford, the diminutive teacher of English at Newnham. She was a late medievalist whose two books had off-centre literary themes, *The Court Masque* and *The Fool.* Duncan-Jones showed that Enid Welsford was a don to the depths of her being. The examiners were setting questions for a paper in the English tripos. 'She prolonged the meeting,' said one of her co-

---

* Eileen Power (1889–1940), director of studies in history at Girton (1913–21), Lecturer, reader and professor (1931) at LSE, renowned for her combination of scholarship and wit in her studies of medieval women, and the wool trade in the fifteenth century. (See page 244)

examiners, 'for three hours with her objections to one question. Of course she won.'

All these women had to struggle to get posts – few of them in the first instance at Cambridge. It was a little easier perhaps in science, because there was less prejudice in labs against women and easier consensus in science about the merit of a line of research. Until the expansion after the Second World War there were few posts available in the humanities: you had to wait for dead men's shoes to step into them. Women students at Cambridge were impaled on Morton's fork: condemned for being unimaginative bluestockings, tireless note-takers in lectures which they reproduced in such a slavish fashion that they never rated more than a modest second class; or they were said to be frivolous sirens on the look-out for a husband and likely to destroy the careers of the most promising of their male contemporaries. No wonder the pioneers of women's education at Newnham and Girton believed women must conform to every shibboleth in observing the proprieties. Students had to be in college by 6.30 and were beset with rules. At Newnham in the early years of the twentieth century they changed into their best dresses for dinner. Attendance at lectures was compulsory and students were reminded that women had 'a right to the kind of happiness that can only come from work'. One year, when Newnham collected only five firsts out of the seventy-nine, Nora Sidgwick, by then Principal, told the girls that they attended too many societies: attendance at once dropped. Not for them the pleasures of their fellow male undergraduates, giving wine parties which ended by twitting the proctors or teasing the porters by running over the sacred grass in the college courts.*

---

* The scale of undergraduate hospitality varied from age to age and college to college. Before 1914 in Cambridge, with whisky at four shillings a bottle, you might help yourself to a cigarette if your friend was out but not to a whisky and soda: that would, of course, be offered you if he was there. In the 1930s you offered coffee to your friends after dinner and, if they called later, tea – and perhaps a biscuit. But such a welcome would have been regarded as beneath contempt at Christ Church, Oxford.

The men sneered at the women students, whose notion of hospitality seemed to be a scrumptious cocoa party after hall dinner, where *everything* could be discussed.

Jane Harrison was one of the earliest women to enter Newnham at a time when all students had to have a chaperon when attending lectures. She resembled a geologist's specimen of rock stratification. At bottom was the granite of one bred in Yorkshire, taking no one on trust, conservative and suspicious, with a keen nose for pretentiousness; on top of this was a rose-red stone of romantic rebelliousness, surmounted by a soft chalk that crumbled under emotional stress. Nothing went easily for her. Her mother died in childbirth, the aunt who began to bring her up and adored her died, her father married her governess, a stern Evangelical who accused her of an entanglement with the curate, and her early trust in Miss Beale, head of Cheltenham Ladies College, turned to ashes when Miss Beale rebuked her for indulging in 'undigested reading'. Her tiny income from her mother's legacy enabled her to compete for a scholarship at Newnham and in her student days she was the animator of a sophisticated group. It was then that the first sign of a syndrome repeated throughout her life appeared. She fell in love with her coach in classics. Unfortunately he was already engaged and, when he married, she was miserable and got a second. That meant she had to go to London and earn a living, which she did by working on classical archaeology in the British Museum and by lecturing.

She dazzled her audience. She wore shimmering green dresses. At Winchester, where she finished her lecture declaiming by heart a chorus from Euripides, the boys leapt on their chairs to cheer her. She next met and fell for the art critic D. S. MacColl. He disapproved of her naive enthusiasm for classical Greek art: he thought her too aesthetic. Gradually he converted her to dig deeper into her sources. But when he proposed she turned him down. Did she fear that his criticism would inhibit her imagination if they lived together? He soon became engaged to another, but that did not stop Jane bicycling through France with him. She wore silk breeches and an apron, which caused a sensation at the Gare St Lazare. Yet when Sutherland MacColl actually married his fiancée her world again collapsed. Twice she applied for the professorship of classical archaeology at University College, London, and mustered a striking list of referees. But the British Museum curators would not support her because one of their own number, a man, was a candidate. In 1898 Newnham offered her a research fellowship and she struck the vein of originality that was to make her name.

She returned to a changed Cambridge. Since 1860 celibacy became no longer enforceable as colleges revised their statutes. Gone were the days when the only married dons were the heads of colleges and a few professors, and when the wives of the heads did not deign to call on the wives of the professors.* Dons were now marrying former students of Newnham and Girton, Jane Harrison found her closest friend, Ellen Crofts, married to Francis Darwin and – unlike Girton, where men were recruited to teach – she found at Newnham a fellowship of women teachers. She noticed that, though some of the wives became ungrudging teachers, they published little; and a don once told her that men didn't expect their wives to understand their work but did expect them to be interested in it because it was theirs. She enthralled the students; her talk was so brilliant; they plotted to sit within earshot of her at meals and to protect her from bores. She smoked cigarettes – she once smoked a pipe on the steps of the Parthenon. She liked good-looking, brainless girls as well as her favourite student, Jessie

---

* The stark masculinity of college life in mid-Victorian times can be exaggerated. Even in those days women were often being entertained in college, the mothers, sisters and cousins of dons who took them sightseeing and arranged dinner parties for their fellow-dons to meet them. They sat next to their host in chapel, and toured combination rooms and cellars, which would have been inconceivable in most colleges fifty years later.

Steward, her first first. But her intimates were men with whom she could try out her ideas. Her closest ally was a fellow of Pembroke, R. A. Neil, with whom she discussed every line of her new book. He asked her to marry him. She accepted. Then he died.

The year after Jane Harrison returned to Cambridge Trinity elected Francis Cornford to a fellowship and he duly became a lecturer in classics. She had already become an admirer of the most influential Greek scholar of her day, Gilbert Murray, and the three of them formed an unofficial research group aimed at confounding what Jane called 'SS' – sound scholars. She often stayed at Murray's house, wrote him teasing and sometimes jealous letters (for reading one of his translations to Bertrand Russell before reading it to her, or for talking to Beatrice Webb about politics while she was 'seething with Orphic eggs and wild bulls and really important things'). But it was Francis Cornford who replaced Neil in her affections. They travelled together, got ill together and worked together. Meanwhile her friend of student days Ellen Crofts Darwin died and her daughter Frances Darwin had a nervous breakdown. Jane had known her since birth; and when Frances recovered and came up to Newnham to read classics she introduced her to Francis Cornford. They fell in love and married.

Francis Cornford was nearly twenty-five years younger than Jane, but after Neil's death Jane had 'drifted into the most beautiful happiness I have ever known . . . bit by bit I came to depend entirely on him'. He never guessed she was in love with him: after all she was so much older than him. She was desolate, she brooded, she again became ill. Her only solace was work. The most curious commentary on the relationship of the Cornfords and Jane Harrison was made by Frances the year before her marriage. She drew, as for a Greek vase, four shadowy figures. The first was herself bending to sacrifice a pig. The second was Francis Cornford holding a pig roughly by the tail. The third was her father hugging a pig; the fourth Jane, statuesque and noble, with her pig on a leash. The pig was a Greek symbol for the vagina.

Jane Harrison's anguish was more intense than ever before, but fortune blessed her. The year the Cornfords married a student came up to Newnham who was to fill Jane Harrison's life for the rest of her days. This was Hope Mirrlees. She regarded Hope as her 'ghostly daughter', and after the war, finding that nearly all her old friends in Cambridge were dead, she left with Hope for France; in the end she left Paris and died in London. Her relationships with men were always intellectual relationships: then her passionate, questing nature suffused them with emotion, over-powering, demanding but neither dominating nor submissive. She knew sexual intercourse was not for her, but her love of men was fierce and deep. There was in her something of that other Yorkshire character in fiction, Catherine Earnshaw, when she exclaims, 'Nelly, I *am* Heathcliff' – the belief that she and her intellectual companions were identical.

What, then, were the problems in ancient Greece which for the most fertile part of her life she worked at in such a frenzy? During the nineteenth century, wearied by the long ascendancy of Latin literature, poets and scholars rediscovered ancient Greece. In Germany the new techniques of criticising the Bible were turned onto Homer and the great tragedians and philosophers. German culture became so influenced by the interpretation scholars put on the Greek classics that Elsie Butler, the ebullient, bright-eyed professor of German at Cambridge during and after the Second World War, wrote a book called *The Tyranny of Greece Over Germany*.* An excellent history of the

* When on the death of Field Marshal Smuts some dons mooted the idea of putting the name of Pandit Nehru forward as his successor, Elsie Butler canvassed the fellows of Newnham stressing to the free-thinkers such as herself how fitting it would be to honour in this way the founder of the secular state of India. To the church-goers she adopted a different argument: 'My dear, he is so very good-looking.'

comparable revival in Britain has been written by the American scholar Frank Turner. The Victorians, he argued, moulded Greek culture to resemble their own society. Thus Grote suggested that Athenian democracy vindicated mid-century parliamentary politics; Jowett Christianised Plato; Gladstone domesticated the ferocity of Homer; and Matthew Arnold denounced Francis Newman's barbaric translation and asserted that Homer's poetry was rapid, 'plain and direct in his matter and ideas . . . and eminently noble'.

None of this stirred Cambridge. There classicists remained dedicated to the editing of texts, a tradition that culminated in the work of A. E. Housman. Richard Jebb was Regius professor of Greek, better known in Cambridge for his outspoken American wife than himself. It was both unkind and untrue of the Master of Trinity (where Jebb was a fellow) to say of him, 'What time he can spare from the adornment of his person he devotes to the neglect of his duties.' It was true that he became the university's member of Parliament and performed many public duties: but there was, after all, his edition of Sophocles. He died knighted and a member of the new Edwardian Order of Merit. His successor, Henry Jackson, too, was made OM but that could hardly have been for his publications. No doubt it was for his geniality, his gift of making college and university business agreeable and harmonious; and he was on the side of reform. Perhaps also because he had been tutor to many who rose in the world and remembered him with affection. These gifts, as well as publications, are welcome in a don but not in our days sufficient for the OM.

It was these placid waters that Jane Harrison disturbed. In her younger days she had accepted the Homeric gods as human beings, only more so, to whom you sacrificed so that they might bless you and bring you good fortune. But had there not been, she asked, an older religion in which you sacrificed to deities and demons to propitiate them in the hope that they would go away and terrorise you no longer? That was why the Furies (Erinyes) were called the 'kindly ones' (Eumenides), why the primitive all-powerful god Meilichios was a snake, as much the king of the underworld as of the earth. Primitive religion reflected the terror that lay beneath the surface of existence. What are rituals? What was religion before it became secularised morality? Why were the ghosts and bogeys of pre-Homeric religion – the Sirens, the Gorgons, the Sphinx – women? Had they perhaps been local heroines in a matrilineal society? As time passed, she suggested, some of these primitive spirits were displaced by male gods – the snake Meilichios became Zeus, Hyacinth Apollo.

Inspired by Nietzsche's *The Birth of Tragedy*, she examined the cult of Dionysus and the maenads who worshipped him and tore Pentheus to pieces for rejecting him as a god. She suggested that when the maenads who worshipped ate the raw flesh of the creatures they had torn apart they were eating their god, a ritual reflected in the Catholic sacrifice of the mass. In ritual you act what you desire, you recreate your emotions; it is only later that in art you represent your emotions. In primitive times the tribe acted or danced the ritual; only later did they divide up into spectators and actors and build theatres. Men imitated war in dance, or lamented the death of the old year and celebrated the birth of spring.

The Dionysiac cult led her on to Orpheus, who had also been slaughtered by the maenads. She showed how the Orphic poems were connected with the cult and contrasted the instinctive religious feeling in the Orphic mysteries with the rational unemotional worship of Zeus and the Olympians. 'Some of the loveliest stories the Greeks have left us,' she wrote, 'will be seen here to have taken their rise, not in poetic imagination, but in primitive, often savage, and I think always *practical* ritual.'

These were some of the conclusions in her most original work, *The Prolegomena to the Study of Greek Religion* (1903). Ever since she visited Greece in 1888 she had been fascinated by the primitive – as indeed artists were to be throughout Europe. Historians, anthropologists and archaeologists were providing more and more evidence of civilisations earlier than Mycenae. There was a revolt against an excessively literary interpretation of Greek culture. Edward Tyler's *Primitive Culture* introduced her to anthropological data (though she was never influenced by James Frazer's *The Golden Bough*). She knew the work of German scholars and reviewed a classic work, Erwin Rhode's *Psyche*. Nor was she working alone in Cambridge. She formed a trio, 'the ritualists', with Gilbert Murray and Francis Cornford. Murray shared her fascination for primitive religion, though unlike her he welcomed the Olympian gods and their myths as a way of bringing order into Greek thought that would finally lead to the triumphs of Greek drama and philosophy. Not for her such sympathy for the Olympians. She called Zeus bourgeois and Apollo a prig. In 1909 she began to study Durkheim and later Bergson. Three years later *Themis* appeared, in which on the evidence of recent archaeological discoveries in Crete she revealed that Zeus had been worshipped originally as a god of fertility. In her last work in 1921 she reiterated that her greatest insight had been the social origin of religion and how religion changes as society changes. Totem, taboo, exogamy reinforce the unity of the tribe, so do initiation rites. Fertility rituals evolve into comedy and tragedy.

She left Cambridge feeling defeated. True, Sheppard had been rejected in his bid to be elected Regius professor. 'I dread the actor-manager in classics – also I think he is barely sane.' Sheppard was not among her enemies. He regarded her with amazement and respect. He wanted us to recognise how like all girls Nausicaa and her handmaidens were, bathing and play-ing ball, how Achilles gave way to emotions that we know only too well, how universal the passions and trials Homer describes are today. She wanted us to see Homer's gods and heroes in their historical setting, to realise how different they were from us, how primitive existence was governed by beliefs and emotions remote from our own. But she had enemies enough – Lewis Farnell* and Andrew Lang (who introduced generations of children to the Greek myths) among them. Most odious was the misogynist William Ridgeway, the only one of her colleagues who refused to subscribe to a farewell token of respect and gratitude. But no one now reads Ridgeway as they do her.

It was indeed a singular tribute to her that Hugh Lloyd-Jones†, who held Gaisford's Regius chair of Greek at Oxford, honoured her by contributing the chapter in *Cambridge Women*. He was the most formidable Greek scholar in post-war Oxford and Cambridge, a generation in which there was hot competition from, for instance, Moses Finley of *The World of Odysseus* fame and the pre-Socratic scholar Geoffrey Kirk. Lloyd-Jones did not hide Jane Harrison's weaknesses. She was too quick to fly to conclusions in linking, say, a new piece of archaeological evidence to her theory of rites. She could be silly. To dismiss the religion of Zeus and the Olympians as she did damaged her reputation.

In ten pages of footnotes containing bibliographical material and scholarly references Lloyd-Jones shows how many continue to consult her work. By 1960 Van Gennep's work on initiation and *rites de passage* regenerated interest. As Lloyd Jones says, all scholars suffer the same fate: their work is soon superseded. But scholars 'stand on the shoulders of their predecessors' and Gilbert Murray's remark that no one can write about Greek religion without being influenced by the work of Jane Harrison seems truer now than when he made it.

There were two other reasons for her disillusionment with

---

* Lewis Farnell (1856–1934), Rector of Exeter, Oxford, author of *The Cult of the Greek State*.
† Hugh Lloyd-Jones, fellow of Jesus College, Cambridge (1948–54), fellow of Corpus Christi College, Oxford (1954–60), Student of Christ Church (1960), Regius professor of Greek, Oxford (1960–89).

Cambridge. What had happened to the carefree yet dedicated students determined to show themselves the equal of men in the tripos? The students now seemed to be keener on hockey. The second reason for her disillusionment was the lack of influence her work had between the wars on research in classics at Cambridge. There was admittedly no one of the stature in anthropology of Malinowski at LSE who might have brought new ideas from the Continent. The same disappointment was felt in 1935 by the Russian émigré Michael (Munia) Postan, when he moved to Cambridge from LSE. He gave his first impressions in a letter to a former colleague: 'The bulk of the dons I have met are dull and provincial. They read little, know less and are smug and conservative in the worst Edwardian manner. They sneer at "fellows with ideas" or tell funny stories about Americans or admire Jimmy Thomas. It is all very painful and explains why so many of the young scientists here turn communist.'

Postan was astonished to find that the medievalists ignored the work of Marc Bloch and none of the lectures on political thought mentioned Marx. Just before the war John Clapham retired as professor of economic history and was succeeded by Postan, who obtained the post by the simple expedient, so the joke ran, of marrying his only rival. Eileen Power was the outstanding medieval economic historian of the day in agrarian and social studies. Postan had first been Eileen Power's student and then her research assistant. She had been plotting for some years to get her former pupil the chair and when offered it said she preferred to remain at LSE. She found LSE intellectually more stimulating than Cambridge and gave dances and parties at her Mecklenburgh Square house. Every time she published an article she went to Paris and bought a new dress. Postan was a European charmer with a seductive Russian accent and a Russian sense of humour, and Eileen Power was not the only woman to find him entrancing. So did a young Oxford graduate who had been appointed to a Cambridge assistant lectureship shortly after Postan arrived in Cambridge.

This was Betty Behrens. Her father, a treasury civil servant, was a Jew and a rationalist who always said that he got more pleasure from his inherited income than he did from his salary. That kind of honesty was ingrained in his daughter. She was taught by private tutors and could not remember a time when she had not spoken French. Her father sent her to Lady Margaret Hall, where she duly got a first in history. Encouraged to travel she learnt German thoroughly and expected anyone with pretensions to being a historian to know it. When, in 1938, she was appointed to an assistant lectureship in history at Cambridge she elected to offer a special subject for finalists on the last twelve years of Charles II's reign. Those undergraduates who chose it as one of the easier options on offer were taken aback by her opening words. 'I shall assume that by Christmas you will all have read Onno Klopp's *Fall des Hauses Stuart.* I'm sorry but it has not been translated. Oh, and I'm afraid that there is no copy in the university library of Sir George Sitwell's *The First Whig,* but there is one in the London Library available to members.'

That was not the only thing that startled her class. As women were not yet members of the university she did not lecture in a gown. She appeared in the smartest of outfits and wore a jaunty hat with a feather. Her voice was squeaky and sometimes shrill but compared with other women dons she was a figure of unparalleled elegance. She was an exacting teacher. 'I see on page 2 you said x, on page 4 you say y. These two statements seem to contradict each other,' her pupil Phyllis Hetzel remembered her saying; and when the strain of the weekly essay became too great and her pupil burst into tears she said, 'Oh, if you don't feel like writing essays, don't.' – The therapy worked. She lived in beautiful rooms with yellow silk curtains and offered her students gin and cigarettes. They dared not do anything but work hard for her. She demanded exactness and evidence; however harsh her criticism, it was never directed at them personally but at their work. If her colleagues in the faculty were irritated by her insistence that one must get things exactly right, her pupils learnt that they could not get away with clever generalisations. One day she was interviewing candidates for admission as one of a committee, when a Miss Bull was followed by a Miss Lamb and then by a Miss Partridge. The next to appear was Miss Goose and, dazed by these representatives of the animal kingdom, Betty broke into irrepressible giggles. But she at once apologised and explained. The imperturbable Miss Goose won a place and went on to a distinguished career in the Home Office. She was secretary to the Committee on the Future of Broadcasting, and when one prestigious professor on the committee tried to bulldoze the committee into accepting her argument, Miss Goose tore the statistics and conclusions to shreds, saying to me, 'Betty Behrens would never have allowed us to get away with stuff like that, would she, Chairman?'

She was one of the few lecturers left to teach history during the war and Herbert Butterfield, the professor of modern history, begged her not to desert. But the Principal of Newnham, a Dame and former civil servant, advised her to go to one of the ministries and promised to restore her fellowship on her return. Butterfield – who regarded the war against Hitler as a disaster as the true enemy was communist Russia – never forgave her. There may have been another reason why she chose to go. In 1940 Eileen Power had dropped dead buying a hat and Postan was a widower working in Whitehall. But by the time Betty was established in London she found he was engaged to Cynthia Keppel, who had been working in the Cabinet Offices. He married her in 1944 and lived a life of great happiness with her until his death.

Betty Behrens stayed in Whitehall until well after the war writing her book *Merchant Shipping and the Demands of War*. It was the best of the Whitehall war histories but she considered the years spent on it a disaster. Other official historians appeared to regard their labours with grave complacency. Oh yes, the evidence lay before them in the files, they could approach it with an open mind, and then in accordance in Geoffrey Elton's principles could blend narrative and analysis in the way that he laid down as the model for professional history. The trouble was, said Betty Behrens, that virtually no one read what they wrote. They were 'solving problems which the most intelligent minds consider irrelevant'. Jonathan Steinberg, a fellow of Trinity Hall, who knew her better than anyone else and was her chosen obituarist, reluctantly agreed with her. Her history of shipping during the war was a work of brilliant analysis. She taught herself statistics, and her power to tell the tale as if she was writing a novel was astounding. But when he took the book out of the University Library he found that only three scholars – among the dozens who had worked on some aspect of the Second World War – had consulted it.

Her work in Whitehall had given her first-hand experience of what government, bureaucracy and its power struggles were like. She had always delighted in the rationality and elegance of the eighteenth century but she always made a point of reminding her readers of the corruption and blinding poverty that were the counterpart to the architectural masterpieces and artefacts of that society. In taking to task a colleague who 'evidently believes that ideas can profitably be studied out of relation to material circumstances', she puts on the line her belief that 'there is always a close connection between the ways in which communities earn their living and the ways in which they think and govern themselves'. In 1967 she published *The Ancien Régime*, on the causes of the French Revolution. It was in popular form with pictures and only 200 pages long, but it was acclaimed at once, translated into a number of languages and sold well in hardback and paperback. She revelled in her success and soon she began to be asked to write for the *New York Review of Books* and acquired an American audience.

The book was to have a sequel. In the preface Betty wrote: 'The writer owes many debts of gratitude ... some to ... Newnham College (whose ways of proceeding have made certain aspects of the Ancien Régime intelligible which otherwise might not have been so) ...' The Principal, the economist Ruth Cohen, was not amused. For years Betty had criticised the college's investment policy (her younger brother was a successful merchant banker); and that was not the only issue on which she was unable to remain silent. Her fellowship was not renewed. It was a petty act, and she was at once offered a fellowship at the graduate college of Clare Hall.

The Ancien Régime emerged from a controversy of some importance. In 1964 the veteran scholar of eighteenth-century France Alfred Cobban attacked the by then accepted interpretation of the French Revolution. This interpretation was the work of a number of French Marxist historians – in particular by Georges Lefebvre and Albert Soboul. Lefebvre maintained that the revolution was the 'crown of a long economic and social evolution that made the bourgeoisie the mistress of the world'. According to Soboul, in the last analysis the revolution happened because 'the relations of production contradicted the character of the production forces'. Cobban argued that the facts did not support these generalisations. The conflicts were between town and country, between rich peasants and poor peasants, and within the bourgeoisie itself. The bourgeois leaders of the revolution were not the few industrialists nor the big merchant capitalists nor the rentiers, but the holders of small provincial offices whose value was declining. The revolution was not in the capitalists' interests: the principal beneficiaries were the soldiers and bureaucrats – and of course the speculators who brought land – as in the days of the *ancien régime*. Cobban was not saying, Behrens argued, that the revolution was simply a change of the individuals who ruled or a decline in industrial and agricultural production. But the great generalisations about class that Lefebvre and Soboul drew could not logically be drawn from the facts. Cobban might have underestimated just how much 'feudalism' still existed in 1789. But Cobban had said, 'If feudalism in 1789 did not mean seigniorial rights, it meant nothing' – and such rights were often owned by the bourgeoisie, who were determined not to relinquish them. Cobban never questioned the multitude of excellent monographs, quoted by Soboul, on different aspects of the social and political conditions of the times. What he questioned was whether the vast generalisations about class and its power flowed from these facts. Are we really to judge a scholar solely by whether he gets the minor facts (such as appear in monographs) right and to ignore that he is unfair or inaccurate or crude when he deals with the major issues?

In her book Betty Behrens, writes Jonathan Steinberg, 'had done to the great Lefebvre, Soboul and Mousnier what she had done to a generation of Newnham girls. She had written in the margins of their tomes, "what do you mean by bourgeois?" . . . and they had not been able to answer.' By 1988 *Glasnost* had penetrated French historiography and Goubert and Furet finally demolished the Marxist interpretation of the French Revolution – having first prudently (as she characteristically added in a letter to me) established good relations with the French intellectual Establishment. Mathiez, Lefebvre and Soboul were accused of having popularised their conclusions, so it was hinted, by employing *Vulgär-Marximus*. As a result the causes of the French Revolution dropped out of the category of problems that the academic élite found interesting. (As indeed did the problem of the rise of the gentry in the seventeenth century that so concerned English historians in the 1950s.) In Britain, too, kings were toppled from their thrones. Whereas E. H. Carr and Isaac Deutscher had been regarded as the authorities on the history of Soviet Russia, Robert Conquest and Leonard Shapiro, who had been unmentionable in their presence, were now proclaimed the experts. This puzzled Betty. In old age she wrote to me asking how in these circumstances could history survive as an academic discipline? No wonder our own historians were assuming the imminent death of history. Surely every serious student must now see that in the age of ideology everything is ideologically slanted.

Yet in the very year – 1966 – that she wrote her defence of Cobban she agreed to marry E. H. Carr. Carr had published in 1939 *The Twenty Years Crisis*. It could be called an apologia for *realpolitik*. International relations, he thought, are governed not by law or diplomatic compromises but by conflicting interests in which the stronger power won. Some regarded his book as a defence of appeasement and a surrender to Hitler. During the war, however, Carr perceived how strong Soviet Russia was: the western powers, he concluded, must copy Russia, plan their economies and accept mass democracy. Between 1950 and 1978 he published a fourteen-volume history of the Soviet Union – of the political and social order that emerged from the revolution. To him the history of the Soviet Union was the transformation through acts of political will of a peasant society into an industrial nation. He later came to be regarded as an apologist for Stalin's regime. He considered that whatever the Soviet rulers did they were not in a position to do otherwise.

Why did she marry him? It was not a happy marriage and they often led separate existences. He was a man who on marriage became a tyrant and he subjected her to all sorts of unkindness. They parted in bitterness. She was sixty-three when she married and reason may have told her that it was time to share her life with someone before she became too old. She never abandoned reason even when she was in love. During the war she had some affairs in London and seems to have approached these with the same remorseless logic as she used upon her pupils' essays. She described the end of one affair in terms of a civil service minute.

> Miss B proceeded to deal with the three alternatives in turn: with regards to a) she said that if Mr X thought her tiresome he should say so. There could only be three possible reasons why he did not say so. These were
> i) he didn't think so
> ii) he was afraid to say so
> iii) that he did not wish to hurt her feelings . . .

The marriage to Carr had, however, one excellent consequence. Carr urged her to write – he himself began a new magnum opus at eighty-five – and the result was her best book, *Society, Government and the Enlightenment*, that no student of the eighteenth century can afford to miss. The problem she set herself was this. Why did Prussia not have a revolution as France did? Both countries had similar constitutions. They were absolute monarchies, both had different provinces each with its own customs, privileges and consciousness and its separate identity. Both were societies divided into orders or estates and also into a number of groups, each with its particular privileges guaranteed by law. Her analysis of Prussia was particularly striking. She could empathise with Frederick the Great, who believed in nothing, preferred his dogs to people and ordered that he should be buried with them, an admirer of Voltaire, a workaholic, working, as Betty did in old age, seven days a week. She corrected many accepted generalisations. Prussian civil servants were often dishonest and Frederick's laws frequently disregarded in the provinces. She also discovered the Prussian novelist Theodor Fontane. She was beguiled by his charm and she appreciated the language his characters used. Their phrases and expressions revealed every nuance of class and status difference. She read novels, particularly the great Russian novels, all

through her life, modern novels too, and made shrewd judgements on them. She thought they made one understand society
better than many monographs. She never read poetry or
listened to music. *Society, Government and the Enlightenment* was
Betty Behrens's best book. It was published in 1985 when she
was eighty-three and it should have been her apotheosis.

It was not. Unlike *The Ancien Régime* it had no illustrations. It
was four times as long and too detailed and precise, too des-
perate to be exact and true for the common reader to sit back
and enjoy the tale. The reviews were complimentary. Nobody
bought it. She was no longer the new name to conjure with in
literary periodicals. She was devastated.

Betty Behrens was by no means a typical don – whatever that
may mean. She had private means, she came from an upper-
middle-class rich family, she lived in style and did not have to
make accommodations to anyone. But like many dons she did
not achieve eminence. She was not a fellow of the British Academy, no university gave her an honorary degree, no foreign
academy honoured her. She was not even a name in *Who's Who*.
No one denied that she was clever and, if they were generous,
that she was a fine historian, superior to quite a number of
staid middle-stump performers in the faculty. But she irritated
her colleagues. She corrected error so vehemently and did not
acquire in her profession friends, let alone allies. She picked a
quarrel with Herbert Butterfield by telling him that his lectures
on the outlines of modern European history, a standard course
attended by very few undergraduates, were inadequate – just
one damn thing after another, no theme, no continuity – so
unlike his excellent highly technical lectures on eighteenth-
century politics. She was right but it was not endearing. She was
a feminist who spurned male clubbability. Jonathan Steinberg
thought too that she 'lacked the intellectual swoop which yields
grand formative ideas . . . she wanted desperately to be an artist
but remained the most skilful of craftsmen'. For such an acute

student of politics she lacked practically every political skill in advancing her career.

There was another reason why she was not more popular. Her gorge rose when she sensed injustice and there was a case of injustice at Cambridge that seemed to her iniquitous: the plight of women dons. At Oxford the college appointed someone as fellow and tutor in the humanities and the university nearly always elected him or her to a university lectureship. There were defects to this arrangement. The colleges tended to appoint men and women prepared to teach sixteen hours of one-to-one tutorials a week in the main subjects of the main schools. Innovation was stultified, new subjects hard for the faculties to introduce, and not enough attention was paid to the ability to research. Had Cambridge science been hobbled by college high tables it could never have followed the lines of research that made it famous. But the Oxford system had one undeniable merit. The women's colleges were treated on the same footing as the men's.

In Cambridge, on the other hand, the faculties appointed the lecturers; and if women were not appointed to these posts, the women dons in their colleges suffered financially. In the history faculty, Behrens pointed out, no woman had been elected to a chair or a readership and only five over the half century had become lecturers. In 1938 there were three, after the war the number fell – in 1974 there were none. Out of fifty-two university teaching officers only one assistant lecturer was a woman. No woman sat on the Appointments Committee and the men on it were indifferent or unaware of the problem. It was not as if the few women who had been appointed had been failures: none had been forced to stop lecturing because her audience had disappeared, 'a fate which, in my experience, was not uncommon among the men'. She did not forget that Harold Temperley, the diplomatic historian, had put her name forward at Cambridge and G. M. Trevelyan backed his judgement. Later she was to write that 'They were prepared, not only to give the women a fair chance, but to hold out a helping hand to them. To the best of my knowledge and belief there has since 1945 been no one with any influence in the Faculty who has wished to do either.'

There was another injustice that did not escape her attention. There were too few women undergraduates in the university. When it was proposed to found a new college for women Marjorie Hollond, the highly groomed economics don at Girton and wife of the Vice-Master of Trinity, opposed the scheme on the grounds there were not enough talented women to fill the existing places at Newnham and Girton. In fact to get a place at either a schoolgirl would have to be as talented as the winners of scholarships at the men's colleges. The atmosphere in the men's colleges was more relaxed: an undergraduate was in trouble only if he consistently failed to turn up for his weekly tutorial. The atmosphere in the women's colleges was more tense, more pedagogic. The determination to show that women could hold their own in the tripos made the dons work their students harder; and every year the women's colleges appeared in the first half-dozen colleges with the highest percentage of firsts and upper seconds.

All this was to change when the men's colleges decided to admit women – first in 1972 King's and Churchill; in 1977 Trinity; and Girton admitted men. Magdalene held out until 1987. Colleges that insisted on admitting only men found that the quality of their applicants plummeted. Newnham remained solely for women. But Betty Behrens noted that not many more women dons were elected in the colleges. Nor were things better in the university. Towards the end of the century only 5 per cent of readers were women, and 6 per cent of professors.

In refusing to remain silent about these inequalities Betty Behrens broke with a long-standing tradition. The women's colleges never protested as institutions against their lot. Not even Helen Cam, an ardent socialist, considered launching a campaign within the university. Nor indeed did Betty Behrens. She was not an organisation woman. But she spoke her mind.

Just as reason had told her to marry so reason told her to leave her cottage and move to a retirement home. She was determined not to be a burden to her friends in old age. It was characteristic of her to choose Swallowfields, once Clarendon's country home. Even there she could not but speak her mind. 'You see,' she said to Phyllis Hetzel, when she thought some regulation in the retirement home bore harder on those feebler than herself, 'I simply cannot bear injustice.' Reason told her that the time had come when she too would become feeble and need help – if only to die. And that she did of a massive stroke on her way to dinner.

CHAPTER THIRTEEN

The Don as
Administrator

The word 'administrator' sounds dingy. It is usually taken to mean the staff who work in the central offices of the university or service the laboratories, libraries and faculties. In fact the senior officers – registrars, secretary-generals, treasurers and so on – have more often than not been college dons. Nearly all dons become involved in the humblest chores of administration – compiling book lists, fixing times for tutorials and demonstrations in the labs and, most time-consuming of all, setting, marking and assessing exam papers. Today dons are overwhelmed by paperwork imposed upon them by government in its desire to make universities 'accountable'. But there are a few who discover they have a talent, perhaps first for college business or in their department, and then find themselves sitting on the central committees of the university.

Such a don was Hugh Anderson, who became Master of Caius in 1912 and later a supremely effective Vice-Chancellor. He was a neurophysiologist but not in the same league as the great mid-century scientists in the physiology lab. Christopher Brooke has left a memorable account of him in his history of Cambridge (1870–1990). Anderson never read a book but he read *The Times* with care every day and took a judicious and cautious view of the way the world was moving. For instance, he supported the admission of women to degrees. The most considerate and welcoming of men, he expected his wife without warning to provide lunch for five, six, or it might be a dozen guests whom he was persuading to support him in some project; and on Sunday after lunch he was home to undergraduates and could draw out the most tongue-tied or galvanise a dour and apparently dull graduate student. He roused them because he could enter into other men's interests. 'A specialised interest in the structure of snails' tongues,' wrote his daughter, 'is, to say the least of it, unusual, but it took him only a few minutes to discover this peculiarity in one of our guests and then he carried on the conversation as if this had always been one of his own particular studies . . .'

Anderson was a member of the Royal Commission of 1922 on Oxford and Cambridge. Asquith was the chairman, and Anderson and G. M. Trevelyan were the two most influential members for Cambridge. The commission abolished the right to vote of all Masters of Arts, non-resident as well as resident. The country parsons were no longer to be entitled to come up and vote on degrees for women. Henceforth the Regent House – all those who taught and researched and all fellows of colleges – was to govern the university by their votes. There was no proposal to make the Vice-Chancellor anything more than a figurehead and chairman of the central bodies.

Anderson's delight and skill in unravelling figures came into their own when he drafted the statutes covering the financial arrangements of the colleges' endowment, external and internal revenue accounts. They were designed to ensure that college income was spent on college purposes and not to enrich the fellows. Government would give a grant to the university. But not to the colleges. As they wished to remain independent they must look after themselves. Anderson spent many hours compiling sheets of figures that would satisfy the college bursars that his plan was fair and equitable. Nor would he allow a secretary to turn his drafts into fair copy. Delegation was a word unknown to him. He worked for hours to provide Trevelyan with all the material he needed to produce the final version of the commissioners' report on Cambridge.

His finest hour was to come. For years the University Library in the Old Schools next to the Senate House had been the centre of controversy. It had to be enlarged: but how? Plans to build around it and on King's Parade were all rejected. Should they excavate beneath the grass beside the Senate House? That too was condemned as inadequate. Eventually a syndicate on which Anderson sat produced the bold scheme of building a new library on Corpus cricket ground opposite Newnham College. Then the inveterate leader of the non-placets spoke. Ridgeway had hitherto been in favour of excavating underground storage but now he confessed to a change of heart. The library must move to a virgin site. But not to the Corpus cricket ground. That was too near Newnham College and women students. The best place was the former playing fields of King's and Clare, used during the war as a hutted hospital and still occupied by huts. Anderson went to work. King's and Clare agreed to sell the site, Anderson called in grandees such as the Duke of Devonshire to back his plan not to have a competition for an architect but to commission Giles Gilbert Scott, who was already building next to the site a court as a memorial to the Clare men killed in the war. Scott drew an elegant classical facade; but where was the money to come from?

At this point a ploy that was to become all too familiar in the ancient universities was conceived. An emissary from the Rockefeller Foundation was touring Europe to discover how medical research could be helped; and Anderson got a fine grant for pathology. When, three years later in 1926, another emissary arrived looking for further medical projects, Anderson floated the idea that Rockefeller might like to build the new library. Mr Rockefeller hummed and hawed. If he gave funds for a library, every other institution would be on his doorstep. Furthermore he disliked Scott's modest design and asked to be shown something more heroic. Scott complied and transformed, as Christopher Brooke puts it, his modest classical features into an 'Assyrian palace' with a tower. Fund-raising continued and in 1928 the design and the Rockefeller bequest were accepted: three days later Anderson died. The man who never read a book was commemorated by a special reading room for manuscripts and rare books being named after him.

The ploy that was to become familiar was to persuade a great benefactor to change tack and give money to a project remote from what he had in mind. Rockefeller was already giving money to pathology and it was put to him that the library project could be camouflaged by integrating it with further subsidies to medical science. To this genial deception he happily agreed. The ploy was worked even more skilfully at Oxford. The Vice-Chancellor, A. D. (Sandie) Lindsay, was a masterful operator who had reorganised the forestry department and raised funds to expand the science departments. It was he who had smoothed the way for the dons to accept the princely benefactions for medical research that William Morris, later Lord Nuffield, had showered upon the university. Morris, who had begun life in the city selling bicycles, had built his car factories on the eastern edge of Oxford and longed to build a college for engineers. This did not suit Lindsay. He had other ideas. A socialist and devotee of Tawney, he saw Morris's offer as an opportunity to develop social studies. Taking the great Oxford administrator Douglas Veale into his confidence, he set to work with him to get Morris to change his mind. Lindsay was wise to do so because Veale was in a class by himself as a university administrator. Dressing up the new college as an institution that would benefit industry, they managed to get Morris to agree, and a graduate college for the social sciences emerged. Later Morris exploded when he found G. D. H. Cole and other left-wing social scientists among the first fellows and rejected the architect's original design because the buildings were not in the gothic style. For some years he would not go near the place and complained he had been fooled. At Cambridge after the war a generous lady, Judith Wilson, offered the university money to found a post in drama, hoping that someone who would direct plays would be appointed. The English faculty trousered the money and appointed someone who had no experience of the theatre and was already a lecturer. The faculty then filled the post vacated with another lecturer.

The post-war years were a golden age for Oxford and Cambridge. Other countries regarded the University Grants Committee as a further manifestation of British political genius – a body able to spend public money without political interference. Indeed members of Parliament who tried to investigate through the Public Accounts Committee how the UGC spent its grant were foiled by Treasury officials. They said it would not be in the public interest to reveal any details. The Treasury itself financed the UGC direct. Nor did it require the UGC to control the universities. Each university planned its own development; and after setting up one new university at Keele the UGC announced that a period of 'consolidation' had arrived. As late as 1958 its chairman was declaring that only a 'small reservoir' of potential university entrants existed.

Then the climate began to change. A committee under Geoffrey Crowther on sixth-form-level education told universities to use their lecture rooms and labs more efficiently and take more students, and Whitehall began to show signs of rebellion. The Treasury's duty is to scrutinise expenditure yet here it was violating its own principles, disbursing not the two millions of forty years ago but fifty-four millions a year. Suddenly the UGC set up a committee to look into teaching methods. Most ominous of all, the Prime Minister announced that Lionel Robbins would be chairman of a committee to cover the whole of higher education. In his report Robbins did not mince words. He criticised the ancient universities for their inability to reach rapid policy decisions and for the 'obscurity which shrouded their financial and administrative arrangements'.

Both universities resembled primitive democracies. The Council or General Board might make proposals, but the whole body of resident dons (Congregation at Oxford, the Regent House at Cambridge) could over-rule them. The colleges were autonomous and controlled admissions and tutorial teaching. So although Cambridge had an expensive veterinary school it had very few students because colleges preferred to take students reading traditional subjects. At all levels naked voting prevailed. The agonies of paralysis produced by this system had to be experienced to be believed. It was a system which might have been planned to perpetuate a civil war in which no side could ever win. Certainly the dons were consulted. Equally certain was the unwillingness of the central committees to put forward proposals that might offend.

In 1961 on the General Board at Cambridge I asked the Council to make an enquiry into university administration. Council appointed a committee to consider what questions should be considered were Council ever to agree to do so. The committee never met. In 1962 I tried again and at the end of the academic year Council appointed a joint committee of Council and General Board. When this committee hinted that fewer matters should be referred to the Regent House the Vice-Chancellor, Sir Ivor Jennings, complained that the committee had become too big for its boots. Had he known that such a major review was likely to be undertaken, he would have opposed the committee being given leave to consider such matters. Yet this came from one who had himself said that 'too many questions are left to the Regent House'. When we presented our report to the General Board it contained a paragraph pointing out that over four years very considerable sums had been spent in fees on plans for the New Museums site but that there was little to show for it. The board ruled that this reference should be deleted: if published, it might give Cambridge a bad name. Alas, if maladministration is suppressed, no wonder pleas to remedy it are dismissed.

In fact the report on administrative reform did not propose that the Regent House should not be able to veto any important proposal. It did not call for a long-term or permanent Vice-Chancellor, although the custom that he held office for only two years meant that as soon as he was conversant with the business he was whisked away. It pointed out that sixty-nine institutions had access to the General Board and proposed to appoint chairmen for groups of faculties who could investigate problems and reconcile interests. They could chase investigations which, unless they were kept moving, got side-tracked. The dons were shocked. That was a proposal to appoint Gauleiters; and the report was blocked by Council and never sent to the Regent House. So was an inconclusive report on college tutorials and university lectures. The two senior officers (Registrar and Secretary-General) were invited to suggest modifications to the Statutes and Ordinances. A year later they reported they could not find time to do so.

Finding time was at the root of many problems. Any important piece of business had to be sent to faculties or colleges for their comments – and as obtaining these comments took at least a term – and as the central bodies did not meet in vacations – and as no controversial issue could be put to the university vote between the middle of May and the middle of October – one had to be pretty nippy at the beginning of an academic year in putting forward a proposal if a decision was to be taken before the year was out. What was worse was that at Cambridge (but not at Oxford) every stage of a complicated building scheme could be challenged by the Regent House. When the university set up a postgraduate medical school the Regent House vetoed a salary differential for the clinical medical practitioners. In effect the dons said: set up the postgraduate school if you wish but we will not allow the doctors in it to be paid more than other dons – even though every other medical school in the country did so. The process of eliciting the mind of the university was fraught with hazards. After a preliminary discussion in the Senate House reports were sent to faculty boards, departments and colleges for their comments. Each regarded the reports from its sectional point of view and protested if its own interests were likely to suffer. The final decision – obtained by consolidating the comments – resembled a Chinese torture. It was death by a thousand cuts.

Cambridge embarked on one reform before Robbins reported. Edward Bridges* was asked to examine the problem of the 'non-fellows'. He proposed a deal. If the university would establish certain teaching posts and funds to help out the colleges, the colleges would undertake to elect to a fellowship any university teaching officer with tenure to the retiring age. The university turned down the first proposal and the colleges the second. They did so on the grounds that they were faced with an unacceptable 'open-ended' commitment: having no control over university expansion and the multiplication of university posts, the colleges protested that they would be swamped. In fact Bridges was more successful than at first appeared. Nearly all colleges increased the number of fellows; two set up graduate satellites; three new graduate colleges were founded; and the Wolfson Foundation provided money to build a graduate college.

The education of humanities graduate students was another bone of contention. (Graduate students in science were well looked after in the labs and got all the direction they needed.) In the humanities they submitted a subject for the PhD, were assigned a supervisor and left to flounder on their own. Some-

---

* Lord Bridges, Secretary to the Cabinet 1938–45, head of the Treasury 1945–56. Hon. Fellow of All Souls and Magdalen College, Oxford. Life peer, 1957.

times the subject lay way outside their supervisor's own field. One of Lionel Trilling's most brilliant students came from New York to research on Dickens. When he submitted his thesis the examiners asked him what periodical literature he had consulted: he had never been told that at that date a bibliography of articles on the Victorian age was published each year in *Modern Philology*. When asked about religion, he said he relied on Weber's concept of the Protestant Ethic: Tractarians, Evangelicals, High and Dry, Low and Slow and all the varieties of Dissent were closed books to him. He had not had much guidance. I asked King's to finance a course of lectures by its librarian on how to use a big library, how to discover copyright and portraits of the dead, etc., but the university refused to continue to finance it and rejected my plea to set up a graduate school where required courses would be taught.

Ivor Jennings was not the only Vice-Chancellor to dislike change. His predecessor, Herbert Butterfield, professor of modern history and Master of Peterhouse, was a radical conservative whose style contained many layers of inference and concealed, as he admitted, 'trip-wires' planted in order to make critics fall flat on their face. His lecture in 1962, *Universities and Education*, gives an insight into his mind. It is a classic example of the adversative style. The adversative style is said to occur on a tombstone in Northumberland, where a family, scorning the falsehoods of lapidary inscriptions, wrote: 'She was temperate, chaste and charitable, but she was proud, peevish, and passionate. She was an affectionate wife and a tender mother but her husband and child seldom saw her countenance without a disgusting frown . . .' A dozen elegant antitheses followed.

In Butterfield's lecture assertions are similarly followed a few pages later by counter-assertions. Universities exist to serve society *but* they must search for truth independent of any immediate utilitarian end. The State has a right to intervene *but* the autonomy of universities must be preserved. More students should enjoy higher education *but* universities must not grow too large. New subjects must be capable of being introduced into the curriculum *but* simply to add them will not radically change our experience. In the great period of Dutch and German universities two centuries ago professors were saved from narrow-mindedness by being closely related to public life *but* professors at the heart of government are dangerous. Research students should be given greater attention *but* undergraduates should not be neglected for their sake. Specialisation ensures that students shall be trained in techniques and those deeper kinds of analysis that give structure to knowledge *but* learning a technique can be so stultifying that we need to invent a technique of not being technical. Specialisation has been caused by the pressure of exams and by universities failing to devise tests to expose cramming *but* it is not in itself evil – the evil lies in the narrowness with which it is handled. Specialists should not push their own subject *but* history offers an unique insight into the humanities, *though* English literature might be more important; *but* we must recall that there is no short-cut to a humanist education. Certainly men should be allowed to train for professions *but* technologists should not be admitted simply because they argue they would gain so much by being in a university. And so on. Butterfield's lecture was an appeal to the academic profession to resist pressure to increase the number of university students quickly because haste is the most pernicious danger in education, and therefore we must not 'attempt to find too swift an adjustment of means to ends'. It was an appeal to resist the introduction of studies that 'reflect current ideas or popular desires . . . and sacrifice long-term values'.

Butterfield was an administrator who combined his work on committees with original research; and his research complemented the conservatism with which he approached university affairs. He was a man with a twinkling eye and seductive manner; he was also a lay preacher and the most original historian of his generation. *The Whig Interpretation of History* argued that historians too often bring presuppositions about the past from the present. Acton and Trevelyan pictured English history as a march of progress towards individual freedom and democracy. But the historian's task is to see the past as it really was, to judge it by its own standards, not by ours. He repeated his disbelief that history was the story of unbroken unilinear progress in *The Origins of Modern Science*. In that book he showed how even the most famous scientists could go off on a wrong track. Galileo might have been right about the movement of the earth around the sun but he was so wrong about so many other matters not merely by the scientific standards of his day that it was hardly surprising he was condemned. Nothing pleased Butterfield more than plotting: he enjoyed academic intrigue, particularly on the board of the history faculty. It was there that he was opposed by another type of administrator. Kitson Clark was also a conservative in politics, Anglican in religion, red-faced, square in shape, with the voice of a bull. He was an innovator. He introduced American history into the syllabus and backed an option that examined colonial history, 'the expansion of Europe', in Asia, Africa and the Americas. He alone took to heart the neglect of graduate students and wrote a handbook for them. He was the kind of don who inspired his students to write books but published little himself. Asa Briggs and W. L. Burn, both leading Victorian scholars, saluted him. He never finished his book on Peel (1929) and not until 1962 did he publish *The Making of Victorian England*. He clashed with the future Regius professor Geoffrey Elton on the structure of the history tripos, and on much else. Elton and Plumb,* on this but on not much else in agreement, wanted the tripos to continue to be in the first two years mainly the study of English consti-

---

* Sir John Plumb, historian, fellow and Master of Christ's (1978–82), professor of modern English history, Cambridge (1966–74).

tutional and economic history from Anglo-Saxon times to the present day. But younger historians wearied of going over this familiar ground and having to keep up with the most recent articles and evidence when they wanted to research and teach their speciality. Kitson Clark became their patron. Perhaps to his own astonishment Kitson Clark came to advocate the German tradition of scholarship, *Lehrfreiheit* and *Lernfreiheit*: the professor teaches what he will, the students learn from whichever professor takes their fancy. Kitson Clark was accused by his colleagues of destroying the central educational purpose of the history tripos. Surely those who took the tripos should at least know the constitutional development of their own country.

Was it for this, or for other personal reasons, that Kitson Clark was never made a professor? Or for lack of publications? He could, it must be said, be tiresome in committee. He could have been elected professor of modern history. But the electors preferred to elect to that chair someone who was already a professor. Some were sad that the electors had not stretched a point and allowed the old bull a few years' fame before he was despatched to the abattoir. Nor did he have better luck in Trinity. Kitson Clark was a bachelor, living in rooms in Trinity above the great gate. He devoted much energy in teaching Trinity undergraduates and sitting on its committees. He hoped to be elected Vice-Master. But no; both vice-mastership and professorship eluded him.

Dons often as they grow older suffer when their colleagues deny them such recognition. Not that their colleagues are necessarily wrong. Dons care that the right man or woman should be appointed: if they allow cosy sentimentality to sway appointments their faculty and university will become third-rate. Charles Wilson was another disappointed man in the history faculty, the author of works on Anglo-Dutch trade and an original history of a commercial company, Unilever, to his credit. Hugh Trevor-Roper, an external elector, persuaded the committee to appoint Wilson to the chair of modern history in succession to Butterfield. He too had ambitions: to be Regius professor, to be Master of Jesus College. But his marriage fell apart; many of his friends sided with his wife; and Owen Chadwick, who had shared Merton House with the Wilsons, was appointed to the Regius chair. (It was an appointment by the Crown which was resented by a number of aspirants who had excellent claims; but Chadwick's exceptional character, so devoid of partisan spirit, and his steady publication of books that arose from patient archival research on controversial themes handled without rancour or bias were qualities that not all the other contestants could match.) In the sixties Charles Wilson opposed the attempts of Peter Laslett* and E. H. Carr to introduce sociological techniques into the teaching of economic and social history. By the seventies Wilson felt he had been marginalised and his views no longer counted on the board. His second ambition also withered. In 1959 Denys Page, the Regius professor of Greek and fellow of Trinity, was brought to Jesus College to be Master when Wilson had been bursar for six years; and when Page resigned in 1973 his hopes again evaporated when a scientist, Alan Cotterill, was preferred. He could not believe that he never had a chance of being elected. The emotional and lyrical side of his nature, so expressive when he played the violin, was not much in evidence when he spoke on college or faculty matters.

National politics occasionally overflowed into faculty politics. Contrary to popular belief the Cambridge history faculty had long forsaken the Whig tradition of Acton and Trevelyan and numbered among its lecturers the university's member of Parliament, Kenneth Pickthorn, and other hammers of liberalism such as the Master of Emmanuel, Welbourne, and Charles

---

* Peter Laslett, fellow of Trinity (1953), historian and demographer, reader in politics and history of social structure, Cambridge.

Smyth (who had the kind of mind that met a suggestion to set as a question in a general paper 'Philosopher Kings' with the counter-proposal that 'Philosopher Queens' would elicit more lively answers).

On the other hand in the faculty of economics and politics after the war a ruthless campaign was fought by the left-wing Keynesians, who were intent on capturing Keynes for socialism against the old-style followers of Alfred Marshall. Using – as Dennis Robertson complained – the most refined psephological techniques, they managed by voting to pack the board and the relevant committees. Richard Kahn, Joan Robinson and Nicholas Kaldor emerged triumphant, and Robertson and Guillebaud slunk hurt into the wings.* From these manoeuvres Dick Stone,† who invented the means of computing the Gross National Product of any country, stood aloof, regarding them with distaste.

How, it may well be asked, did Cambridge flourish if these antediluvian forms of government and murderous rivalries supervened? They could be overlooked because the fifties and sixties were a period of unbroken expansion. Buildings arose, posts multiplied, new proposals could be accepted if they could show they were academically respectable and inconvenienced no one. They could be overlooked because of the prestige of Cambridge science. Most of the scientific departments were buzzing with new lines of research, radio-astronomy, cosmology – steady-state theory versus big bang – the conversion of the

---

* Sir Dennis Robertson (1890–1963), fellow of Trinity, professor of political economy, Cambridge (1944–57). Richard, Lord Kahn, fellow of King's (1930–89), professor of economics, Cambridge, who wrote a famous article on the 'multiplier' that is at the heart of Keynes's *General Theory*. Joan Robinson (1903–83), fellow of Newnham (1964), professor of economics, Cambridge (1965); member of Keynes's circle. Nicholas, Lord Kaldor (1908–86), LSE (1932), fellow of King's (1949–86), professor of economics, Cambridge (1966); a notable Keynesian economist and a socialist. Claude Guillebaud, fellow of St John's College.

† Sir Richard Stone, fellow of King's, professor of finance and accounting. Director of Department of Applied Economics (1945–55).

Cavendish from nuclear to solid state physics – Alex Todd's*
empire in organic chemistry – the Nobel Prizes in physiology
and the realisation that biology had acquired a new dimension
through the work of dons in Perutz's lab – none of this was
much affected as the budgets of the research councils grew and
the pharmaceutical industry recognised the value to themselves
of the Cambridge biologists. Apart from matters like college
admissions no one in Whitehall much cared about Cambridge
governance.

It was Oxford that was criticised. Industry complained that
so few Oxford graduates got their hands dirty in industry. The
left regarded it as the bastion of privilege, although it was educating almost as many potential Labour cabinet ministers as
those who thronged the Conservative front bench. Oxford was
far better attuned to Westminster than Cambridge and, when
Robbins reported, it moved at once. Congregation accepted a
recommendation to set up a commission under Oliver Franks,
the Provost of Worcester.

The world saw Oliver Franks as a wartime civil servant,
Britain's ambassador in Washington and a banker, but he
thought of himself as a don, preferred to live in Oxford and,
whenever the right vacancy occurred, took it. No university
administrator has ever equalled Oliver Franks's stature. Elected
a fellow of his college (having rowed in the boat) to teach
philosophy, he said he would leave after ten years and departed
in 1937 to the chair of moral philosophy at Glasgow. During
the war he went to the Ministry of Supply and, though a tempor-
ary civil servant, became permanent secretary of the department. In 1945 plum after plum was dangled before him, but
he returned to Queen's as Provost, only to be appointed
ambassador to Washington at a vital time for Britain. His friend-

* Alexander, Lord Todd, life peer (1962), Master of Christ's (1963–78), professor of
organic chemistry, Cambridge (1944–71); OM.

ship with Dean Acheson – they met secretly over cocktails for four and a half years – covered the days of the Marshall Plan, the Korean War and the drafting of the NATO agreement. On his return the shower of plums, including the editorship of *The Times*, continued, but he opted to become chairman of Lloyds Bank. In Whitehall he was hailed as an 'alpha triple-plus mind'. In Washington his skill at summarising discussions was praised by Truman; whatever task he was given he surmounted; and he was a public servant without a peer. (Yet oddly enough, he let others draft even the most important despatches: drafting was not his forte.) His direction matched his judgement. He was austere but not a stuffed shirt: twice he chaired committees to liberalise the Official Secrets Act, and twice his proposals were rejected. Oxford wondered how he would set about his task.

Franks astonished the dons by insisting on taking evidence in public. As the headlines in the press blared, as one professor complained that the university did not provide him with a typewriter let alone a secretary and another denounced the colleges as self-perpetuating oligarchies, Franks was deluged with protests: why wash Oxford's dirty linen in public? But Franks realised that this was the way to educate his electorate – because in the end what he proposed would have to win the approval of the dons. He placated them by stating his unequivocal belief in college autonomy and university democracy, and tried to harmonise the conflicting interests of the colleges and the university. His task was harder because Asquith in 1923 had been indulgent to his old university and allowed Oxford colleges to retain far more powers than the Cambridge colleges. He foresaw the difficulties colleges faced when the university relentlessly expanded ('Oxford should not acquire intellectual empires in a fit of absent-mindedness'): but he urged all colleges to elect forty to forty-five fellows and the richer ones to subvent the poorer to enable them to do so. He urged them to make their entry meritocratic and eliminate the idle offspring of loyal old graduates: he even suggested a two-tier system of entry to help the maintained schools but this never got off the ground. He recoiled from establishing postgraduate centres: those creatures must remain embedded in the colleges. He failed to persuade Oxford to allow Council to govern partly through decrees. Council therefore proposed that Congregation could over-rule a decision of Council only if fifty dons petitioned for a postal vote. The General Board was reduced in size and was no longer to be a collection of delegates from faculties and departments. But on one important issue he carried the day. Oxford consented to appoint the Vice-Chancellor for four years instead of two – and to elect him.

Franks heartened the dons by stating that Oxford was a great international university. He rubbished Robbins's recommendation that Oxbridge should be cut down to size and made less attractive. Franks stigmatised this as 'superficial and timid'. In Table 330 of his report he showed that Oxford and Cambridge dons were not sunk in port but more productive than other university teachers. In 1963–4 55 per cent of their dons published one or more books, whereas the average for British universities was 34 and for Berkeley, California, 40 per cent. The differential for articles in learned periodicals was similar. Why punish success? And yet Franks missed a chance to blow the trumpet for Oxford's scholarship. No one would guess from the report that Oxford, at least in the fifties, led the world in analytic philosophical enquiry, and that it was Mecca for American graduate students in philosophy. Why was it, someone might ask, that economists from Oxford pullulated in Whitehall yet the more renowned school at Cambridge had less influence in public affairs? What tendencies were visible in the research of those who worked in, or were associated with, the school of Modern Greats? Oxford had a galaxy of chairs and posts in the old scholarly disciplines of the humanities: ancient oriental languages and studies; archaeology; theology; Celtic, Anglo-

Saxon and Romance languages; military history; and the Bodleian was a unique jewel: what number of research students did these studies and facilities attract? Were all of the older scientific departments and institutions still in the forefront of research and comparable in renown with Oxford chemistry, biochemistry and low-temperature research? And the history school and the classical scholars – how had they contributed to knowledge?

Had he done so Franks might in this last instance have pointed out that Cambridge had to import from Oxford both Denys Page and Roger Mynors to fill the chairs of Greek and Latin. Although the Cambridge history school was in some ways more lively than Oxford's, the figures of Hugh Trevor-Roper and A. J. P. Taylor were far better known to the reading public: Trevor-Roper by his account of the last days of Hitler, which has scarcely been challenged since that day despite masses of material becoming available, and also by his examination of the evidence for the rise of the gentry before the Civil War, which soon every scholarship candidate had to master.

Alan Taylor had an even larger public. His appearance on radio with Bob Boothby, Michael Foot and W. J. Brown led the BBC to ask him to give a series of lectures on television – which he did without a note. None of this affected the meticulous study he made of diplomatic sources, and his finest book was *The Struggle for the Mastery of Europe, 1848–1918*. He was later to change his mind on the causes of the Second World War, with disastrous effect. But his volume on modern Britain in the Oxford History series was an astonishing *tour de force*, and, as always with his writing, paradoxical and controversial.

Oxford moved sedately after the Franks Report. His proposal for a council of colleges with power to coordinate the affairs of the colleges by majority vote was rejected. The power of Council to govern by decree was voted down. Since seventeen bodies reported to the General Board, Franks proposed that super-faculties should be set up: Max Beloff led a party that rejected that piece of managerial good sense. Congregation still ruled and was not slow to challenge Council. One weary Vice-Chancellor at the end of his four-year term spoke of the 'fairly unrelenting struggle to sustain what was best in Oxford'. Council was given to looking over its shoulder in guessing what Congregation would do. When the issue of admitting women to the men's colleges arose, Council only permitted a handful of colleges to act, put a brake on the numbers they could admit and proposed that no other colleges could follow suit for a few years. But the Sex Discrimination Act of 1975 broke the power of the university to dictate to the colleges.

Oxford accepted that the regulations for admitting students would have to be changed if boys and girls from the maintained comprehensive schools were to have a chance of a place. Among the changes, to Max Beloff's dismay, a pass in Latin was no longer required for matriculation. For years management studies had been dismissed as another name for bad economics. In the early sixties Oxford refused an offer by the UGC to fund this subject. Not until 1999 was management studies truly accepted. Nevertheless 'swimming against the tide,' wrote Oxford's historian Michael Brock, 'was judged an unacceptable indulgence' – much like the early years of the New Labour government of 1997. Nevertheless Oxford was not afraid to repel proposals from semi-official bodies. A committee had been set up to consider changes in the shape of the academic year: should there not be two rather than three terms, or should there be four terms? Brian Flowers was the chairman and in 1993 wrote, 'there were many responses which varied from Oxford's crisp "Sod off!" to Cambridge's more elaborate "Sod off, please!"'

Lacking a Franks Commission, Cambridge remained unconvinced of the need to reform its administration. When the absurdity of refusing to pay clinical staff a differential was remedied other absurdities took its place. For instance, at a time when centrifuges could be had for the asking by scientific departments (and they are not cheap), the professor of music's request for a piano was refused. In disgust Thurston Dart resigned and was at once offered a chair in London. In 1985 a report on efficiency, commissioned by the Vice-Chancellors Committee, came before Cambridge. The response was icy. What was meant by efficiency? No definition was given. Therefore the report could be disregarded. Eventually a large number of dons revolted and called for an enquiry into the governance of the university. At the end of that exercise Cambridge accepted that by the end of the century the Vice-Chancellor should hold office from five to seven years and that he should not be head of a college. The Council should have executive power on urgent business; and the Regent House could debate an issue that was not specifically put to it by Council only if a hundred dons signed a petition.

One of the most professional and successful among Vice-Chancellors, Eric Ashby, used to say that academic staff should not complain that the University Grants Committee was interfering with their academic freedom because the chairman of the UGC and the larger part of its members were fellow-academics. They were the bulwark against direct governmental control. One such chairman came from both Oxford and Cambridge. This was Fred Dainton, the son of a master mason in Sheffield who could barely read. As a boy he was made to read to his father and after a few paragraphs analyse what he had read. Fred got a first in chemistry at Oxford, went to Cambridge for his PhD. In his first tutorial at Oxford 'Tommy' Thompson at St John's had torn up his essay and told him to write it again. In the first tutorial he gave at Cambridge he tore up an essay on 'The kinetics of the hydroen chlorine reaction' and told his pupil to do it again. He had found the treatment worked.

For fifteen years he ran physical chemistry at Leeds, and then accepted the vice-chancellorship of Nottingham because the new medical school there gave him the chance to integrate the pre-clinical courses with the clinical. He was off on the road as an administrator – for the nation as well as his university. First he was asked to join the Council for Scientific Policy, then to suggest how the national libraries might be rationalised. (His recommendation to stop the 'swing away from science in the schools' by stopping sixth-form specialisation and insisting that every boy and girl studied all the main subjects across the board was rejected.) Then he ran into the first rumblings of student unrest. He had always treated students as equals: now he found they regarded the Vice-Chancellor as their enemy. Fred was a Yorkshireman. If that was how they felt, he was not going to waste his time with such oafs. He accepted a chair at Oxford and became chairman of the Council on Scientific Policy.

Almost at once he ran up against Victor Rothschild. Rothschild was director of the think tank that Heath had set up when he became Prime Minister. When he had been chairman of the Agricultural Research Council Rothschild had spent time insinuating into Lord Salisbury's ear the message that fundamental research was essential for agriculture and the council should not be asked to run veterinary stations. Now after a spell as scientific adviser to Royal Dutch Shell he was not so sure. Research on the physiology of the cow was never-ending. What was needed was research into specific problems – and it was for the consumer, the farmer and the ministry to identify the problem. Considerable sums were spent on scientific research but how little despite the assertions of the scientific Establishment ever trickled into industry? He therefore proposed that the Council for Scientific Policy should be wound up and scientific research money given under contract to those in industry who put forward requests or ideas. University scientists rose in wrath, Fred Dainton at their head. The usual miserable compromise was struck: the only beneficiaries were the Civil Service departments concerned, who pocketed the money which had hitherto gone to the research councils. Dainton became a Whitehall favourite, the natural choice as chairman for academic institutions, of the Postgraduate Medical School at Hammersmith, of LSE's library and of the British Library Board, where he saw off a well-orchestrated attempt to keep open for all readers the great reading room at the British Museum: of the thirty-three most vociferous supporters of that proposal he found that only fourteen had readers' tickets. When made a life peer he made blunt speeches in defence of academic freedom and was inevitably made chairman of the House of Lords Library and Computing Committee. Since he died the committee has rarely met.

It was in 1973 that he became chairman of the University Grants Committee. On his second day in office he was told that all university building must stop at once. The oil crisis had struck. He managed to exempt halls of residence from the rule and his next task was to see that no university went bankrupt. Inflation soared to 30 per cent. The quinquennial system – by which universities were financed on a five-year rolling grant – collapsed. Coming from Sheffield (where later he became Chancellor of the university) he was, if not a supporter of the independent republic of South Yorkshire, a strong supporter of Labour, and he made up his mind to show Margaret Thatcher, who was then Secretary of State for education and science, that he was not a yes man. When she came to meet the Vice-Chancellors Committee he pointedly went and sat with the Vice-Chancellors instead of by her side. That was a mistake. He was not the spokesman for the universities. That was the role of the chairman of the Vice-Chancellors Committee. His role was to advise his minister and he was responsible to her. The incident was not lost on her when she became Prime Minister.

CHAPTER FOURTEEN

'Down with Dons'

In mid-twentieth century the dons regarded themselves with marked self-satisfaction. A fellowship in a college gave them status, and when they appealed for funds to create new colleges or satellites of old ones for the non-fellows, donors came forward. When the civil servants and Cambridge engineering dons scuppered Winston Churchill's plea to create an institution that would rival the Massachusetts Institute of Technology, Jock Colville (Churchill's private secretary during the war) saw his chance. He gently steered the money to Cambridge. He proposed to found a new undergraduate college whose entry should be biased towards scientific and technological studies. True to form, some dons denounced such a departure from a traditional college, but this time good sense prevailed.

The colleges retained their prestige because they were educational centres, not merely social institutions giving hospitality to visiting students from overseas. They, and not the faculties, controlled admissions to the university; their tutors and directors of studies determined what subject an undergraduate should read and what papers he should sit for in his examinations. Above all they arranged the tutorials to which he went each week. The colleges were the link to parents and alumni. Some, sinking below the Plimsoll line under the weight of their own dignity, still fussed about students climbing into college after midnight. But the modern college tutor usually worried more about students heading for a nervous breakdown. The degree to which dons watched over their students never ceased to astonish European observers accustomed to the anonymity and freedom of a continental student's life, whereas an undergraduate was beset by absurd regulations. But only a tiny minority criticised the tutorial system as a waste of scholars' time and an infringement upon the student's freedom to learn on his own as he liked. Undergraduates identified themselves with their college rather than the university. Even more loyal were the college servants, the old breed of clerks, butlers and porters still willing to work for lower wages than they could get in a large industrial city because the colleges, with their circle of fellows and students and retainers, and their special customs and traditions, resembled families.

They differed just as real families do. One college might be rent with quarrels, the dons voting against each other in caucuses of age and class and calling. Another might be a cosy womb, a third an amorphous society devoid of any particular character. There were dim colleges, fubsy places, rigidly pious in observing any academic ritual, places which delighted in niceties of precedence through which younger fellows were taught their place and were edged into sycophancy towards the Master and the seniors, places where general ideas were never discussed and the intellect and imagination withered. There were small colleges like Peterhouse, whose intellectual influence was out of all proportion to their size. There were self-confident, self-critical ones like Balliol. Rich or poor, their individuality was preserved by their financial independence; and why should they not be self-assured when the fellows governed themselves?

College meetings were still characterised by a certain formality. Gowns would be worn and college officers addressed by the name of their office. It was they – bursars, tutors, deans and the like – who ran the colleges – except that at Oxford the head of the college might take a hand in admissions. College politics were inconsequential: there were never recognisable parties, only a series of shifting ad hoc alliances. For many dons the college stood at the centre of the universe, and any request or new ordinance laid down by an outside body – the university or the UGC – was to be treated with contempt.

Self-government was at the heart of a don's life. A sizeable part of that life was spent in voting: voting in college meetings, voting on faculty boards or in the Senate House on university affairs, voting on appointments committees, on syndicates, delegacies and on bodies of all sizes and descriptions. Standing or ad hoc committees sprouted: what better way of involving the fellows in governance? On going to a committee a don was not particularly concerned to come to a decision: what he enjoyed was making points and voting. Two dons rarely agreed upon a remedy. The time wasted in committee in deciding, for instance, what colour and kind of flowers should bloom in the window boxes next spring could be considerable. The custom – followed in Whitehall and business – of the chairman taking the sense of the meeting and, unless there was strong dissent over his summing up, taking a decision was rarely observed. Efficiency was not a word that crossed many minds. But then why should it when the prosperity of the fifties and early sixties carried the colleges along floating with the current?

In mid-century dons found themselves busier than before the war. They advised departments in Whitehall and foreign governments, they administered big science for the nation. They acted as consultants to industry, advised investment trusts, conducted polls, ran theatres and worked for cultural agencies such as the British Council and the Arts Council; they wrote reviews for the Sunday newspapers and weekly periodicals, they were televised, they organised experiments in education and filled seats on countless national and local committees – they were involved in society to a degree unthinkable to a don at the beginning of this century. Belloc's lines were rewritten:

Remote and ineffectual don!
Where have you gone, where have you gone?

The vacations were not golden oases reserved for research or leisure but crammed with activities. Being a don was more than a job. It was a way of life. It gave a man security yet freedom from routine. Not for him the office, the long journey to work, the separation of work from family and friends. If he would never be rich, he was at least his own master.

Oxford and Cambridge were universities of many mansions. If a fine scholar was sufficiently determined not to be seduced by college rituals, or devoured by family life, he could devote himself to his subject and end honoured by his colleagues, elected an FRS or FBA, the recipient of doctorates from other universities, accepted as a savant of international renown. But for the don whose special gift lay in teaching there ran another path as a college director of studies or tutor, and his income was likely to be comparable to that of a reader (the grade below professor). For many dons, moreover, there was something attractive in the college blend of research, teaching and amateur administration. On university and college committees a don would find himself in the role of amateur architect, financier, estate manager, catering consultant or wine merchant; or as an arbiter on some delicate point of aesthetics or morals. He lived in surroundings compared to which any other city whose university tempted him to move appeared so often shabby and ugly. That was why so few moved.

They did not move because they were part of a self-confident society. When the Nuffield sociologist A. H. Halsey and Martin Trow,* the Berkeley, California, expert on higher education, surveyed British universities, they found that in the sixties only

---

* Halsey and Trow published *The British Academics* in 1971, but the surveys quoted were made at an earlier date.

8 per cent of dons would be prepared to move to an equivalent post elsewhere in Britain. Whereas 47 per cent in the civic universities wanted to move to Oxbridge. Two-thirds of all university teachers would rather accept the less well-paid post of university lecturer and fellow of a college at the ancient universities than a readership in London or a chair at the most august civic, or the most dashing new, university. Over half the Oxbridge dons were educated at public schools or direct grant schools; nearly three-quarters of them were the sons of professional, managerial or business men; over three-quarters of them were recruited from Oxbridge itself.

Around 1960 most dons favoured expanding the universities but feared the consequences. Halsey and Trow found them timid and conservative. One other admission had to be made. Academic distinction by itself did not bestow the gift of a cultivated sensibility. Dons were not intellectuals. Most dons were professional men and women enjoying the rituals of their club, uninterested in the arts or indeed in general ideas. How many visitors dining at high table and expecting to be dazzled by the conversation were first bewildered and then bored by unintelligible university gossip. There were few iconoclasts. Long ago one fellow of Trinity Hall had once petitioned the Lord Chancellor to set aside an election on the grounds that he was a member of the college and his rival was not. He lost his case. The Lord Chancellor ruled that a man must not only be of decent character but also likely to be a good colleague. Charles Crawley, the historian of that college, commented: 'It is perhaps rash at any time for a possible fellowship candidate to circulate satirical epigrams about senior members of the university, including the senior tutor of his own college.' Ah, well.

There was, however, one book published in 1964 that questioned this sublime self-satisfaction. It was written by two young fellows of King's, Jasper Rose and the physicist John Ziman. Not that it was satirical. *Camford Observed* surveyed the culture of the ancient universities dispassionately; but it was also critical. First about admissions and the influence on English education of the scholarship exams (was 'Write a Eulogy on Wine' really a testing subject for an essay?). The authors described the marvellous advantages of college life and tuition for dons and undergraduates alike, but didn't the endless parties make one wonder whether one was at a carnival or a finishing school? For the first time they took the lid off the sizeable discrepancy in the earnings of the dons – to say nothing of the perks, free dinners, free rooms and the rest – and those of their colleagues in the civic universities. When fellowships were advertised how seldom did an applicant from a civic university succeed? – yet how often when a chair was advertised was a professor from Redbrick preferred, suggesting that the promise of the young internal candidate years ago had not been fulfilled. Oxbridge dons were more independent than the academic staff in Redbrick; there was less toadying to departmental heads: there the professor ruled supreme, not at Oxbridge. At the same time Oxbridge snobbery opposed any development that could be called vocational. Technology, agriculture, estate management, oriental languages, veterinary science languished, and the teachers in such subjects waited in vain for college fellowships; or because colleges were reluctant to admit students to read such subjects and called for more posts in history and English. Oxford and Cambridge lost out in the post Robbins bonanza to the civic universities that were willing to take in more students.

It was in their description of the central bureaucracy that Rose and Ziman found it impossible to restrain their gift for satire. 'It is a bureaucracy with a sort of many-stalked cauliflower for a head. Like a cauliflower it looks brainy – but has no mind of its own.' Dons, they concluded, 'will not vote *for* change unless it is the only hope of survival; they will vote solidly *against* it if it seems in any way to threaten anything of substance they

value. Too much power is offered to an intransigent minority.'
Nothing was more extraordinary in the dismissal of the outside
world by Oxford and Cambridge than their lack of interest in
education – in the primary and secondary schools in their own
country, even in the way in which their examining boards for
GCSE performed. Many young dons earned extra money
examining at Advanced Level, but where in the university did
a body exist that considered the impact of these exams on the
maintained schools?

As may be imagined, the authors' comments on the central
bureaucracy stirred the hornets to reply. Ivor Jennings, no
longer Vice-Chancellor, wrote me a fulminating letter: how
could I have allowed two young fellows of my college to write
such a book? I replied that at King's no one supposed that it
was part of the Provost's duties to censor what the fellows wrote.
No doubt he suspected me of putting them up to it; and indeed
the criticisms they made Jennings had heard me make over
the years on the General Board and throughout the university.
Jennings need not have feared. The trouble-makers were soon
on their way, Jasper Rose to teach on a new campus of the
University of California and John Ziman to a chair in the physics
department at Bristol.

It was not until the seventies that the grave complacency of
the ancient universities was to be jolted. 'Student unrest' struck
universities all over the western world. Oxford and Cambridge
escaped the worst excesses of the student militants that made
Essex notorious. At the Polytechnic of North London the Director was assaulted, the staff terrorised and the governors so
intimidated that some connived at the disruption. Only cour-
ageous members of staff like Caroline Cox and John Marks told
the public the truth. Unlike the London School of Economics
Oxford and Cambridge were not liable to be invaded by militants from all over the metropolis. The movement began by
demands to be represented in the governance of the university,

in particular on those bodies that were concerned with student affairs, e.g. the library or halls of residence. But the militants had other fish to fry – the destruction of the capitalist system with all its hypocrisies, of which the universities were a part. The university authorities were bewildered and surprised by the tactics and hostility of the militant students. They were also caught on the hop by the Latey Committee's recommendation (accepted by the government) that the age of majority should be lowered from twenty-one to eighteen. That meant that proctors and tutors could no longer claim to be *in loco parentis*: indeed the Privy Council in the interest of natural justice required universities to set up a quasi-judicial body to consider cases of ill-discipline and on top of that a court of appeal against sentence. The days when a college told an undergraduate to go down, i.e. be expelled for a year or permanently, and he went down without question, had gone.

The powers of the proctors and tutors therefore melted away. They began to resemble the giant Pope at the entrance to the Valley of the Shadow of Death, able only to sit in his cave grinning and biting his nails. At Oxford in 1964 the proctors took action against some undergraduates for damaging the car of the South African ambassador. In revenge the junior proctor's telephone number was circulated as being the premises of a nest of call-girls; since an American air-base was nearby, he got little sleep. The hint of malice in this response was an augury. Nevertheless, Oxford moved sensibly and by 1969 Professor Herbert Hart's committee proposed a new disciplinary set-up and met the reasonable demands for students to be represented on certain university bodies. Council endorsed Hart and the Privy Council assented to the new statutes in 1971. At the end of 1973 the militant students made their bid. They occupied the Examination Schools for a week. They next invaded the Indian Institute, which they had been warned not to occupy. To their amazement they were met with strong-arm resistance and were thrown out. A month later they attacked the new university offices and were again seen off, being no match in a roughhouse for the proctors' men and university police. Eighteen men were charged before the new disciplinary court, all found guilty and expelled for a year. On appeal only one got off more lightly. Oxford emerged with credit.

There was, however, one college in which trouble was always brewing. This was Balliol. Ever since Lindsay's time as Master it had been a citadel of the left, and when Lindsay's successor retired he had been succeeded by the Marxist historian Christopher Hill. Hill distanced himself from the Dean and others responsible for discipline; but whenever he supported them, the militant students pilloried him as a traitor. The fact that Balliol's walls were covered with graffiti might not have been known so widely outside Oxford but for the fact that the *Spectator* published a series of letters by 'Mercurius Oxoniensis'. The pseudonym was widely believed to conceal the identity of Hugh Trevor-Roper. Mercurius described Oxford's politics in magnificent seventeenth-century prose. He compared Balliol's wall to 'an extroverted privy-house: the scribblings which there, through shame, are writ inwardly being here shamelessly publish'd to the world'. One week Mercurius surmised that the Master had been hanged by the fanatics and 'hustled to his grave at midnight, very obscurely . . . The Proctors have forgiven the young men who hanged their Master, as doubtless ignorant of the statutes against murther.' Donnish bravado, however, equally heightened the tension. When Hill was away on sabbatical leave his deputy invited his old Balliol contemporary, now Prime Minister, to dine in college. It was not the most tactful hour to choose since Heath had just signed a naval agreement with the apartheid South African government. The gates were locked and police massed in the quad to make way for the Prime Minister and fellows to pass to the senior common room from the Master's Lodgings. In the riot that followed Anthony

Kenny* said to Heath, 'I expect you're quite used to this kind of thing.' 'Never seen anything like it before in my life.'

Cambridge was, as ever, slow to respond to the students' requests for representation on committees. In 1970 there was a riot surpassing anything at Oxford. The Greek Tourist Board organised a dinner at the Garden House Hotel. It was at the time when the colonels had seized power in Athens and some 200 students, marshalled by a loudspeaker in a fellow's rooms in Peterhouse, descended on the hotel and broke up the dinner party. The police were late on the scene and by that time the deputy proctor had been hit on the head by a brick and taken to hospital. Two policemen were injured. Six students came up before Melford Stevenson, a judge noted for his severity who lived in a house called 'Truncheons'.† They got six months and two others were sent to reformatory. The judge said the sentences would have been stiffer but for the fact that a 'group of dons had been an evil influence upon them'. Two years later the General Board refused to endorse some changes in the regulations for exams in the faculty of economics. Masses of students occupied the Old Schools, and the university asked a well-known judge, Lord Devlin, to look into the matter and report. To ask someone eminent to issue a report after a fracas was by this time a well-worn device to defuse matters. Devlin made the unastonishing recommendation that students should to some degree have representation on university bodies.

The student demonstrations of the late sixties and seventies did the universities immense harm. Here were students supported by more than adequate grants for residence and tuition out of the tax-payers' pocket, rioting and smashing university property. And when the few were hauled before disciplinary bodies their teachers hastened to put forward excuses for their

---

* Anthony Kenny, fellow and Master of Balliol (1978–89), philosopher.
† Sir Melford Stevenson, Justice of the High Court (1951–79).

behaviour. The academics who sat as judges on the disciplinary bodies were confounded by barristers briefed to defend the students, their fees paid from Student Union funds, again provided by the tax-payer. Vice-Chancellors found themselves in a legal morass. The courts would refuse applications for an injunction to expel students occupying buildings, and the Vice-Chancellor became engulfed in legal niceties. The dons, too, lost public support. They were seen – though this was truer of staff at the civic universities – as either unreasonable in not being willing to hear sensible student requests or, more often, as feeble, divided and vacillating in dealing with the militants. Too often the academic staff were split between those refusing to agree to any demand, however reasonable, those who tried in good faith to find common ground and negotiate a settlement, and the small minority who made common cause with the students and regarded the disturbances as an opportunity to humble the Vice-Chancellor and his minions. The vacillations caused by these divisions did not escape the notice of Mercurius Oxoniensis. The high table, he declared, was divided between 'young ninnies, crying for novelties and old jellies quaking and yielding to them'.

When Melford Stevenson had accused a group of dons for being an evil influence upon the Cambridge undergraduates, the Vice-Chancellor at once denied that any such group existed. But now a new voice was to be heard among the dons declaring that donnish culture was at the heart of the matter. This was the voice of John Carey, Merton professor of English at Oxford, who published an article entitled 'Down with Dons'.

'The most obnoxious thing about dons,' he began, 'is their uppishness.' Living their working life among the young, who can be counted upon to know less than they do, they are likely to acquire a high opinion of their own abilities. When a young don said he wondered whether compared to miners dons were paid too much, Hugh Lloyd-Jones supposed that he could never have done any worthwhile teaching or research. Had Lloyd-Jones ever considered, asked Carey, that his own contribution to the community was 'of uncommonly little consequence?' Would not a little humility be in place for dons since 'their avocations and their maintenance at the public expense is notoriously difficult to justify...' Years of self-esteem had, as it were, blinded the professor 'to his economic value'.

Carey next spot-lit Bowra. He praised him for not allowing administration to deflect him from scholarship. His breadth of knowledge was a reproach to modern dons with their narrow specialisation. 'He inspired others to creativity which is any teacher's most important job.' But Bowra the man he thought detestable. He was bumptious and insolent. What was he doing much of the time but advertising his own superiority to the lower middle classes, the grammar school boys, and the earnest? If we ask why students began to rebel against the rules of the university was it not because Bowra and his like had for long jeered at authority? How did he square this with the domineering way in which he exercised his authority in the years when he was Warden of Wadham and Vice-Chancellor? When Bowra justified undergraduates appealing to the Privy Council about proctorial authority by saying that they were entitled to do so, did he ask himself why 'gilded sprigs from the foremost families' should exercise this right? Was that not 'a grandiose and typically donnish sense of the university's place in the scheme of things'? It was on a par with those letters to the press signed by dons 'gravely informing some foreign government that the way it deals with its refractory minorities does not tally with donnish notions of freedom'. A don had as much right as a budgerigar to prate about such matters. He lived in a protected environment in which all his wants were catered for, and the majority of his fellow-citizens would abolish him at once if they had a free choice since they received no direct benefit from universities.

John Carey might have recollected that, at the height of the reputation of the German professoriate, Nietzsche had said that professors were both complacent and resentful. Professors behaved as if they were the new priesthood. In Germany they kowtowed to the Emperor but patronised their fellow-citizens. In Oxford and Cambridge the world of getting and gaining was often the target. Jenifer Hart remembered Isaiah Berlin dissuading her husband from practising as a barrister. The only point of doing so would be to earn fame and money and 'the death of the soul it produces is automatic and inevitable'. Carey was furious that dons despised those who sought power or made money. What right had the dons to think they were indifferent to all the suffering in the world?

> Ah Love! could thou and I with Fate conspire
> To grasp this sorry Scheme of Things entire,
> Would we not shatter it to bits – and then
> Re-mould it nearer to the Heart's Desire!

The dons resented the Scheme of Things even more when the militant students regarded the university as being itself part of a corrupt society. John Carey's dons carry a lot of Nietzsche's baggage.

Carey was a master at fouling his own nest and his diatribe *The Intellectuals and the Masses*, which accused intellectuals, as Orwell had done, of snobbish disdain for ordinary people, bred publicists like Paul Johnson vilifying intellectuals throughout the ages, and politicians like Margaret Thatcher and Norman Tebbit, who were to enjoy clipping the dons' wings. Odious as the Merton professor's sneer was at Bowra for 'hob-nobbing' with undergraduates, he was certainly endowed with prophetic gifts. In the late seventies, as Britain's economy declined, people began to question the assumption that the nation's prosperity was linked to the universities. Did Oxford and Cambridge nur-

ture competitive businessmen? Had the glittering, epigram-
matic speakers at the Union, the nursery of statesmen, climbing
the ladder to careers at Westminster, performed all that well
when they ruled the country? Alex Todd used to chide government for not realising that money spent on fundamental
research kick-started a 'spin-off' to industry; but this was hardly
true of the myriad labs in many universities or even in polytechnics. Soon journalists and academics themselves began to criticise liberal assumptions. In America Martin Wiener connected
Britain's economic decline to English culture. The cultivated
classes despised industry, and Oxford and Cambridge were
geared to producing gentlemen, not businessmen. Sheldon
Rothblatt showed how long it took for Cambridge to sanction
a faculty of engineering and how few sons of businessmen went
into industry. In the eighties Correlli Barnett wrote a series of
polemics about the deplorable record of British management
and blamed university culture. Economic historians dissected
him but none of them had his talent for self-advertisement.
He and Wiener were to influence the incoming Conservative
governments.

Margaret Thatcher's governments challenged the culture of
the universities. The dons saw themselves as the successors to
the boffins and code-breakers in the war, as part of a civilised
welfare state. Edward Boyle, that politician turned Vice-
Chancellor, used to defend universities by claiming that they
were 'pushing back the frontiers of knowledge' – that blush-
making phrase. The dons prided themselves on teaching a
student body with the lowest drop-out rate in the world. They
saw themselves as the guardians of civilised values who should
not be judged by solely commercial considerations. Now they
were being told that commercial considerations came first.
Government saw them as shielded from the tough competitive
world in which business and industry had to survive. Nine-tenths
of their costs came from public money so their costs must be

cut. Government no longer trusted the universities. It ignored them and did not consult them to suggest alternative ways of saving so that mass higher education could be financed. The older dons, many of them dedicated Conservatives like Robert Blake at Oxford, turned to the Tory grandees for help. They were no longer there. The old Christ Church alliance with Westminster had vanished. The grandees had been supplanted by Margaret Thatcher's supporters.

The universities now received letters telling them by how much their grant would be reduced. The only course for most of them was to urge academics to take early retirement regardless of whether a particular department could afford to lose so many senior teachers. The UGC had never been geared to plan higher education, nor did it exercise financial control: so government replaced it with a Higher Education Funding Council, which allocated grants across the whole of the multitude of institutions. Its members were predominantly businessmen, not dons. In 1970 the staff:student ratio was 1:8, in 1990 it was 1:17. The unit of resource (a term of art that expressed the income from fees plus the average amount of income per student that came from government sources) fell from an index of 100 in 1970 to 40 in 1990. In 1995 the capital programme was cut by 31 per cent. The Department of Education showed not the faintest interest in the effect of these policies.

A further indignity followed. Universities were told they must be made accountable. This was at first puzzling. In 1967 they had foolishly resisted the Public Accounts Committee's request that the Comptroller and Auditor General should look at the UGC's account and, if he saw fit, those of individual universities. They bleated that to do so would damage morale, undermine the UGC and infringe academic freedom. But in that year £211 million had been poured into universities and of course it was right to monitor a sum of this size. But why should there now be a further demand to make universities accountable? In only one case, on the Cardiff campus in Wales, had there been a scandal. When was there last an outcry about the low standard of teaching? When was there concern about the low standard of British research? There never had been any such outcry. The air was thick with rhetorical questions.

Why then did the Conservative government call for accountability? The demand sprang from a deep contradiction in Conservative philosophy. In principle they opposed State investment, State management, the corporate State. The market was the best arbiter. Keith Joseph, at one time Secretary of State for Education, believed in market forces. In business the market is the brutal judge of efficiency. No profits, and the business folds. In a market economy universities would be free to choose their levels of fees, intake of students, the courses they would offer. Oxford and Cambridge might charge high fees, yet if parents still believed it was worthwhile for their children to go there, they would thrive. Other institutions could pack in students at lower unit costs and thus survive. Some might go to the wall if they failed to find a market. This was the model Max Beloff advocated. He had left his chair at Oxford to become the first Vice-Chancellor of the independent University of Buckingham and gloried in receiving no grant from the State.

But what would happen if students made the 'wrong' choices? What if few were attracted to science or if philosophy and archaeology were abandoned because they could not be made cost-effective? The marketeers quivered. Conservative governments, however much they paid lip-service to the market, were not going to allow universities to price their services. They would not be allowed to float in the market and find out what the public was prepared to pay to go there. So the Higher Education Funding Council was set up to dictate to universities what they should do as money got shorter. Since the market was 'imperfect' and could not guarantee that universities were efficient, government imposed an elaborate system of review. The work of every department in every university was to be assessed every three years. The assessors were to be the academic staff in rival or allied departments in other universities.

An enormous burden of administering this new system fell upon the universities. In 1994 a survey showed that 33 per cent of a don's time in term was taken in administration: only 20 per cent was left for research. The waste of time was prodigious. The dons complained that what with having to raise funds for their research, from foundations and business, and what with having to produce convincing evidence that their research was valuable, they had little time left actually to do any research.

Visiting British universities a few years after this regime of accountability had been operating, Martin Trow was struck by a new phenomenon in British academic life. The dons had become liars. Vice-Chancellors had said that if swingeing cuts were imposed, standards would fall. Now that they had been imposed no Vice-Chancellor said openly that the quality of teaching and research in his university had fallen. To admit to a decline would be to invite outside inspectors to recommend that some departments should be closed down. Yet how could standards not have fallen when fewer academics taught vastly more students? Whitehall, however, presented this as a triumph of 'higher productivity' or 'efficiency gains'. The dons were encouraged to become cheats as well as liars. They became adept at misinterpreting directives from the Funding Council. They soon realised that the torrent of paper flowing into the council and its agencies was so voluminous that the information, right or wrong, they filled in on the forms could never be checked by the 'quality assessment agency'. In order to bump up the ratings in a department, its head would try to lure someone from another university to join it just before the day of assessment so that his publications could be added to the rest and thus obtain a higher rating for the department. The quantity, not the quality of the publications counted. Universities entered an era in which articles that could be published quickly ousted the book that might take five years or more of research. The truth is that many admirable teachers have no aptitude for research and turn out worthless articles. Interdisciplinary research suffered: no single department could get credit for it. Trow sensed another change. The universities used to trust the UGC. Trust had disappeared. 'It seemed at times,' wrote Trow, 'as if we were observing dealings between a small dependency and a foreign power.' Enter the inquisition, exit loyalty.

One Cambridge don wrote perceptively about these changes. Stefan Collini described how bibliometrical methods were forced upon universities and suggested that the government agencies and vice-chancellors were to blame, for allowing the *quantity* of books or articles published instead of their *quality* to be the measure of a don's or a department's worth. His analysis of the folly, the contradictions and the degradation of all these exercises in 'productivity' or 'accountability' was masterly. Had this come about, he asked, because the Department of Education and Employment and the Higher Education Funding Council don't understand what scholarship in the humanities is? Or because they do understand the damage they are inflicting and are indifferent to it.

Collini's satire would have had even greater force if he had not suffered from a well-known donnish illness – inwardness. He did not pick on the biographer's neglect of Sparrow's contribution to bibliography and late Latin verse. He accused his book of bearing 'little trace of recent scholarship about the topics it touches'. He later admitted that all he meant was that the biography did not analyse the politics and social life of the period. How true of what he himself has written. There is scarcely a word about the demands people make for a better health service, for better schools and teachers, for a mass of welfare schemes and the reduction of crime, violent crime. Nor, to come nearer to the universities, about the decision to increase the numbers in post-eighteen education. How far further education should go, what value many of the courses in it achieve, is problematic; but the question should be considered. Such matters, and unemployment, are troubling all major European countries. Dons spit at the name of Margaret Thatcher and few spit further than Collini; and with good reason. But Collini never addresses the problems she and her two successors as Prime Minister have had to face. He does not even address the problems of diseconomies in university governance. He ends by being a lobbyist who does not understand politics.

The Conservative governments went beyond accountability and reducing grants. They had been compelled to pay academic staff who were forced to retire early a sum for breach of contract since their contract of service ran to the retiring age. So they insisted that all new contracts – including those involving promotions from a lectureship to a chair – should contain no guarantee of employment to a retiring age. Meanwhile the salaries of academics in relation to other occupations continued to fall – lower and lower. A. H. Halsey recorded that in 1929 the salaries of dons were 3.7 times greater than the average in manufacturing industry. In 1989 they were only 1.5 times greater. The relative status of dons had declined; and with it their prestige. Students, too, were to be worse off. They were forced to take out loans to cover their maintenance costs. Even worse, government slipped a clause, not once but twice, into Education Bills which would have permitted the Department of Education to question the content of courses and in other ways infringe academic freedom. This aroused impassioned debate in the House of Lords, where on one occasion Michael Swann, a former Vice-Chancellor of Edinburgh and chairman of the BBC, and on another Roy Jenkins, by then Chancellor of Oxford, led the opposition and induced the government to drop or reword the clause.

It would have been impossible for the Conservative governments to convince the universities that mass higher education could be financed only by cutting the costs of existing institutions. It was comprehensible enough that they did not 'consult' universities before issuing their dictates. Instead they sent a junior minister, Robert Jackson, to visit a few universities and face the flak. But those he visited found themselves treated like the awkward squad on the square being bawled at by the regimental sergeant-major. But even he – for he did not lack courage – would have found it hard to explain the most perverse decision of all that they later took – perverse in that it went counter to Conservative principles. They announced that all polytechnics and numbers of colleges of further education should be entitled to call themselves universities. All were to be funded through the Higher Education Funding Council and inspected for quality of teaching and research under the same terms. It was not the name that stuck in the gullet. In America men and women 'go to college', be it in Cambridge, Mass., or Oxford, Mississippi. It was the abolition of the principle that different institutions, aiming at different levels and kinds of higher education, ought to be differentiated. The binary principle that Tony Crosland and his sagacious civil servant adviser Toby Weaver established when they created the polytechnics was now abandoned. In 1950 there had been twenty-two vice-chancellors; in 1993 there were 102. The Vice-Chancellors Committee was effectively castrated. It now spoke in a medley of falsettos.

The dons too were changing. In 1991 Peter Snow published *Oxford Observed*, an exceptionally well-written account of the city as well as the university and the various cultures that flourished within each. He could spare only one chapter for the dons and amused himself by depicting new typologies, much as Tuckwell and his predecessors had done in the past. There were the 'Denim dons', survivors of the student radicals in the seventies teaching post-structuralism and various forms of Marxism; and the 'Glitterateurs' writing best-sellers and appearing on TV, often revisionist historians out to shock the left and win large advances from publishers. There was the 'Nine-to-five don' whose wife was not prepared to accept a life in which her husband remained in hall. Most dons now were dissidents united in hatred of the Thatcher years and very few still posed as 'Enterprise dons' willing to support Margaret Thatcher's revolution. The account he gives of college business suggests that little had changed. Yet the dons no longer inhabited a stable and autonomous world. They had to bend to the political winds.

If dons in Cambridge had been asked what was the most striking change of the nineties it would have been the virtual end of the male college. As one after the other of the men's colleges admitted women, the culture of college society became transformed. It could hardly have been different at Oxford.

No euphoria greeted the end of eighteen years of Conservative rule. The dons no longer regarded politicians with hope. Nor were they wrong to do so. The days when half the Labour Cabinet would have been at Oxbridge had gone. More typical was Tom Levitt, one of the new Labour MPs. He had taken his degree at Lancaster and went to Oxford to train as a teacher. 'The male-oriented public school ethos was so evident that I was grateful I had not been there as an undergraduate. All my worst prejudices about the place were confirmed.' He had a point. Only one or two colleges in the ancient universities made a deliberate attempt to identify talent in the comprehensive schools and then by intensive dedicated teaching turn the promise into performance so that in their last year the State school undergraduates could show themselves the equal in the first class of the boys and girls from independent schools.

The new minister for higher education in the Labour government was Tessa Blackstone, head of Birkbeck College, London. She had first hit the news as a young member of the think-tank in the seventies, when Kenneth Berrill was its chairman, and had written a report proposing that the British embassy in Paris, the splendid house of the Princesse Borghese, Napoleon's sister, should be sold off and the embassy cut its costs and move to less ostentatious quarters. In 1998 she announced that the government would abolish Oxford and Cambridge colleges' fees. The £35 million that would be saved would be distributed to other universities. If the colleges then charged top-up fees to recoup their losses the universities would be penalised. Oxford and Cambridge were to learn that whereas the previous government had chastised them with whips the new government, like Rehoboam, would chastise them with scorpions.

In terms of equity the dons had no reply. At University College London, academics gave tutorials in addition to their lectures and examined as part of their duties. The tutorials might well be in groups of two or three students, though were probably not as frequent as those at Oxbridge. That may well have been the case in other universities throughout the country whereas at Oxford and Cambridge the colleges paid those who gave tutorials an extra sum of money.

The dons – the old Oxbridge lobby – replied in a debate in the House of Lords. Yes, Oxford and Cambridge must plead guilty to the charge that they were élite institutions. So were the Grandes Écoles in France, or the Max Planck institutes in Germany but they, like Imperial College or LSE in Britain, were specialist institutions. Only a dozen or so universities were world class, and of those ten were in North America. None on the Continent, where universities admitted vast numbers of students who rarely met academic staff: many of them dropped out. Ralf Dahrendorf* spoke of the almost universal decline of continental universities since the 1960s in the wake of mass higher edu-

---

* Ralf Dahrendorf, KBE, held professorships of sociology at Hamburg, Tübingen, Konstanz, LSE (1958–69); Director of LSE (1974–84), Warden of St Antony's College, Oxford (1987–97). Life peer 1993.

cation. Students came to Oxford from the Continent to escape mediocrity at home. 'Almost nowhere else in the world are the chances for students and teachers to meet and inspire each other as great as in the ancient universities' – and this from a loyal student and later director of LSE. Oxford and Cambridge remained in the world-class category because they emphasised the importance of talking and writing in tutorials rather than reading and taking notes in overcrowded lecture rooms. Yes, the tutorial system cost more; but to study at Harvard cost three times more than to study at Oxford. Others spoke of their amazement at being taught in tutorials face to face by men and women whose books they had read at school. In one sense the colleges were more efficient: fewer undergraduates dropped out. Graduate employment was not much more than a third of the national university average. The richer colleges offered out of their own funds research fellowships, another link in the chain between attracting school leavers with high A Levels to excellence in research. Excellence breeds excellence, said a Cambridge scientist, pointing to the succession of Nobel Prizes in several departments. Jack Lewis, the first Master of the new Robinson College, contrasted Cambridge science with other universities he had known: departments were not isolated empires: the colleges were another asset in mixing dons from different disciplines.

To counter Tom Levitt, the head of another new college for mature women students told the tale of three women who had all been told they would never fit into such snob surroundings. One said, 'I am a scouser off the streets and my teacher said Cambridge was for rich kids. She said: "Give me a match and I'll burn the place down tomorrow."' The student disregarded her teacher, applied and was accepted. All three succeeded and one got a PhD. Time and again speakers referred to the infinite blessing of the college tutorial, where a student met his teacher face to face and trained his mind. Roy Jenkins reminded the

government that 'Britain, as a medium-sized country without
too many recent successes to its credit, is peculiarly lucky to
possess one quarter of the small number of outstanding world
universities'. Their lovely buildings and surroundings attracted
students and scholars as well as tourists. They did not wish in
the twenty-first century to become intellectually empty shells as
– so some might think – had happened over the years to Sala-
manca in Spain and Coimbra in Portugal. Over six years' strenu-
ous effort Oxford had raised from private and other sources a
gross sum of £340 million. But it would take far more than that
to produce an annual income to meet the annual deficit of £19
million.

The speeches in the House of Lords fell on deaf ears. It
looked as if the ancient élite universities, recognised as Britain's
most prestigious, were at last to be cut down to size. But Roy
Jenkins had foreseen what a Labour government might be
tempted to do, and in October 1997 he had sent the Prime
Minister a memorandum on the subject. When the blow fell in
March 1998 he sent a stiff note to Downing Street complaining
that the promised consultation that, so he understood, the
Prime Minister had promised, had not taken place. Other
influences were brought to bear: the Rector of Lincoln, Eric
Anderson, who had been Blair's housemaster at his Scottish
public school Fettes, warned him of some of the consequences.
As a result the two Vice-Chancellors were invited to go to the
Department of Education and Employment, and an instruction
from Downing Street was sent to the department insisting that
any settlement must be reasonably satisfactory to the two universities. The Vice-Chancellors, briefed by some wily college
bursars, began the interview with the department and the
Higher Education Funding Council by wondering whether the
government had taken into account when coming to their
decision that a number of colleges without endowment would
go bankrupt and close if they lost their fees. Would there not

be an outcry, would not students suffer? What about the costs
of organising the admission of students? Those costs fell on the
colleges and not the university, as would be the case elsewhere.
Or, for that matter, the costs of the welfare of students? What
about the sums the colleges had to pay to repair their crumbling
ancient buildings, on their gardens and avenues, the delight of
millions of tourists? Did the government want to force Oxford
and Cambridge to charge top-up fees and admit more overseas
and fewer home students and repeat the errors which had made
the great civic grammar schools such as Manchester, Bristol
and Birmingham join the independent schools? It looked for
a moment as if Oxford and Cambridge were going to escape
like Houdini from the trap the egalitarians had planned. But
not quite. At the end of the negotiations the colleges were to
lose only 22 per cent of their fees; and the loss would be spread
over ten years. As part of the bargain the richer colleges would
have to agree to finance the deficits of the poorer colleges.

Had nostalgia won? Certainly. The dons of the twenty-first
century are going to find their way of life changed and greater
difficulty in persuading younger men and women to follow them
when the reward for following the life of the mind is to accept
such financial hardship. Nostalgia, however, is the mother of
loyalty. Oxford men and women will have their own memories.
So will every Cambridge graduate: of a light burning late into
the night in a lab where a scientist is setting up an experiment;
of a library or a lecture where illumination first dawned; of a
room in a college, of talk and the gaiety of friendship; of sunset
on the river while rowing in an eight back to the boathouse; of
a play, or a concert, or a poetry-reading, or of teachers and
preachers. But it would be odd if he did not associate these
memories with the tender beauty of the place, and with the
dignity and the domesticity of its buildings. One of its greatest
dons, E. D. Adrian, Vice-Chancellor, Chancellor and sometime
Master of Trinity, once said: 'The time may come when the

colleges may become alms-houses for the old and cafeterias for the young: but it will always be something to have fallen asleep to the sound of the fountain playing in Trinity Great Court.'

The Intellectual Aristocracy

Family connections are part of the poetry of history. They call to mind the generations of men and women who were born, married and died, and perhaps bequeathed to their descendants some trait of their personality, some tradition of behaviour, which did not perish with the passing of the years but persisted in their grandchildren and their grandchildren's children, and so made the past immortal. But family connections are most important to the social historian when they reveal some caucus of power or influence, such as the Whig cousinhood, which moulds the country's culture.

The inter-marriage between these families is not an easy process to follow. To relieve the tedium of collating it, let us imagine that we are riding in a hunt, and having started a fox in the Pytchley country, we pursue it on a 200-mile point straight across the Midlands, ending on the edge of the Beaufort. So in our pursuit of this class we will start from one family and move into the country of the neighbouring hunt only if one of its members is related to the antecedent family. Some intellectual families – Moberlys or Headlams – will lie off the line we hit but it is astonishing how many we will ride through, particularly if we follow the scent into the twentieth century.

Let us begin by drawing a covert in the Macaulay country and see how Rose Macaulay descended from the ancestor of the famous Macaulays who was a minister in the Hebrides. Rose

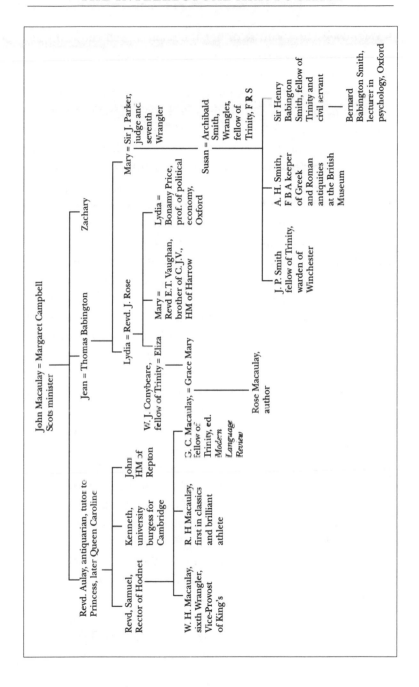

was a novelist and satirist of her times and a well-known figure in London literary society. Her father was a scholar; her uncle, W. H. Macaulay, was a magnificent figure of a don; her great-uncle a headmaster. She is also descended from the Conybeares and Babingtons. The Conybeares were for generations parsons and scholars descending from an Elizabethan schoolmaster. There was the Revd John Conybeare, who defended revealed religion against Matthew Tindal in a book which George Washington always liked to have by him; there was the Revd J. W. E. Conybeare who wrote a life of Alfred the Great, and another Conybeare who was a fellow of University College, Oxford, an Armenian scholar who married a daughter of Max Müller. In recent times a Conybeare was a master at Eton for nearly fifty years. William Daniel Conybeare was an excellent palaeontologist, but he was one of those appalled by the implications of German theology. His son W. J. Conybeare, a noted *Edinburgh* reviewer, married a daughter of Lydia Babington, who was taught by her father to read each morning a chapter of the Old Testament in Hebrew and a chapter of the New Testament in Greek. It was this Conybeare who was the grandfather of Rose Macaulay. Her first cousin, 'Beetles' Babington, was professor of botany at Cambridge at the same time as another cousin, Churchill Babington, was professor of archaeology. Churchill's range was wide: he was also expert in ornithology and numismatics and won praise for 'his able defence of the English clergy in the seventeenth century against Macaulay's aspersions'. The achievements of the Macaulay-Babington connection are displayed in the first table.

But we must turn to Zachary, the brother of the Revd Aulay and Jean Macaulay, if we are to get the run for which we were hoping. Everyone knows that his eldest son was the historian Lord Macaulay, but one tends to forget that his youngest son, Charles Zachary, married a daughter of 'Radical Dick' Potter, a founder of the *Manchester Guardian*. Here the pace begins to

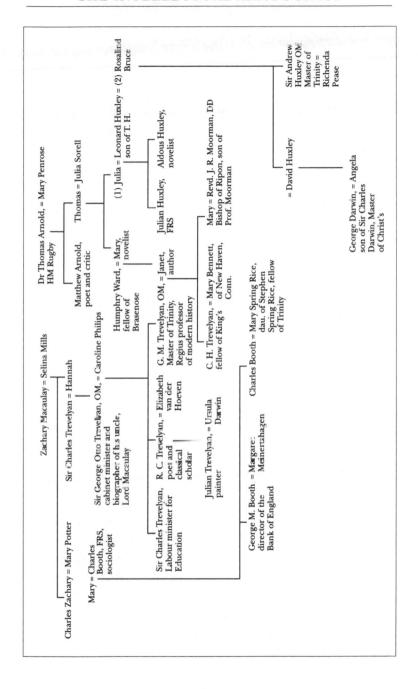

quicken. Their daughter Mary married Charles Booth, the author of *Life and Labour of the People of London*, one of the greatest sociological studies of Victorian times. With Charles Booth we ride into a new country, the families of radical Liverpool, into the Rathbones and Cromptons. Henry Crompton, professor of history at University College, London, and a sponsor of the First International; as were the chemist Sir Henry Roscoe, FRS, and the economist W. S. Jevons, FRS. One of Booth's uncles collaborated with Stephenson in building the *Rocket* and another was secretary to the Board of Trade. Charles Booth's third son married the daughter of Stephen Spring-Rice, fellow of Trinity, one of whose granddaughters was the wife of Professor C. M. Robertson, the son of D. S. Robertson, Vice-Master of Trinity and professor of Greek at Cambridge. The main connection, however, follows through Charles Booth's wife. Her cousins were the nine Potter sisters who spread their enveloping wings over radical and socialist society at the end of the last century. The most famous was the eighth, Beatrice Webb. The eldest, Laurencina, married Robert Holt, gazetted a baronet by Lord Rosebery, who misread his humorous letter of refusal and was compelled by Holt to cancel the honour. The second, Catherine, married Leonard (later Lord) Courtney, second Wrangler, fellow of St John's and Financial Secretary to the Treasury. The fifth, Theresa, married C. A. Cripps, later the first Lord Parmoor, whose eldest son was bursar of Queen's, Oxford, whose younger son was Sir Stafford Cripps and whose daughter married Sir Jack Egerton, FRS, professor of chemistry, London. The seventh, Margaret, married a cousin of L. T. Hobhouse, local government reformer, who was the grandfather of Theresa Clay, the zoologist. The youngest of the nine sisters, Rosalind, had married Malcolm Muggeridge, publicist, polemicist and scourge of these intellectual families. The link with the next family, however, is the fourth Potter sister, who married a banker, Daniel Meinertzhagen.

Meinertzhagen, too, was liberally supplied with daughters. The eldest married her second cousin, George Macaulay Booth, the son of Charles and a director of the Bank of England. The second married Hubert Warre-Cornish, son of the Vice-Provost of Eton. She was thus sister-in-law to Sir Desmond MacCarthy, whose daughter married Lord David Cecil – who as professor of English literature, Oxford, could count a fellow of All Souls and a senior Wrangler among his ancestors. Her youngest sister married A. F. R. Wollaston, explorer, naturalist and fellow of King's, of whom Keynes wrote that he 'could unlock hearts with a word and a look and break down everyone's reserve except his own'. The third Meinertzhagen girl married Robert John Grote Mayor.

Here the scent leads back to Cambridge, for the Mayors are a celebrated academic family. J. E. B. Mayor was professor of Latin, a man of vast learning and minute accuracy who, at the age of six, 'revelled in Rollin (in default of Plutarch)'. He was in the great tradition of dons. He wrote much but rarely the books on which he was working and ought to have written. He collected a library of over 18,000 volumes and during the long period in which he was University Librarian never left Cambridge for more than eight days together. He addressed Germans on 'Why I Am a Vegetarian', never consulted a doctor from the age of twelve to eighty-three, and boasted that he could dine every day off a penny halfpenny; he was also adamant in never taking exercise for its own sake. Lexicography and the deliberations of the Old Catholics were among his passions, and at the age of eighty-two he learnt Esperanto. One of his brothers was third Wrangler and a master at Rugby. Another, the third to be elected a fellow of St John's, became professor of classics at King's, London, and married a niece of John Grote.

Grote was professor of moral philosophy at Cambridge. He founded a club at his vicarage in Trumpington at which animated discussions took place. His brother George was the banker and philosophical radical who wrote the notable history of Greece. John Grote's great-nephew, Robin Mayor, was senior Classic in 1890 and a fellow of King's, who retired in middle age from the civil service to devote himself to philosophical speculation; his brother was a master at Clifton. His son, Andreas Mayor, entered the British Museum and his daughter became the second wife of the scientist Lord Rothschild, FRS, fellow of Trinity and first head of the Central Policy Review staff in the Cabinet Office. Rothschild's elder daughter by this marriage became a professor at the Massachusetts Institute of Technology and later a fellow of King's. She married the economist Professor Amartya Sen, Master of Trinity. His younger daughter was a lecturer in English literature at Queen Mary College, London.

But we must hark back to Zachary Macaulay to establish the well-known connection between the Macaulays, Trevelyans, Arnolds and Huxleys.

From this we can see that Mrs Humphry Ward, the novelist, was the granddaughter of Dr Arnold of Rugby and niece not only of Matthew but of William Delafield Arnold of the Indian Civil Service and author of *Oakfield*, and of William Forster, minister for education in Gladstone's first administration. Her father was distinguished mainly for losing academic posts by his propensity to oscillate between atheism, idealism and the Anglican and Roman Catholic faiths. When he was being received as a Roman Catholic in Hobart his wife was so furious that she threw a brick through the glass window of the church. Her cousin married the modernist theologian of the early twentieth century, Bishop Barnes of Birmingham, whose son became an ambassador. Her grandmother's family were also scholars. Mrs Arnold's brother married 'Mrs Markham', author of children's history books, otherwise Elizabeth Cartwright Penrose, daughter of the doctor of divinity who invented the power loom and niece of the agitator for parliamentary reform in the eighteenth century. Their son, Francis Cranmer Penrose, FRS – the middle name indicated the descent from the great archbishop – was an art historian, architect and surveyor of St Paul's Cathedral. His daughter, Dame Emily Penrose, took a first in Greats and became Principal in succession of Bedford, Holloway and Somerville Colleges. Julian Huxley, FRS, and Aldous Huxley were both grandsons of T. H. Huxley, 'Darwin's bulldog'. With this last name we ride out of the Macaulay country and over the Darwin-Wedgwood land. They are connected by three marriages. The Nobel Prizeman Sir Andrew Huxley, OM, professor of physiology at University College, London, and later Master of Trinity, was the half-brother of the zoologist and the novelist. He married the granddaughter of the first Lord Wedgwood, whose grandfather was Charles Darwin's brother-in-law. His elder brother's daughter married George Darwin, the eldest son of Sir Charles Darwin, Master of Christ's. So at last Darwins and Huxleys are kinsmen. Julian Trevelyan, son of R. C. Trevelyan, married (though the marriage was later dissolved) Ursula, a great-granddaughter of Charles Darwin.

Now we are in open fields and the pace is tremendous. The descendants of Josiah Wedgwood of Maer, son of the founder of the pottery, provide one of the most remarkable examples of the way in which a great intellectual connection attracts to it in each generation distinguished brains from other families. Omitting the master potters among the Wedgwoods who carried on the craft, we find that in the first generation Josiah Wedgwood had the following brothers-in-law: Robert Darwin, FRS, son of Erasmus; Sir James Mackintosh, the Whig philosopher who was attacked by James Mill in his *Fragment on Mackintosh* and who admitted that he could 'no more learn to play the game of life than that of whist'; and J. C. Sismondi, the Genevese economist who propounded the theory of over-production and the increasing poverty of the working classes. Josiah's own brother, Thomas Wedgwood, was the pioneer photographer.

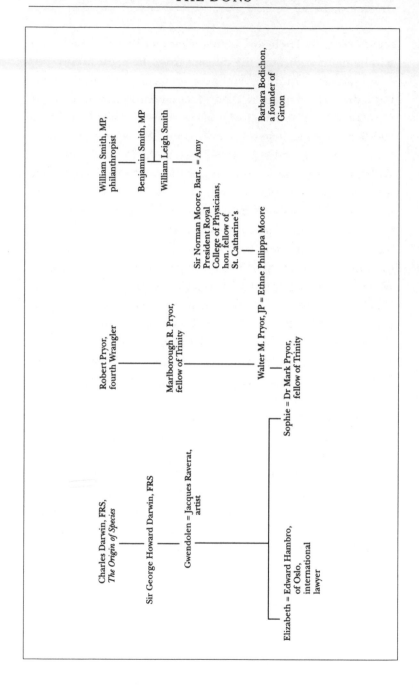

The second generation contains Charles Darwin himself; the etymologist Hensleigh Wedgwood, fellow of Christ's, and Henry Allen Wedgwood, barrister and author. These generations found their chronicler in Darwin's daughter, Henrietta Litchfield, and the third generation glow with life in the pages of *Period Piece*, written by Darwin's granddaughter Gwen Raverat. It contained the mathematician Sir George Darwin, FRS, Sir Horace Darwin, who made scientific instruments, the botanist Sir Francis Darwin, FRS, and Leonard Darwin, president of the Royal Geographical Society. Another Wedgwood became a civil servant and yet another secretary to the Charity Organisation Society. By the end of the century a daughter of Sir James Rendel, FRS, the civil engineer, and a daughter of the civil servant, the first Lord Farrer, had married into the family. And later in life Farrer did the same.

The grandchildren and great-grandchildren of Charles Darwin have extended the intellectual affiliations of the family. Three of his second eldest son's children have played a part in this extension. The eldest, Sir Charles Darwin, FRS, Master of Christ's and director of the National Physical Laboratory, married a daughter of F. W. Pember, Warden of All Souls. It was his son who married a Huxley. The second, Gwen Raverat, who was the wife of the French artist Jacques Raverat, had two daughters, one of whom married Dr Mark Pryor, zoologist and fellow of Trinity.

The Pryors are an example of a family, by origin Quaker, who conformed and sent their sons to Cambridge. On his mother's side Mark Pryor descended from William Smith, MP, adherent of the Clapham Sect, who worked in Parliament to abolish slavery and religious disabilities. He was the son of the Clapham city merchant who sent a present of tea to Flora Macdonald when she was imprisoned in the Tower. We shall meet this family again, but for the present we can pause only to note that Amy Leigh Smith's marriage to Norman Moore was fostered by her aunt, Barbara Bodichon, who was the friend of George Eliot and the prime founder of Girton. Moore was a scholar as well as a brilliant doctor: he contributed 459 biographies to the *DNB* and wrote a history of St Bartholomew's Hospital. So poor as an undergraduate that he lived largely on bread and marmalade, he was unjustly deprived of his scholarship and sent down by his college for brawling – though he had in fact refused to brawl – but such was the outcry that he was reinstated and cheered on getting his degree.

The third and youngest daughter of Sir George Darwin became the wife of the surgeon and bibliographer Sir Geoffrey Keynes.

His elder brother John Maynard, Lord Keynes, claimed to be the first son of the marriage of a fellow of a college with a graduate of Newnham – his father was Registrary, i.e. senior administrative officer, at Cambridge. The year 1882, in which they married, was the date when the university statutes were reformed to permit any fellow of a college to marry. Their grandson, Richard Keynes, professor of physiology, Cambridge, married the daughter of Lord Adrian, OM, Nobel Prizeman and Master of Trinity. Two of his sons were elected fellows of Trinity.

Sir Horace Darwin's younger daughter married the treasury official Sir Alan Barlow, whose father was a physician to three sovereigns and President of the Royal College of Physicians. Sir Alan's niece married Carl Winter, fellow of Trinity and Director of the Fitzwilliam Museum. His son, Professor Horace Barlow, fellow of Trinity and then of King's, was related through his grandmother to Lord Farrer. Lord Farrer was brother-in-law to the Hon. Sir Steven Runciman, fellow of Trinity, whose mother obtained a first-class in the history tripos of 1890. His nephew Garry, Lord Runciman, businessman and sociologist, and his great nephew David were both fellows of Trinity. Farrer was also brother-in-law to Lord Bridges, son of the Poet Laureate and

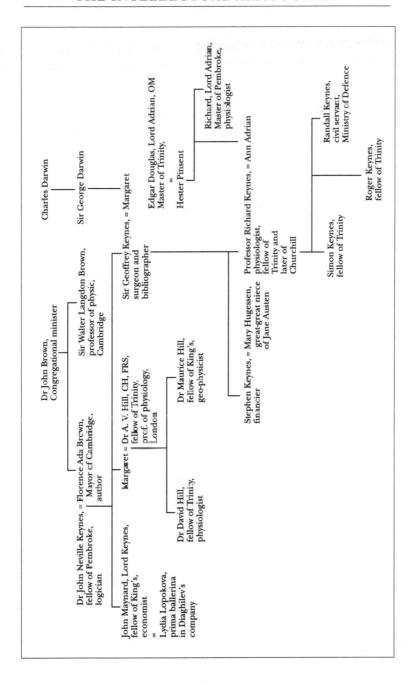

permanent secretary to the Treasury. Bridges was chairman of a committee at Cambridge from 1960 to 1962 to study how the colleges could be persuaded to elect to fellowships those university readers and lecturers who were without them. Few of the colleges accepted his recommendations.

Sir Francis Darwin was the father of Bernard Darwin, who wrote fourth leaders for *The Times* and had an encyclopaedic knowledge of golf, cricket and the works of Dickens. His son, Robin Darwin, was Principal of the College of Art. Sir Francis was also the father, by his second wife, of the poet Frances Cornford, who married Professor Cornford, fellow of Trinity. Their eldest son was John Cornford, the young communist intellectual, who was killed in the Spanish Civil War. John's son was professor of politics at Edinburgh and then became Director of the Nuffield, and later the Paul Hamlyn, Foundation. Mrs Cornford's mother was not only a fellow of Newnham; she was also cousin of Henry Sidgwick, the prototype of the new academic class. Sidgwick's grandfather was a Yorkshire cotton spinner, his father a clergyman and grammar school headmaster who was last Wrangler in 1829, and he himself was a Rugbeian who resigned his fellowship of Trinity in 1869 on the grounds that he could no longer conscientiously sign the Thirty-Nine Articles. Later, when professor of moral philosophy, he took the lead in promoting university reform and women's education. He married the sister of A. J. Balfour and thus became related to the physicist, Lord Rayleigh, FRS, who had married another sister, and to Professor F. M. and Gerald Balfour, fellows of Trinity. Eleanor Sidgwick became Principal of Newnham. Sidgwick's brother Arthur was second Classic, became a fellow of Corpus, Oxford, and was the father of the partner in the publishing house of Sidgwick and Jackson and of a daughter who was a lecturer at Birmingham University. His cousin Alfred was a philosopher. Sidgwick's youngest sister married her third cousin. This was E. W. – later Archbishop – Benson and father

of the trio of Benson brothers, A. C., E. F. and Father Hugh
Benson.

The following Wedgwoods are cousins of the Darwins: Dr
Ralph Vaughan-Williams, OM, whose maternal grandparents
were a Wedgwood and a Darwin; the novelist Arthur Wedgwood;
Sir Ralph Wedgwood, railway director, and his daughter, the
historian Dame Veronica Wedgwood, OM; and Irene Gosse, a
Wedgwood through her mother and second wife (though the
marriage was later dissolved) of Philip Gosse, son of Sir Edmund
Gosse, critic and author of the greatest of Victorian autobio-
graphies (about his Nonconformist childhood), *Father and Son.*
Finally there were the children of the first Lord Wedgwood,
who married the daughter of the judge Lord Bowen: his son, the
artist and second baron; his fourth daughter, the anthropologist
Camilla Wedgwood; and his eldest daughter Helen, who married Michael Pease, the geneticist son of the secretary and
chronicler of the Fabian Society, E. H. R. Pease, father of Sir
Andrew Huxley's wife.

The Peases lead us into the Quaker country.* E. H. R. Pease
is an interesting example of the way in which the Society of
Friends breeds that kind of non-conformity which is the hall-
mark of an intelligentsia. The senior branch of the family produced members of Parliament, businessmen and bankers; the
cadet branch to which he belonged was for the most part content to live quietly on its patrimony. But comfortable mid-
Victorian philanthropy, or even the activity of his uncle Albert
Fry, prime founder of Bristol University College, was not enough
to satisfy this young man who, earning £400 a year on the Stock
Exchange, which was more than he spent, with a small capital
of his own and handsome prospects, suddenly decided to

---

* The families which descend from two seventeenth-century Quakers, Charles Lloyd and
Robert Barclay, include Bells, Bevans, Birkbecks, Buxtons, Chapmans, Foxes, Frys, Galtons,
Gurneys, Hanburys, Hoares, Hodgkins, Lubbocks, Peases, Peleys, Wakefields and Words-
worths.

become a cabinet-maker, and study the theory of socialism. He ended by becoming secretary to the Fabian Society and to Sidney Webb, at £100 a year. Among these Quaker families the inter-marriages are so frequent that the scent is hard to follow. E. H. R. Pease's mother, for instance, was Susan Fry, sister of the judge Sir Edward Fry, who married Mariabella Hodgkin, sister of Thomas Hodgkin, whose wife was Lucy Anna Fox, sister-in-law of Sir Joseph Pease, the grandson of the man who built the first railway between Stockton and Darlington and who was first cousin to the grandfather of E. H. R. Pease. Here the fox is beginning to run in circles like a hare. Among those families perhaps the best covert to draw is the Hodgkins, where we will find a straight-necked one.

Thomas Hodgkin was a successful banker with a taste for archaeology and history, and he had the good sense to resign from his bank to write a history of early Britain. But his fame rests on one of the most splendid pieces of historical description in the English language, *Italy and Her Invaders*. Three of his ancestors were fellows of the Royal Society: Hodgkin of 'Hodgkin's disease'; Luke Howard, friend of Constable, the meteorologist who first classified clouds; and Isaac Fletcher the astronomer. Thomas's elder sister was the mother of Roger Fry, and of Margery Fry, Principal of Somerville; his younger sister married the architect Alfred Waterhouse, whose daughter became the wife of Robert Bridges, the Poet Laureate. Thomas Hodgkin's second son, the Anglo-Saxon historian, became Provost of Queen's, Oxford. Among his grandsons were the Bishop of St Albans, who married his cousin, the sister of Mr Charles Bosanquet, Rector of King's College, Newcastle, and kinsman of the philosopher Bernard Bosanquet; and the Nobel Prizeman Sir Alan Hodgkin, OM, Master of Trinity and President of the Royal Society, married the eldest daughter of the American Nobel Prizeman Peyton Rous, who was a foreign member of the Royal Society and an honorary fellow of Trinity Hall. Their son, Jonathan, FRS, molecular biologist, was elected professor of genetics at Oxford.

And now the chase has led to Oxford – to another famous sisterhood, the daughters of A. L. Smith, Master of Balliol – noted in childhood for the prickly woollen stockings and thick serge petticoats they wore. Alan Hodgkin's mother married in her widowhood the eldest son of the Master. He had been a fellow of All Souls and of Magdalen and became Rector of Edinburgh Academy. Her brother-in-law by her first marriage, Robert Hodgkin, Provost of Queen's, was also her brother-in-law by her second marriage as he was the husband of the third daughter of the Master. Smith's eldest daughter married Sir Harold Hartley, FRS, fellow of Balliol and chairman of British European Airways. The second daughter, Molly, married first a Barrington-Ward, who was a fellow of All Souls, and brother of the editor of *The Times*; and second Sir Frederick Hamilton, who made his fortune in South Africa. The fourth daughter, Miriam, married Sir Reader Bullard, the ambassador who was the son of a wharf foreman. The sixth daughter, Rosalind, was the wife of Murray Wrong, fellow of Magdalen and son of the historian of Canada, and, second, of Sir Henry Clay, Warden of Nuffield. The youngest daughter, Barbara, married the brain surgeon Sir Hugh Cairns. The youngest son of the Master, Hubert Smith, was the chief agent of the National Trust.

The grandchildren of A. L. Smith include: Thomas Hodgkin, fellow of Balliol, who married Dorothy Crowfoot, OM, FRS, tutor of Somerville; Edward Hodgkin, foreign leader writer on *The Times*; Sir Julian Bullard, fellow of All Souls and diplomat; Oliver Wrong, professor of medicine, University College, London; David Cairns, the music critic, and his brother John, professor of microbiology at Harvard; and Anthony Smith, broadcaster and naturalist. One granddaughter married an official in the International Monetary Fund, another Lord Shore, Labour cabinet minister, and father of a lecturer at Goldsmiths' College, and a third Murdoch Mitchison, fellow of Trinity and professor of zoology at Edinburgh. Murdoch Mitchison and his brothers Denis and Avrion, both professors in the University of London, came of a long line of scientists. Their mother was the novelist Naomi Mitchison, descended from the Haldanes.

The Haldane–Burdon-Sanderson marriage is of peculiar interest. The Haldanes can be traced back to Bishop Burnet and they number among them many lawyers, physicians, sailors, such as Duncan of Camperdown, and soldiers such as Abercromby of Aboukir. James Haldane's father and uncle gave up their naval careers to spread Evangelicalism in Scotland, and for similar reasons Robert Burdon, after a brilliant Oxford career, threw up his post as secretary of presentations, disgusted at the way in which Church patronage was conducted. His uncles were the great maritime lawyer Lord Stowell, and the die-hard Tory Lord Chancellor Lord Eldon. Some members of Eldon's nepotic succession could certainly not be accused of Toryism. A later successor to the woolsack, Lord Haldane, was not only a brilliant Secretary for War and a Hegelian philosopher but Lord Chancellor in the first Labour administration, while his niece, Naomi, married a Labour MP, G. R. Mitchison.

Murdoch Mitchison's sister married Mark Arnold-Forster. His grandfather was Hugh Arnold-Forster, PC, MP, the second son of William Delafield Arnold, and had been adopted by his uncle, who brought in the Bill for compulsory elementary education in Gladstone's first administration. Hugh Arnold-Forster married Mary Lucy Story-Maskelyne. Her sister was the wife of the scientist Sir Arthur Rücker, Principal of London University, and her father was professor of mineralogy at Oxford, where he was a prime mover in establishing the study of the natural sciences. Her great-grandfather, Nevil Maskelyne, was a fellow of Trinity, Astronomer Royal and author of *The Nautical Almanac*. Nevil's sister was the mother-in-law of Henry Strachey and sister-in-law

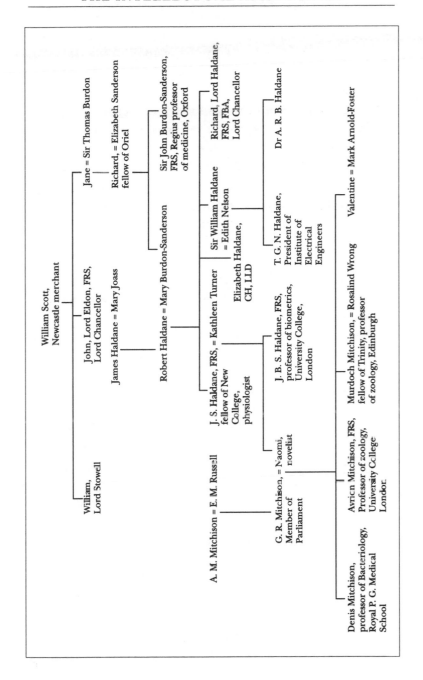

of Robert Clive. Mary Story-Maskelyne's father, brother-in-law, maternal grandfather, paternal grandfather, paternal great-grandfather, uncle and uncle's father were all fellows of the Royal Society.

The Peases, who led us to the Hodgkins, will also lead us to the Butlers, another Cambridge family of public servants and scholars, in that the only daughter of Joseph Beaumont Pease married Sir Cyril Butler. The Butlers descend from Weeden Butler, the friend of Burke, through his son George Butler, senior Wrangler, fellow of Sidney Sussex and headmaster of Harrow. The following are notable among his children and descendants:

1. George Butler, fellow of Exeter, Principal of Liverpool Collegiate Institution, *m.* Josephine Grey, who worked in the cause of women's rights.

2. A. S. Butler, professor of natural philosophy, St Andrews, *m.* Edith Bolton.

3. Arthur S. G. Butler, Wrangler, permanent examiner to the Civil Service.

2. Charles Butler, relief worker.

1. Spencer Perceval Butler, double first in classics and mathematics, barrister and public servant, *m.* Mary Kendall.

2. Sir Cyril Butler, public servant and a founder of the Contemporary Arts Society.

2. Sir Spencer Harcourt Butler, Governor of Burma.

2. Sir Montague Butler, Governor of Central Provinces, India, Master of Pembroke, *m.* Ann Gertrude Smith, daughter of George Smith, Indian correspondent of *The Times*, who was great-nephew of the Rector of the Royal High School, Edinburgh, in Sir Walter Scott's day.

3. R. A. Butler, Master of Trinity, fellow of Corpus, Chancellor of the Exchequer, *m.* Sydney, daughter of Samuel Courtauld, industrialist and connoisseur.

2. Arthur Francis Norman-Butler, Wrangler, Inspector of Schools, *m.* Sibella Norman.

    3. Edward Norman-Butler *m.* Belinda Ritchie, granddaughter of Sir Richmond Ritchie and Anne Thackeray, whose father was W. M. Thackeray; also granddaughter of Charles Booth.

    3. Susan *m.* Sir George Abell, viceregal secretary in India, director of the Bank of England.

2. Ralph Butler, fellow of Corpus Christi, Cambridge.

2. Sir Geoffrey Butler, MP, fellow of Corpus Christi, university burgess.

2. Isabel *m.* Sir Henry Erle Richards, fellow of All Souls and Chichele professor of international law, Oxford; legal member of the Viceregal Council.

    3. Audrey Richards, reader in social anthropology, Cambridge.

    3. Enid *m.* Geoffrey Faber, fellow of All Souls, publisher and author.

        4. Tom Faber, fellow of Trinity and then of Corpus Christi, Cambridge.

    3. Katharine *m.* Eric Beckett, fellow of All Souls, legal adviser to the Foreign Office.

        4. Philip Beckett, lecturer in agricultural science, Oxford.

2. Margaret *m.* Alan Macpherson, solicitor, uncle of R. F. Macpherson, fellow of King's and Registrary of Cambridge, whose aunt was a fellow of Girton, and whose second cousin, George Rylands C. H., was a fellow of King's.

Alan Macpherson's great-grandfather was Principal of Aberdeen University, his grandfather Sub-principal and professor of oriental languages and his cousin, H. M. Innes, fellow of Trinity. One of his aunts married the 13th Sir John Peter Grant and hence became a niece of Lady Strachey, the wife of General Sir Richard Strachey, FRS;

another aunt married a brother of Maria Edgeworth.

1. Arthur Gray Butler, fellow of Oriel, first headmaster of Haileybury, *m.* Harriet, niece of Maria Edgeworth.

   2. Harold Edgeworth Butler, professor of Latin, London, *m.* Margaret, daughter of A. F. Pollard, fellow of All Souls, professor of history, London.

      3. David Butler fellow of Nuffield, *m.* Marilyn Speers, professor of English, Cambridge, and later Rector of Exeter College, Oxford.

      3. Christina *m.* Sir Howard Colvin, fellow of St John's and reader in architectural history, Oxford.

      3. Honora *m.* Norman Addison, master at Eton.

1. Louisa *m.* Sir Francis Galton, cousin of Charles Darwin by Erasmus Darwin's second wife.

1. Henry Montagu Butler, senior Classic, headmaster of Harrow, Master of Trinity, *m.*

(i) Georgina Elliot.

   2. Agnes *m.* E. W. Howson, fellow of King's, master at Harrow.

   2. Edward Butler, master at Harrow.

   2. Arthur Hugh Butler, librarian of the House of Lords.

   2. Maud *m.* Bernard Morley Fletcher.

(ii) Agnata Frances Ramsay, daughter of Sir J. H. Ramsay, FBA, whose brother was professor of humanity, Glasgow. She was placed alone in the first division of the first class classical tripos, 1887.

   2. James Ramsay Montagu Butler, fellow of Trinity, Regius professor of modern history.

   2. Gordon Butler, obtained a first class in classics and history; died in the First World War.

   2. Sir Nevile Montagu Butler, ambassador to the Netherlands, father-in-law of Sir John Elliott, Regius Professor, Oxford.

Three connections in this list of achievement are of particular interest. The first is the link through Geoffrey Faber to his great-uncle F. W. Faber of the Oxford Movement, which, unlike the Clapham Sect, has produced few notable descendants. The second is the relationship of the Master of Pembroke (the father of Rab Butler) to Sir George Thomson, Master of Corpus. Lady Butler as a member of the Smith clan was the sister of Janetta, wife of the philosopher Professor W. R. Sorley, fellow of Trinity and then of King's, and mother of Charles Sorley the poet and of Joan, who married a professor of literature at Aberdeen. One of her grandfathers was a first cousin of J. E. B. Mayor and the other a professor of Sanskrit at Oxford. Three of her sons are professors and so is one of her sons-in-law. She was also the sister of the Very Revd Sir George Adam Smith, the Old Testament scholar, who married a daughter of Sir George Buchanan, FRS. One of Lady Butler's sisters was the first woman to be elected a fellow of University College London, another the first woman to be elected a member of the British Physiological Society. One of Sir George Adam Smith's daughters married Ian Clarke, a master at Stowe who was related to the Anderson connection (Elizabeth Garrett Anderson, pioneer in obtaining medical education for women); and to Lord Bryce. Another was Janet Adam Smith, literary editor of the *New Statesman*, wife successively of the poet and critic Michael Roberts, and of a headmaster of Westminster. Her two sons and daughter by her first marriage all became professors. Another married Sir George Thomson, FRS and Master of Corpus, whose son became an ambassador and whose son-in-law was a fellow of St John's. The Master of Corpus was the son of the great physicist, J. J. Thomson, OM, Master of Trinity; and Lady Butler was his wife's aunt.

The third connection also relates to a head of Cambridge colleges. Bernard Morley Fletcher, the husband of Maud, was the brother of Sir Walter Morley Fletcher, FRS and fellow of

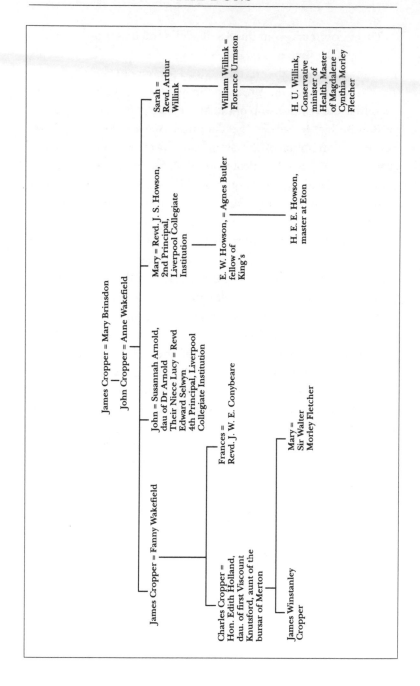

James Cropper = Mary Brinsdon
|
John Cropper = Anne Wakefield

James Cropper = Fanny Wakefield

Charles Cropper =
Hon. Edith Holland,
dau. of first Viscount
Knutsford, aunt of the
bursar of Merton

James Winstanley
Cropper

Frances =
Revd. J. W. E. Conybeare

Mary =
Sir Walter
Morley Fletcher

John = Susannah Arnold,
dau of Dr Arnold
Their Niece Lucy = Revd
Edward Selwyn
4th Principal, Liverpool
Collegiate Institution

Mary = Revd. J. S. Howson,
2nd Principal,
Liverpool Collegiate
Institution

E. W. Howson, = Agnes Butler
fellow of
King's

H. E. E. Howson,
master at Eton

Sarah =
Revd. Arthur
Willink

William Willink =
Florence Urmston

H. U. Willink,
Conservative
minister of
Health, Master
of Magdalene =
Cynthia Morley
Fletcher

Trinity, and their niece married Harry Willink, Master of Magdalene. And this brings in another family, the Croppers, in that Sir Walter married Mary Cropper. The Master of Magdalene's grandmother was a Cropper; and the mother of E. W. Howson, who married Agnes Butler, daughter of the Master of Trinity, was also a Cropper. One of the Croppers married a daughter of Zachary Macaulay and on her death the widow of her brother, H. M. Macaulay; another married a son of Lord Brougham, a third a daughter of Dr Arnold, and a fourth J. W. E. Conybeare, so that Lady Morley Fletcher and Rose Macaulay both shared an uncle. Another Cropper married a daughter of Dr Arnold and adopted an Arnold niece, who married Edward Selwyn, fellow of King's, headmaster of Uppingham and Principal of Liverpool Collegiate Institution. Nor are these links with Clapham surprising because the family descends from James Cropper, a Quaker who was prominent in the anti-slavery movement; and through the Croppers and Butlers the ties between Trinity, Corpus and Pembroke are certainly strong.

Though this fox would run much further we had better hack back to the Babingtons, where there is a gap in the hedge for us to jump into the Vaughan country. The Vaughans descend from an alchemist who was a fellow of Jesus, Oxford, and the twin brother of the poet, Henry Vaughan the silurist. The alchemist's son became a fellow of the Royal College of Physicians and by the end of the eighteenth century the family was already established in the front rank of the professional classes. At that time there were five Vaughan brothers, one President of the Royal College of Physicians and doctor to George III, another an eminent judge, a third Warden of Merton, a fourth fellow of All Souls and a diplomat, and the fifth, the Revd E. T. Vaughan, a double first and fellow of Trinity. The judge had the following notable descendants:

1. Henry Halford Vaughan, fellow of Oriel, Regius professor of modern history, Oxford, *m.* Adeline Jackson.

   2. W. W. Vaughan, headmaster of Wellington and later of Rugby, *m.* Margaret Symonds.

      3. Dr Janet Vaughan DBE, Principal of Somerville College.

   2. Millicent *m.* Sir Vere Isham, Bart.

      3. Sir Gyles Isham, Bart, actor, notable president of the OUDS.

1. Hester *m.* Francis Hawkins, MD, brother of the Provost of Oriel and of Caesar Hawkins, FRS.

By a second marriage:

1. The Revd Charles Vaughan *m.* Jane Coote.

   2. Louisa *m.* H. A. Perry, fellow of King's and colonial judge.

   The Revd E. T. Vaughan also married twice. T. H. Green, the Balliol Idealist philosopher was his grandson through his first marriage. By his second marriage he had:

1. The Revd Edward Thomas Vaughan *m.* Mary Rose, daughter of Lydia Babington Rose.

   2. C. E. Vaughan, master at Clifton and professor of English at Cardiff, Newcastle and Leeds.

1. C. J. Vaughan, senior Classic, fellow of Trinity, headmaster of Harrow, Dean of Llandaff, *m.* Catherine Stanley, sister of Arthur Stanley, Dean of Westminster.

1. Edwin Vaughan *m.* Henrietta McCausland.

   2. Ileen *m.* Sir Henry Stuart Jones, professor of ancient history, Oxford, and Principal of Aberystwyth College, University of Wales.

1. General Sir John Vaughan, later *The Times* correspondent.

1. The Revd David James Vaughan, fellow of Trinity, philologist, liberal theologian and founder of Leicester Working Men's College.

The E. T. Vaughan connection will lead to the Russian scholar Sir Bernard Pares and to his son Richard, historian and fellow of All Souls. It will also lead to the brother-in-law of T. H. Green, John Addington Symonds, whose daughter married W. W. Vaughan, headmaster of Wellington and later of Rugby, the son of a Regius professor. But the most rewarding line to follow is that of C. J. Vaughan. A favourite pupil of Dr Arnold at Rugby, where his academic triumphs won him the name of 'Half-Holiday Vaughan', he re-established Harrow as a school not only by raising the numbers, which had fallen below seventy, but by creating an excellent staff of assistant masters and transmitting to his scholars his own passion for accuracy and the delicacies of language. He had a winning way with boys – all too winning. When John Addington Symonds was a boy at Harrow he discovered that Vaughan had seduced one of his friends: he later told his father, who forced Vaughan to resign the headmastership and threatened him with exposure if he ever accepted major ecclesiastical preferment. He was as good as his word and only after the elder Symonds's death did Vaughan dare to accept the deanery of Llandaff, where his ordinands were known as 'Vaughan's doves'. Vaughan had married the sister of his Rugby school friend, Dean Stanley, the cousin of Kate Stanley. Kate Stanley's mother was one of the founders of Girton who said, 'So long as I live there shall be no chapel at Girton.' She herself married the son of Lord John Russell and thus was the mother of Bertrand Russell, OM. Earl Russell descended on both sides from great aristocratic families; yet he was one of the few aristocrats who successfully transplanted himself to the rock garden of the intelligentsia without a sigh for the more luxuriant flower beds of the nobility. 'Non-conformity' is not a middle-class monopoly. His son Conrad was professor of history at King's College, London, and spoke on the front bench of the Liberal Democrat Party in the House of Lords. Through his grandfather's marriage Conrad, Earl Russell, can claim descent from the eighteenth-century historian William Robertson.

One of Kate Stanley's aunts married the brother of Julius Hare, the liberal Anglican theologian; and Hare married the sister of F. D. Maurice. Since the time when Henry Maurice was ejected from his living under the Act of Uniformity to the day when General Sir Frederick Maurice was removed from his post as Director of Military Operations by Lloyd-George, the Maurices have sacrificed their careers to their duty to tell the truth as they see it. Joan Robinson, professor of economics at Cambridge was the General's daughter.

The youngest daughter of John Addington Symonds, Dame Catherine Furse, was the wife of Charles Furse, the portrait painter (whose great-niece married the Prime Minister, Neville Chamberlain). Furse was a nephew of William Cory (Johnson), the uncle of the colonial official, Sir Ralph Furse, who married Sir Henry Newbolt's daughter, and was himself the uncle of Roger Furse, the stage designer. All these were cousins of Sir Compton Mackenzie. We could follow the Furses, as W. T. J. Gun did, through their Symonds blood and connect them with the Hills, a family of civil servants and savants of which perhaps the most famous was Sir Rowland Hill, and see how one grandson of the Johnsonian scholar, George Birkbeck Hill, is a professor of medical statistics and how another married a daughter of Ernest Rhys, the editor of Everyman's Library. Or we could follow the Furses on another scent. A sister of the portrait painter married Cecil Lubbock, a director of the Bank of England. He was the son of Frederic Lubbock, who married a daughter of John Gurney of Earlham: one of Cecil Lubbock's brothers was for long a master at Eton, another was Percy Lubbock, author of *The Craft of Fiction*, another was a fellow of Peterhouse. The youngest brother took as his wife a great-granddaughter of the Bonham-Carter who married Florence Nightingale's aunt and was the father-in-law of A. V. Dicey. The Lubbocks descend from the astronomer Sir John Lubbock, FRS, whose eldest son,

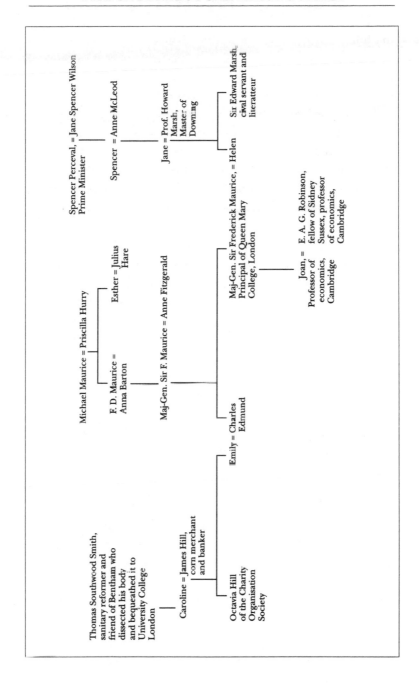

the first Lord Avebury, FRS, Vice-Chancellor of London, married as his second wife a daughter of the anthropologist General Pitt-Rivers. Another Lubbock married a daughter of Lord Boyd-Orr, and another married Paul Vellacott, headmaster of Harrow and Master of Peterhouse.

Or we can return through the Venns to the Gurneys – to a distant branch of the Quaker family who had made their name in the eighteenth century as shorthand writers. One of the members of this family was the mother of C. F. G. Masterman, double first in the natural and moral sciences, and Liberal cabinet minister. He married a Lyttelton and his daughter was the wife of Richard Braithwaite, professor of moral philosophy at Cambridge. One of her great uncles was headmaster of Haileybury and then of Eton, and another Lyttelton married C. A. Alington, headmaster of Eton and Dean of Durham. Alington was the father of a fellow of University College, Oxford, and father-in-law of the Revd J. C. V. Wilkes, late Warden of Radley, of Sir Roger Mynors, professor of Latin at Oxford, and of his brother Sir Humphrey, fellow of Corpus and Deputy-Governor of the Bank of England. George Lyttelton was for long a master at Eton and his son was the jazz musician, whose first wife was a Gaskell, and sister of the bibliographer Philip Gaskell, fellow of King's and later librarian of Trinity. His mother was a cousin of Philip Noel-Baker, Labour minister, and was the sister-in-law of Alec Penrose, fellow of King's, whose brother Lionel was professor of genetics at University College, London. Philip Gaskell himself married the daughter of a fellow of Emmanuel and a fellow of Girton.

One of John Addington Symonds's daughters was the mother of an editor of the *Spectator*, St Loe Strachey. His wife wrote: 'the Stracheys are most strongly the children of their fathers not of their mothers. "It does not matter whom they marry," said one of St Loe's aunts to me when I was quite young, "the type continues and has been much the same for three hundred years."' This was not a view which Barbara Strachey endorsed.

Her mother, the chronicler of women's emancipation, was a Pearsall Smith and Barbara took after the masterful women of that family. Indeed her father, Oliver, a notable cryptographer in both world wars, and her uncles Lytton and James could not be said to be paragons of masculinity, whereas her Strachey aunts such as Pernel, the Principal of Newnham, or Pippa or Dorothy, the wife of the painter Simon Bussy, appeared – at least on the surface – to be made of sterner stuff. On the Pearsall Smith side Barbara's grandmother had married Bernard Berenson, her great-aunt was Bertrand Russell's first wife and the old maid of that generation was her great-uncle Logan Pearsall Smith. Barbara's brother Christopher, the first professor of computation at Oxford, was in voice and manner every inch a Strachey.

Barbara Strachey's cousin Julia, the author of that amusing and melancholy novel, *Cheerful Weather for the Wedding*, married first the Bloomsbury sculptor Stephen Tomlin and, on his death, Lawrence Gowing, the painter and Slade professor of fine art at University College, London. Their aunt married the son of Sir Alexander Rendel, whose sister, as we have seen, married into the Wedgwood family. (Another editor of the *Spectator*, Wilson Harris, was also connected to the Rendels.) Sir Charles Strachey married a sister of the literary critic Sir Walter Raleigh, and his sister Winifred married an Indian administrator, Sir Hugh Barnes. The daughter of this marriage, Mary St John Hutchinson, had two children: the elder married Lord Rothschild. On the dissolution of that marriage, she became the wife of the novelist Rex Warner. The younger child, Lord Hutchinson, QC, married the actress Peggy Ashcroft, though the marriage was later dissolved. Sir Hugh Barnes married again and by his second marriage produced a pro-consul of a new cultural medium. Sir George Barnes was the first director of the BBC's Third Programme and became the first director of television. His wife came of impeccable academic stock.

Those who are still up with the hunt may feel that the time has come to hack home. In fact hounds have come full circle back to perhaps the most famous of all the evangelical connections. The Clapham Sect Evangelicals were dedicated to the abolition of slavery. As part of that struggle they despatched to the tropics missionaries who were to alter the course of British colonial history; and their enthusiasm for humanitarian causes sent ripples across the surface of English life and inspired such people as Shaftesbury and Florence Nightingale, herself a descendant of a member of the Sect. What brought them together? Wealth, certainly, for many of them had acquired or inherited fortunes made as bankers or merchants. Tory politics was another unifying influence; some were members of Parliament, others pro-consuls in India or the colonies; philanthropy, of course, united them; and above all Evangelicalism.

They had begun to inter-marry before they settled in Clapham. William Wilberforce's maternal aunt had married a Smith and both families were partners in Baltic trade. He and Henry Thornton shared an aunt, and in addition his grandfather had married a Thornton. The Thorntons were linked through the Sykeses to the Babingtons, and Thomas Babington's son married a niece of Henry Thornton's wife. One of Babington's sisters married Thomas Gisborne and Babington himself married the sister of Zachary Macaulay. Zachary Macaulay's daughter married Sir Charles Trevelyan. Another son of Thomas Babington married Eleanor Elliott, a granddaughter of the Revd Henry Venn,* whose son John led the Clapham Sect in prayer. A granddaughter of Babington married the Revd Charles John

---

* Henry Venn was a famous cricketer. After playing victoriously for Surrey against All England a few days before ordination he gave his bat to the first comer saying, 'I will never had it said of me, Well struck Parson.' But the old Adam rose up in his descendants and his great-great-grandson, J. A. Venn, bowled out the great Australian player Victor Trumper twice – using a bowling machine invented by himself and his father the logician.

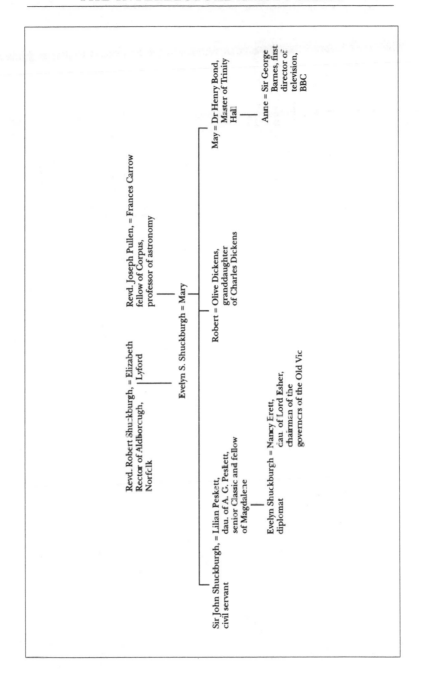

Revd. Robert Shuckburgh, = Elizabeth
Rector of Aldborough,   Lyford
Norfolk

Revd. Joseph Pullen, = Frances Carrow
fellow of Corpus,
professor of astronomy

Evelyn S. Shuckburgh = Mary

Sir John Shuckburgh, = Lilian Peskett,
civil servant   dau. of A. G. Peskett,
                                 senior Classic and fellow
                                 of Magdalene

Robert = Olive Dickens,
            granddaughter
            of Charles Dickens

May = Dr Henry Bond,
        Master of Trinity
        Hall

Evelyn Shuckburgh = Nancy Erett,
diplomat   dau. of Lord Esher,
                               chairman of the
                               governors of the Old Vic

Anne = Sir George
          Barnes, first
          director of
          television,
          BBC

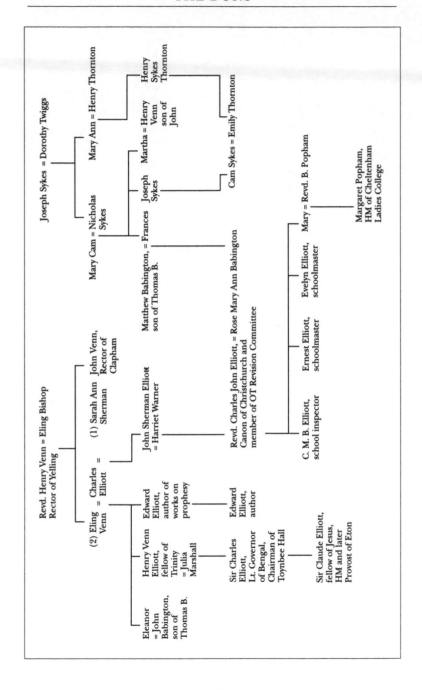

Elliott, whose mother was a great-great-granddaughter of Isaac Newton's mother.[*]

The link to the Stephens is through the Venns – a notable academic family in that J. A. Venn, the President of Queen's and editor of *Alumni Cantabrigiensis*, represented the ninth generation to graduate from Oxford or Cambridge. James Stephen, a Master in Chancery, met and became fast friends with the Rector of Clapham, John Venn, the catalyst of the Clapham Sect. James bred a generation of academic lawyers and writers. His second child was 'Stephen on Pleading', whose son and grandson edited successive editions of his *New Commentaries*. The Master in Chancery's fourth son was the author Sir George Stephen, and his second daughter the mother of Edward Dicey, editor of the *Observer*, and of A. V. Dicey, professor of law at Oxford and author of *Law and Public Opinion in England*. His third son, Sir James Stephen, was the *Edinburgh* reviewer, professor of modern history at Cambridge and colonial undersecretary who drafted the Bill to free the slaves in the British Colonies. It was this third son who married Jane Venn, the daughter of the Rector of Clapham. Their first child was Sir J. Fitzjames Stephen, high court judge, *Saturday* reviewer and author of a powerful attack on Mill's liberalism entitled *Liberty, Equality, Fraternity*. He had the following children:

Katherine Stephen, Principal of Newnham
Sir Herbert Stephen, clerk of assizes and legal author
J. K. Stephen, fellow of King's, parodist and author of *Lapsus Calami*
Sir Harry Lushington Stephen, Indian judge, *m.* Barbara Nightingale.

Barbara Nightingale was a great-granddaughter of William

---

* Tables I and J show the connections between the Elliotts and Venns and hence between them and the Stephens.

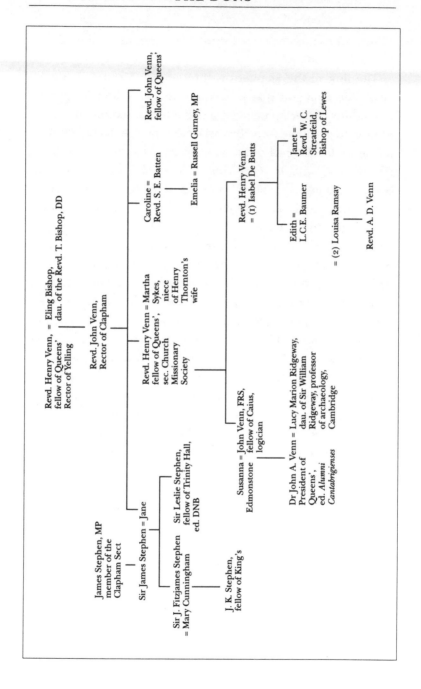

Smith, MP; her great-aunt was Florence Nightingale's mother; her aunt married the poet A. H. Clough; Clough's sister was the first Principal of Newnham; and his daughter was also head of that college.

The second of Sir James Stephen's sons was Leslie Stephen. Leslie Stephen married first a daughter of Thackeray and, second, Julia, the widow of the publisher Herbert Duckworth. Julia was a daughter of one of the beautiful Pattle sisters. She was thus a niece of Julia Margaret Cameron, the photographer, and of the wife of the Prince of Wales's tutor and mother of H. A. L. Fisher, Warden of New College and president of the Board of Education under Lloyd George. H. A. L. Fisher's wife numbered among her great-uncles F. H. and A. C. Bradley, and one of his nephews was Professor Adam Curle of Exeter University. Fisher's sister married, first, F. W. Maitland, the constitutional historian, and, second, Sir Francis Darwin; her daughter by her first marriage married Gerald Shove, fellow of King's and economist. Nor does this exhaust Julia Stephen's relations. Her sister married Henry Halford Vaughan, professor of history at Oxford, who retired to write a *magnum opus* which he was believed to have destroyed in scholarly despair. It was he who was the father of the headmaster of Rugby whom we have already met.

Julia Stephen had two families. George Duckworth, her son by her first marriage, married a daughter of the fourth Earl of Carnarvon (father of the discoverer of Tutankhamun's tomb). Two of the fourth Earl's granddaughters successively married Evelyn Waugh. By her marriage to Leslie Stephen she had Vanessa, the wife of Clive Bell; Thoby, who died when still a young man; Virginia, the wife of Leonard Woolf; and Adrian, who as we saw married Karin Costelloe, the sister of Ray Strachey. Their elder daughter married the Nobel Prizeman, the chemist Richard Millington Synge, kinsman of the Irish playwright.

Vanessa Bell's second son, Quentin, was professor of the history and theory of art at Sussex University and wrote the biography of his aunt Virginia. He married the daughter of A. H. Popham, keeper of prints and drawings in the British Museum. His wife was a daughter of the Fabian, Lord Olivier. Vanessa's daughter, Angelica, was the second wife of David Garnett. David Garnett's grandfather was keeper of the printed books in the British Museum, his father an editor and tireless counsellor of young authors, and his mother, Constance Garnett, by her translations virtually introduced Russian literature to England. One of Angelica's daughters married the son of Ralph Partridge, the author and friend of Lytton Strachey, and of Frances his wife. Frances Partridge was the sister of Tom Marshall, professor of sociology at London, and of Ray, the first wife of David Garnett. David Garnett's elder son, Richard, became a publisher and married the offspring of the union between Professor Bruce Dickins and the daughter of Professor Sir Herbert Grierson.

Thus, if we recollect that E. M. Forster was a great-grandson of Henry Thornton and that Duncan Grant was a cousin of Lytton Strachey, all the members of the original Bloomsbury circle except Saxon Sydney-Turner and H. T. J. Norton, fellow of Trinity, have already appeared in the families we have examined; and so have the first five Principals of Newnham and nine out of the ten Masters of Trinity in the twentieth century.

Here, then, is a sketch of a new social group emerging in society. The process, though it may have been exhausting to follow, is in no way remarkable. A similar study could be made of the families of brewers. Still, aristocracies which seem to be secure can vanish overnight if society rejects the credentials by which they have established themselves or if they lose self-confidence; and in the 1960s some of their children who might have been expected to excel abandoned the goal of a fellowship and with a sigh of relief dropped out. 'Where is Bohun, where's Mowbray, where's Mortimer? Nay, which is more and most of all, where is Plantagenet? They are entombed in the urns and sepulchres of mortality,' mused Sir Ranulphe Crewe on the medieval nobility. Whether the names of these families will continue to appear among the holders of fellowships and chairs in the twenty-first century remains an open question; but some of those who will hold them will surely be able to trace their descent back to those mentioned above as, for instance, quite a few of the intellectual aristocracy could claim the fifteenth-century Duchess of Norfolk as a remote ancestor.

Index

THE DONS

Beckett, Katherine, Lady (*née* Butler), 323
Beckett, Philip, 323
Beecham, Audrey, 166
Beecham, Sir Thomas, 177
Begin, Menachem, 215
Behrens, Betty (Mrs E.H. Carr), 245–55; *The Ancien Régime*, 252, 247–8; *Merchant Shipping and the Demands of War*, 246; *Society, Government and Enlightenment*, 251–2
Belinsky, Vissarion Gregorievich, 219
Bell family, 317n
Bell, Clive, 113, 339
Bell, Kenneth, 137
Bell, Quentin, 339
Bell, Vanessa (*née* Stephen), 180, 339
Belloc, Hilaire, 280–1
Beloff, Max, Baron, 201, 203, 274, 293
Ben Gurion, David, 215
Bendern, Patricia de, 224–5
Benjamin, Walter, 229
Bennett, Joan, 205
Benson, Arthur Christopher, 18, 105, 107, 114, 180, 317
Benson, Edward Frederic, 317
Benson, Edward White, Archbishop of Canterbury, 316
Benson, Sir Frank, 174
Benson, Father Hugh, 317
Bentley, Richard, 79, 85, 125
Berenson, Bernard, 333
Bergner, Elisabeth, 177
Bergson, Henri, 241
Berlin, Aline, Lady (*née* Gunzbourg), 225
Berlin, Irving, 214
Berlin, Dr Lev B., 218
Berlin, Sir Isaiah: games, 147; relations with Bowra, 152, 154–5; on Bowra's love of honours,

162; talk, 193, 209–10, 212, 222; and All Souls, 199–200, 203, 211–12, 226, 228; background and career, 209–10; honours, 210, 222; character and interests, 211–13; affection for, 213–14; wartime post in USA, 214; Zionism and Jewishness, 214–16; ideas and writings, 217–22, 228–32; visits Russia, 217–18; reputation, 222; political views, 224, 229; women and marriage, 224–5; love of music, 225–6; as head of Wolfson College, 226–8; criticised, 228–31; influence on Hart, 290; *Jewish Slavery and Emancipation*, 215; *Two Concepts of Liberty*, 220
Bernal, John Desmond, 2, 131, 133
Berrill, Sir Kenneth, 299
Besicovitch, Abram, 85
Betjeman, Sir John, 138, 152, 164, 168, 194, 198
Betjeman, Penelope, Lady, 166
Bevan family, 317n
Beves, Donald, 184
Bible: literal truth questioned, 64–6
Birch, Frank, 175, 177–8
Birkbeck family, 317n
Birrell, Augustine, 68 & n
Bishop, Adrian, 165
Blackett, Carmen, 234
Blackett, Patrick Maynard Stuart, 129, 133
Blackie, John Stuart, 72
Blackstone, Tessa, Baron, 299
Blair, Tony, 301
Blake, Robert, Baron, 292
Blake, William, 95
Bloch, Marc, 244
Bloomsbury group, 21, 102n, 113, 164, 340

Blunt, Anthony, 125, 151n, 157, 191
Boase, Thomas, 138
Bodichon, Barbara, 314
Bodley, George Frederick, 21
Bohr, Niels, 129, 131
Bonney, Thomas George, 206n
Booth, Charles, 308, 323
Booth, George Macaulay, 309
Booth, Mary (*née* Potter), 308
Boothby, Robert, Baron, 150, 166, 183, 194, 273
Bosanquet, Bernard, 318
Bosanquet, Charles, 318
Bowden, Frank Philip, 122
Bowen, Charles Synge Christopher, Baron, 317
Bowen, Elizabeth, 166, 212
Bowra, Sir Maurice: Wadham salon, 138, 152; background and career, 139–43; as Warden of Wadham, 139, 143, 152, 154; views and values, 140, 144, 148–50, 152–4, 168–9; writings, 141–5, 157; as President of British Academy, 144; Sparrow on, 144, 193–4; talk, personality and manner, 145–8, 156, 162, 164, 169, 193; friendships, 149–52, 155–6, 164; envy, 154–5; on Isaiah Berlin, 154–5; fear of blackmail, 156; university administration and appointments, 156–61; craving for honours and recognition, 162–4; social unease, 164, 223; sexual life and interests, 165–7; encourages Berlin, 209–10; Berlin mimics, 212; writes hoax details for Berlin's *Who's Who* entry, 222; Berlin on, 223; Carey on, 289

344

INDEX

INDEX

Strachey, Jane Maria, Lady
(*née* Grant), 20
Strachey, Lytton, 12, 113,
115, 180–1 & n, 185,
190, 192, 333, 340
Strachey, Oliver, 333
Strachey, Pernel, 333
Strachey, Philippa, 333
Strachey, Ray, 339
Strachey, General Sir
Richard and Caroline,
Lady, 323
Strachey, St Loe, 332
Stravinsky, Igor, 223
Stubbs, William, Bishop of
Oxford, 74, 88–9, 91, 93
student unrest (1970s),
284–7
Sumner, Benedict
Humphrey, 198–9
Swann, Michael, Baron, 297
Swift, Clive, 175
Swinburne, Algernon
Charles, 71–2, 74, 144
Sydney-Turner, Saxon, 340
Sykes family, 334
Sykes, Christopher, 194
Symonds, John Addington,
74, 329–30, 332
Synge, Richard Millington,
339

Tait, Archibald Campbell,
Archbishop of
Canterbury, 62
Talmon, Jacob, 219
Tatham, Edward, 8
Tawney, Richard Henry, 57,
222, 259
Taylor, Alan John Percivale,
137, 222, 273
Tebbit, Norman, Baron,
290
Temperley, Harold William
Vazeille, 253
Temple, Frederick,
Archbishop of
Canterbury, 64, 66, 101
Tennyson, Alfred, 1st
Baron, 69, 102
Thackeray, William
Makepeace, 323
Thatcher, Margaret,

Baroness, 277, 290–2,
296, 298
Thirlwall, Connop, 79
Thomas, Hugh, Baron, 87
Thompson, Hepworth,
83–4, 96
Thompson, 'Tommy'
(chemistry tutor,
Oxford), 275
Thomson, Sir George
Paget, 123, 325
Thomson, Sir Joseph John,
121–8, 130, 133, 325
Thomson, Rose, Lady (J.J's
wife), 125, 132
Thornton family, 12, 14
Thornton, Henry, 12, 334,
340
Tilley, Arthur, 105
Tillyard, Eustace
Mandeville Wetenhall,
186
Tindal, Matthew, 306
Tizard, Sir Henry, 134 & n
Todd, Alexander Robertus,
Baron, 2, 270 & n, 291
Tolstoy, Count Lev, 219
Tomlin, Stephen, 333
Toscanini, Arturo, 226
Toynbee Hall, London, 11n
Toynbee, Arnold, 72
Toynbee, Philip, 224
Tractarians, 29, 49, 51–2,
64, 68, 88
Trevelyan family, 12, 310
Trevelyan, Sir Charles, 77,
334
Trevelyan, George
Macaulay, 1–2, 20, 84–8,
98, 134, 185, 253, 257,
266, 268
Trevelyan, Julian, 311
Trevelyan, Robert Calverley,
311
Trevelyan, Ursula, 311
Trevelyan-Northcote Report
(1853), 15
Trevor-Roper, Hugh
(Baron Dacre), 11, 87,
201, 268, 273, 286
Trilling, Lionel, 264
Trinity College, Cambridge,
79–81, 83–7, 100, 115,

123–32, 134, 204; admits
women, 254
Trollope, Anthony, 12, 16,
70; *Barchester Towers*, 7
Trotsky, Leon, 224
Trotter, Coutts, 84
Trow, Martin, 294–5; *see
also* Halsey, Albert Henry
Truman, Harry S., 271
Trumper, Victor, 334n
Tuckwell, William, 1, 7, 35,
298
Turgenev, Ivan, 219, 225,
230
Turner, Frank, 240
Tyler, Edward: *Primitive
Culture*, 242

Unitarians, 14–15
universities: Newman's idea
of, 53–6, 59; funding,
192–4
University College London,
299
University Grants
Committee (UGC), 260,
275, 277, 292–3, 295
Urquhart, Francis Fortescue
('Sligger'), 78, 137

Vaughan family, 327–9
Vaughan, Revd Charles and
Jane (*née* Coote), 328
Vaughan, Charles Edwyn,
328
Vaughan, Charles John and
Catherine (*née* Stanley),
328–9
Vaughan, Revd David
James, 328
Vaughan, Revd Edward
Thomas and Mary (*née*
Rose), 327–9
Vaughan, Edwin and
Henrietta (*née*
McCausland), 329
Vaughan, Henry, 327
Vaughan, Henry Halford
and Adeline (*née*
Jackson), 328, 339
Vaughan, Dame Janet, 328
Vaughan, General Sir John,
329